'The best Minister of Sport we never had!'
ALAN JOHNSON MP

'As this book shows, Tom also carries a knockout punch when fighting his corner for boxing and sport of all kinds.'
LENNOX LEWIS

'Lord Pendry has been an inspirational figure in the UK Olympic movement and in particular, the sport of artistic gymnastics in the UK.'
NELLIE KIM, OLYMPIC GOLD MEDALLIST

'Tom has given so much over the years. His love of sport is legendary ... now read about this fascinating man and his life.'
DAME MARY PETERS, CH, DBE, OLYMPIC GOLD MEDALLIST

'Lord Pendry is an absolute stalwart of sport in Parliament. He has enormous experience that he brings to everything he is involved in with humour, compassion and determination when needed.'
CHARLOTTE LESLIE MP, CHAIRMAN OF THE ALL-PARTY BOXING GROUP

'Perhaps Tom's greatest legacy was managing to include just two key words in the Labour manifesto: Olympic bid. The rest is history and the millions who enjoyed London 2012 owe Tom a debt of gratitude.'
PAUL WILLIAMSON, DIRECTOR OF TICKETING FOR LONDON 2012

'He was the best Sports Minister we never had! He certainly should have held the office and had he done so it would have been with distinction. A man of conviction, consistent support for the athletes, a passion for sport and a dedication to improve recreational facilities across the country.'
LORD MOYNIHAN, FORMER CHAIRMAN OF THE BRITISH OLYMPIC ASSOCIATION

'As the foundation's first chairman and now its president, Tom's enthusiasm for its work and the good that football can achieve through it remains undimmed.'
RICHARD SCUDAMORE, EXECUTIVE CHAIRMAN, THE PREMIER LEAGUE AND FOOTBALL FOUNDATION TRUSTEE

'Some politicians fail to understand the beautiful game – Lord Pendry is certainly not one of them. His understanding and support for the game at all levels is exceptional.'

SIR ALEX FERGUSON

'Tom would have made the ideal Sports Minister but, nevertheless, his contribution has been so outstanding that the PFA were minded to recognise his achievement with a special presentation at our 2015 annual awards dinner.'

GORDON TAYLOR OBE, CHIEF EXECUTIVE OF THE PROFESSIONAL FOOT-BALLERS ASSOCIATION

'Tom and I were members of the Labour League of Youth in the 1950s and we have trodden the same paths ever since, arriving at different times in Parliament – determined to change our world for the better!'

BARONESS BOOTHROYD

TAKING IT ON THE CHIN

• Memoirs of a Parliamentary Bruiser •

LORD PENDRY

Biteback Publishing

First published in Great Britain in 2016 by
Biteback Publishing Ltd
Westminster Tower
3 Albert Embankment
London SE1 7SP
Copyright © Thomas Pendry 2016

ISBN 978-1-78590-027-3

10 9 8 7 6 5 4 3 2 1

A CIP catalogue record for this book is available from the British Library.

Set in Adobe Caslon Pro

Printed and bound in Great Britain by
CPI Group (UK) Ltd, Croydon CR0 4YY

ACKNOWLEDGEMENTS

I am indebted to a number of people who have assisted me in writing this book. In particular, my former parliamentary assistant Gee-Hae Kim, who bore the brunt of the workload, her very able successor Blerina Hashani, and Ian Hernon, himself an accomplished author, for advice on a range of areas which as a novice were greatly appreciated.

I am also grateful to those among my friends, colleagues and family who never ceased to badger me to speed up the process of completing the book in a reasonable time schedule. Both my daughter and my son thought they could have written a better book – with hindsight perhaps I should have let them try!

As I have mentioned in another page, my debt of gratitude extends to my researchers and assistants over the years, Paul Williamson, Tim Payton and Philip French, for their hard work and expertise, without which I would never have been able to attempt to bring together some of their endeavours in a book form.

Finally, whenever I needed to have my memory jogged for relevant dates, the House of Lords Library Research Department came up trumps. Without naming names, they all showed diligence and professionalism that I am sure the Bodleian Library would find it hard to match.

CONTENTS

CONTENTS

INTRODUCTION

BY IAN HERNON

Tom Pendry remains a colourful figure in a parliamentary estate dominated by the grey and the drab. His refreshingly clubbable presence makes a welcome change from policy wonks of all parties, but his fondness for fun is underpinned by a genuine socialist commitment to making life fun for the majority, not just the privileged few. And underpinning that is a passionate commitment to sport that has marked most stages of an eventful life.

Among political memoirs, this book is unique in its sheer span, covering the full spectacle of post-war Labour politics, in government and out of power, veering from glittering promise to abject disappointment and, he hopes, back again. He has been a Far East Air Force boxing champion, a bruiser, a national service intelligence recruit in Hong Kong and a heavyweight politician whose career as young activist, agent, parliamentary candidate, MP, whip, minister, shadow Sports Minister, privy counsellor and peer has spanned sixty years. His memoirs throw new light on successive governments and great, epoch-making events, and are a mixture of light and shade, irreverent wit and deeply serious intent.

From his success as the first promotion of the 1970 intake, Tom's Westminster career proved a rollercoaster as others leap-frogged him into the wrong jobs due to the tightness of Labour's majority from 1974 to 1979. During much of that time he was a senior whip, helping to sustain successive governments. His grasp of parliamentary procedure and eye for detail was renowned, but generally he shunned the boring and mundane.

For the political anorak, all the great post-war figures have walk-on parts in this book: Nye Bevan, Clem Attlee, Bessie Braddock, Philip Noel-Baker ... through to more contemporary characters such as John Prescott, John Smith, Jack Cunningham, Roy Mason, Denis Howell and Dennis Skinner. For the less politically obsessed reader, there are broadcasters/writers Peter Jay, Dennis Potter and Brian Walden, artists L. S. Lowry and Harry Rutherford, and many from the world of sport, including Seb Coe, Tessa Sanderson and Lennox Lewis, and boxing promoters Frank Warren and Frank Maloney (the latter having undergone a sex change in 2015). Not forgetting such one-off characters as Father Patrick McGovern, a pugnacious Hong Kong Jesuit, and Sister St James, a ferocious Labour-supporting nun.

His achievements are lasting and include: introducing a key piece of legislation giving much-needed support to youngsters caring for elderly and infirm loved ones; as shadow minister of sport, opposing the creation of a 24-hour news service, which led to the successful fight to keep sport on Radio 5; playing a major part in the UK's anti-apartheid campaign on the international sporting stage ahead of the release of Nelson Mandela; serving in Northern Ireland at a pivotal period of the peace process. And, perhaps his lasting legacy, putting sports high on the agenda ahead of Labour's 1997 election landslide. As he points out:

'Britain is a sporting nation – there are few, if any other, countries in which so many people participate, watch and debate so many sports so often – and Labour is the party of sport.' That provided much of the impetus that made the London 2012 Olympics and Paralympics such a resounding success.

In the process, he helped kick-start the careers of Tony Blair, Roy Hattersley, Jonathan Powell and, bizarrely, cinema and country and western legend Kris Kristofferson. He is less proud of his involvement in the career of James Purnell. And his greatest disappointment, which still rankles, came when Blair failed to give him the Sports Minister job he coveted and that most leading sports commentators reckoned should have been a shoe-in.

Tom's memoirs are packed with characters and incidents. Some are dark. He took up the constituency case of a local GP complaining of cuts in drugs funding – Harold Shipman, Britain's most prolific serial murderer. And he arranged the helicopter search for Moors murderer Ian Brady's missing victim. In both cases, his correspondence with serial killers makes fascinating reading. He also played a major part in the extradition of runaway Hong Kong police chief Peter Godber, who had absconded with what today would be millions of pounds.

Then there are more light-hearted, some would say bizarre, incidents described with characteristic gusto. Such as when he dislocated his shoulder showing Muhammad Ali how to punch at a Savoy meal, almost hitting the World Heavyweight Champion's wife in the process. Or his foreign travel, where glittering diplomatic occasions were disrupted by the effects of food poisoning. Or when he was asked to write an alternative to then-Poet Laureate Sir John Betjeman's poem to celebrate a royal wedding.

And then there are the stories from Tom's earlier years, during which the first Nazi parachutist to land in Britain during World War Two was captured in a shed in his Ramsgate back garden. He and his siblings were evacuated during the Luftwaffe's blitz on the Channel ports and it was mixing with Geordies in his wartime home in the north-east that turned him into a lifelong socialist – memories of the Jarrow hunger march were still vivid. He became a Labour activist while he was underage – forcing a party rule change. And he saw his promising football career stymied by a knife stuck in the turf.

During an astonishing lifetime – which isn't over yet – Tom has mixed with Prime Ministers and Presidents, sporting legends and crooks, civil rights leaders and trade union barons, TV stars and artists, pub brawlers and writers. But, throughout his humanity, his sense of fun and his sincerity has shone through.

Ian Hernon
Deputy editor of *Tribune*
Spring 2016

CHAPTER 1

THE FORMATIVE YEARS

CHILDHOOD

I was born in St Peters, Broadstairs, in 1934, on the very same street as the former Prime Minister Ted Heath. My family – parents, five boys and one girl – moved along the coast to Ramsgate when I was a small child. It was a very dramatic time for that town. The Battle of Britain raged above our heads and, according to the local library record of that time, the war's very first German bombing took place over Ramsgate. Prior to that first aerial bombardment, however, the Pendry family witnessed warfare in our back garden in May 1940.

On hearing the air-raid warning for the first time, we scuttled to our newly built Anderson shelter in the garden – not for a moment realising that we were within hours of becoming part of the war's history. As we waited for the 'all clear' siren, we were conscious that there was a great deal of noise and activity outside. Once the siren had signalled the end of the blitz, we emerged from the shelter to see a flurry of activity among the police, air-raid wardens and Home Guards. Clearly something significant had happened while we had been in our shelter. We then discovered that a German airman had landed in the cornfield next to our house after his plane had been shot down. He had sought shelter in a shed at the back of our garden before being apprehended. Many years later I discovered that the airman was from a Luftwaffe reconnaissance aircraft sent over to see the lay of the land before the much heavier bombing that was to follow a month or two later.

My father, Leonard, was a navy man in the First World War and took part in the Battle of Jutland, known at the time as the Battle of Horns Reef, a ferocious duel of naval juggernauts in which the British lost more ships than the Germans but succeeded in bottling up the German fleet. My family has always treasured a letter he sent home, which was published in *The Times*, dated 13 June 1916, signed simply 'a seaman'. It reads:

At last I have a chance to write a few lines just to let you know that I came out of last Wednesday's memorable and glorious set-to. No mistake, I've got what I joined for, and more besides. Of course, being a light cruiser, I don't suppose you will have heard much about our little squadron, but we were there – right there – and the Germans knew it, too. The same time, it's a wonder we are here, for the enemy's battle cruisers are not exactly what we were designed for, but it points at the desperation to get at the enemy at all costs, which is the motive of all our lads in action. Everything worked admirably aboard. Cool and calm was everyone. We are to be considered one of the luckiest ships in the Navy after this, as shells of all calibre were bursting all around us. We were close handy when the ————— blew up. It was worded round that it was one of our ships, which redoubled the energy of the lads. It is said we have the blame of a Hun battle cruiser, and furthermore one of those beloved creatures (the Zepp). Of course, the truth will come out eventually, and we shall hear who really killed Cock Robin. Up to now it is the little Yarmouth with her 6 in. aboard her. Anyway, the papers are gradually revealing all. I received letter and cigarettes, which came in very handy … The news of your shift to new quarters comes like another victory. You could not have done better – splendid, in fact. You had best name it Jutland Villa, in commemoration of the conflict and our safe return. Well, I must say goodbye, as this leaves me in the pink of condition. I don't think there will be another naval battle this year.

Talk about British grit and understatement!

I well remember queuing up for our gas masks at St Luke's Parish Church Hall in Ramsgate. My very first recollection of that event was being extremely jealous that my younger brother Brian, who was eighteen months younger than myself, was deemed to be qualified for a gas mask in the shape of Mickey Mouse. As I had just turned five, I was considered too grown up for such a mask and therefore received a mature one like the rest of my family. That did not seem fair to me.

I was too young to really appreciate it at the time, but our family – like all our neighbours – were facing real dangers as Hitler's Luftwaffe prepared to 'soften up' our corner of Britain ahead of his planned invasion.

Our evacuation from what was fast becoming the front line was for me a very distressing event. I was with my three brothers, Eric, Terry and Brian, and my sister Elizabeth. My eldest brother Jack was already in the Eighth Army. I can remember when we were assembled with the entire school of St Augustine's Junior, waiting to be given the details of our removal from our homes. With our newly acquired gas masks strapped to our shoulders, we were lined up before our headmistress Sister Patricia. I vividly recall a mountain of chocolates in front of her, which were to be given to us evacuees, and my ever-greedy eyes were focused on a solitary red bar of chocolate. I prayed that I would be rewarded with it when my turn came in the queue. When it did, however, my avariciousness was met with disappointment when I discovered that all the other chocolate bars were milk. I had picked the solitary plain chocolate bar. I find it strange now how in all the tension surrounding us youngsters I thought this to be the most bitter experience on that day.

With limited knowledge of where we were heading, the school proceeded to Ramsgate railway station where we learnt that we were bound on a train to London en route to Stafford in the East Midlands. Also on board were many survivors from the Dunkirk evacuation who had been ferried to Ramsgate harbour that very day. Many of the soldiers were in terrible shape, a lot of them on stretchers laid out on the forecourt of the station. Even at my tender age, I remember witnessing two different kinds of women. The first set comprised of those from the Salvation Army, who were tenderly comforting the soldiers with tea and biscuits. The second group were only interested in acquiring souvenirs, badges, helmets and other memorabilia from soldiers who had just witnessed and barely survived one of the worst battles in wartime history. That contrast has stayed in my memory ever since and even to this day I contribute to the collection boxes of Salvation Army men and women when observed in pubs selling their paper the *War Cry*.

Overall, the 'little ships' made 4,200 trips from Ramsgate, the chief evacuation port, to rescue men from the Dunkirk beaches. Fifty years later, on 24 May 1990, around eighty of them gathered at Ramsgate and Dover to repeat the historic cross-Channel journeys. But, in 1949,

42,783 soldiers were transported from Ramsgate railway station, carried by eighty-two southern rail special trains.

To be honest, the feelings I had at the railway station observing the wounded soldiers and the souvenir hunters, bad as they were, did not compete with the tears of having to leave my mum. I was truly the cry-baby of our family and when boarding that train even my younger brother Brian seemed to be braver than I was. Although upset, it didn't taint my recollection of a truly memorable trip to London. As the train slowly crawled through every station along the way, masses of people would throng the banks in great numbers to applaud these brave soldiers. I remember at some stage we probably thought it was for us! The soldiers were showered with fruits from the 'Garden of England' – apples, pears, cherries – and sandwiches. Luckily for us, the soldiers shared them with us evacuees.

Arriving via London at Stafford, the Pendry siblings were separated for the first time. My sister was billeted in one place, young Brian in another, Terry in yet another, and I had the misfortune to be with Eric, who, with the absence of Jack, was 'acting head brother'. As it turned out, I was too difficult for him to handle and he soon handed me over to my sister. She wasn't too well-pleased either, having been stuck in a family with youngsters of her age group, but she was certainly more understanding of my homesickness than Eric.

My anxiety vanished when our mother was able to leave Ramsgate and come to Stafford once my father had been posted to work in Cornwall under the Essential Works Order – he was a skilled coach builder who had left for the sea before he finished his apprenticeship. I vividly remember waiting at Stafford railway station and the moment I saw a familiar-coloured dress coming down the steps and my mother at last emerging in full view. I shed more tears, but this time they were tears of joy. Since our departure, my mother had been desperately trying to ensure that we could all live together under one roof. Fortunately, one of her brothers in the county of Durham managed to get a house that we could all stay in, at Swalwell near Blaydon-on-Tyne. Finally, we were a family once more, and the next few years were happy ones spent growing up together.

Despite this, however, we were also struck with sadness and tragedy when I was eleven years old. My youngest brother Brian, a year younger than me, jumped off the school bus before it had stopped – he fell backwards and was killed. I was on that bus with my other brother Terry and it was the most heart-breaking thing that one could ever experience. Brian was by far the brightest member of the family. My mother was devastated when I ran from the bus to tell her that Brian had had an accident, not realising then how bad it would turn out to be.

THE 1945 GENERAL ELECTION

Throughout my time in Durham I was overwhelmed by the generosity of Geordies. I still believe that they are the most big-hearted and caring of people and our family owe a great deal to them. I discovered that they were prepared to share their last slice of bread with us evacuees. I also had the good fortune to hear from them stories of their experiences working in the coalmines. I would sit at the feet of many learning all about socialism and the problems that they had experienced from 'the wicked colliery owners' and equally wicked Tory governments, none of which in their view respected them as the valuable workers and people they were. They couldn't wait for a government that would be more sympathetic to the work that they did. Their teachings influenced my decision to become a socialist, and my political journey really began here, at the tender age of eleven, with the 1945 general election.

During that election, I went backwards and forwards on my bike with my rosette, then green and white (strangely, the Tories were red then), between the committee room and the polling station. I felt compelled to help and generally felt that I was making a real contribution to a Labour victory. Before the results were announced, we, as a family, had returned to Ramsgate. The results were delayed to accommodate postal ballots from armed forces members scattered around the world, and when they were finally declared, I was staying with my Uncle Tom, whom I was named after, at the Chislet Colliery Miners Welfare Club near Canterbury, which he managed. The atmosphere was electric as the *Daily Herald*, with the glowing headline 'LABOUR IN POWER', passed from person to person. I really felt I had done my bit in the Blaydon constituency, which Labour had won by a majority of 18,089. I was allowed to stay up late to celebrate the victory – with soft drinks, I promise!

The general election held on 5 July 1945 was exciting even for an eleven-year-old. We had all sensed there was something massive happening, that there was a change in the air.

It was a landslide 145-seat victory for Clement Attlee's Labour Party over Winston Churchill's Conservatives, who were deeply shocked given the heroic status of their leader. That margin reflected the voters' belief that the Labour Party were better able to rebuild the country following the war than they. During the war, Labour had played a full part in the defence of the realm and the defeat of Nazism under men such as Attlee, Herbert Morrison and Ernest Bevin at the Ministry of Labour. Labour promised jobs for all, decent housing, a National

Health Service and a cradle-to-grave welfare state. The report was a bestseller and Labour eagerly adopted it. Churchill also blundered badly when he accused Attlee of seeking to behave as a dictator, complete with his own Gestapo, in spite of Attlee's sterling service in his own War Cabinet. That did not go down well with returning veterans. Nor did the memory of the Conservative's 1930s policy of appeasement.

It was thought by many that the new breed of education officers, many hailing from the working class and educated in grammar schools, were instrumental in their classes in encouraging books from the Left Book Club (Michael Foot, J. B. Priestley, Bernard Shaw and other left-wing authors). They discussed 'what form a post-war government should take' and many have thought that the strong socialist influences found in the works of the Left Book Club had helped secure Labour's landslide win.

The subsequent assembly of the House of Commons, after what was often dubbed the 'khaki election', was spectacular, with members sporting their uniforms with a variety of ranks and medals. It was reported that when Major John Freeman, MP for Watford, seconded the King's Speech (from the government benches), it brought tears to Churchill's eyes to see a British Major wearing a Desert Rat logo in those circumstances. John went on to be a very successful MP, becoming financial secretary to the War Office, Under Secretary of State for War – leading a UK defence mission to Burma in 1947 – and parliamentary secretary to the Ministry of Supply.

In 1948, the charismatic Aneurin Bevan spearheaded the National Health Service, which was considered to be the most prized achievement of the Attlee government, but, in 1950, Hugh Gaitskell, as Chancellor of the Exchequer, proposed to impose charges in the NHS for dentures and spectacles. Harold Wilson and John Freeman supported Bevan and resigned as ministers, although Freeman was more concerned with the issue of German rearmament. Freeman was urged not to resign and offered preferment, but he refused the offer and went through with his resignation. I think, without doubt, those resignations affected the unity of the Labour Party in the eyes of many. In the subsequent general election in 1951, Labour was displaced and another Churchill government came into being. Although Freeman survived that election with the slimmest of majorities, 508, he decided not to continue in Parliament for the subsequent election, which took place in 1955. Without him as the candidate, Labour lost in Watford.

He became the assistant editor of the *New Statesman*. He also presented the unique TV programme *Face to Face*, where only the back of his head was in view, which had the effect that all the focus remained on the interviewee. It was a very hard-hitting interview technique, which made Gilbert Harding, a very aggressive interviewer himself, cry openly upon being examined by Freeman. It also led the way for future interviewers like Jeremy Paxman to employ similarly aggressive techniques. Although having a successful parliamentary and diplomatic career, as British High Commissioner in India and British ambassador in Washington, many would argue his greatest contribution and higher public profile was his subsequent media career.

BOXING AND OTHER SCHOOLBOY SPORT

By the end of the war, however, back in Ramsgate, I had discovered another form of fighting – this time in the ring. And it was all thanks to my brother Jack. For my eleventh birthday, in June 1945, he took me to the Tottenham Hotspur football ground to see Bruce Woodcock knock out Jack London in the sixth round to win the British and

Empire titles. Doncaster-born Woodcock had begun his career in 1942, winning all of his first twenty bouts, all by stoppage. This set him up for his first title bout at White Hart Lane. Woodcock was about two stones lighter than London, but was more nimble and was able to evade many of London's attacks, building up an early points lead. London started to come back at him with body punches, but in the sixth round Woodcock caught him with a left hook to put him down. He got up but was put down twice more, finally being counted out. Many years later I discovered that Bruce Woodcock was, when he won that title, living and working in my future constituency of Stalybridge and Hyde, in the town of Dukinfield.

Recognising my enjoyment of this event, my brother said that if I joined Ramsgate Boxing Club he would buy all the gear for me – the shorts, the boots, the vest – the lot. Inspired by the fight I had just witnessed, I jumped at that opportunity and proceeded to box as a schoolboy in the 'mosquito' weight division (Juniors had odd weights named after insects and animals). The training I had was great, and I also had the opportunity to be taught at school by a Benedictine priest who had won a public school boxing trophy when he attended Dulwich College many years prior. However, if I were to become a Bruce Woodcock, then I would, of course, have to put on a few pounds and carry a heavier punch.

Many years later I explained my love of school boxing and its benefits to youngsters during a House of Lords debate, in which some peers claimed it was harmful. I said:

I wish to illustrate the beneficial side of competitive sport, particularly boxing at school and amateur levels. Certainly at these levels, boxing is not harmful, yet some of my so-called friends, knowing that I started my boxing at school, think that it did do some damage to me, as I finished up a Member of Parliament and a Peer of the Realm.

At this point my friend Lord Hoyle cheekily intervened: 'We have thought that for years!'

Not deterred by that intervention, I continued:

Boxing in schools promotes skill development and a structured pathway leading to competition and coaching. Some who contend that boxing is a dangerous and inappropriate sport for youths are, in my view, so misinformed. Boxing is not only about fisticuffs and strength but is a sport based principally on skill, structure, rules and discipline. It is also a sport that appeals to both boys and girls, and is less dangerous than many sports as defined by Sport England. Intersport boxing competitions have taken place in various schools near where I was an MP, in Manchester, but also in London, the south-west and other areas of the country. I argue that in those schools, competitive boxing increases fitness levels and promotes a healthy lifestyle. Many teachers have witnessed increased motivation in disengaged students, improvements in self-confidence and self-esteem, greater enthusiasm and positive behaviour. Boxing teaches both girls and boys about the value of respect, sportsmanship and self-worth.

In that 2014 debate I also responded to the then Sports Minister, asking:

What planet is Helen Grant on when she advocates young girls to take up more feminine sports like cheerleading, ballet and roller-skating to make them look 'absolutely radiant'? Tell that to Nicola Adams, the boxing gold medallist, or Gemma Gibbons, the silver medallist in judo, or indeed our speakers today: the noble Baronesses Lady Heyhoe Flint, Lady Massey and Lady Grey-Thompson, the greatest Olympian of them all. They are all feminine and all radiant and exceptional sportswomen.

My other schoolboy sporting passion was the 'beautiful game', football, which ran in our family history. Schoolboys and girls the world over who are football fans have heroes, and I am no exception. As an evacuee in Durham I was made aware of certain uncles and cousins on my mother's side who were sporting heroes from that time. One was an 'uncle' and a former England international footballer who played for Blackburn Rovers when they last won the FA Cup in 1928. His name was Austen Fenwick Campbell – the poshest name of any football player surely before or since – although in fact his fans knew him as 'Aussie' Campbell. I also had a cousin who played for Charlton Athletic, Queens Park Rangers and then Southampton, called Joe Mallett. At school I happily swapped cigarette cards with their faces on them and it wasn't until a few years after that bragging of mine that I was informed by doubting friends that in the north-east it was well known that 'uncles' and 'cousins' did not always mean real blood relatives, but rather family friends. I have yet to discover whether I was given false information – I doubt my family were out to deceive me. Nonetheless, I still have those cigarette cards to this day.

Another footballer, certainly not a 'relative' but who did become my hero at that early age after seeing him play at St James's Park was the famous Newcastle United centre forward Albert Stubbins – a tall, ginger-haired, goal-scoring giant of a man. In 1947, he was transferred to Liverpool for what was at the time the second-highest transfer fee of £13,000 and as such my allegiance went with him to Anfield. He played for England when the great Tommy Lawton was unavailable. Years later I was on the top table at a Football League dinner with Bobby Robson, the great former England manager and a Newcastle supporter in his schooldays, and there we discovered that we both had in Albert the same childhood hero. We were then overheard by the *Times* sports editor, Tom Clarke, and others around us, who proclaimed that they too were Stubbins fans. Tom Clarke thought that this was too good a coincidence to ignore – our common appreciation for this great footballer – and asked if I would organise a luncheon for Albert in his honour at the House of Commons, with his newspaper paying his fares and hotel expenses. This I readily agreed to and proceeded to arrange.

It was a splendid event, with the toast to Albert proposed by Ronald Allison, director of corporate affairs at Thames Television. Geoffrey Green, football correspondent of *The Times*, wrote of his precious memories of seeing our guest of honour wearing the magpie shirt of Newcastle United half a century before. He went on:

Those were the days of wartime football but rich in individuals. It was pure theatre to see 'Wor Jackie' Milburn breeze down the right wing – his position then – and watch Albert Stubbins at centre forward hammer in the nail from the cross. Their relationship was instinctive. They echoed the combination of Hulme and Drake of Arsenal in the 1930s. At one stage Albert scored 250 goals for Newcastle in 228 appearances; in 1940/41 he scored hat-tricks in four successive matches; he played for England in wartime internationals and eventually in 1946/47 the north-east said farewell to Albert's copper head as Liverpool procured him. At once they won the League.

I still proudly possess the commemorative menu for that event. On it is scrawled: 'Tom – What can I say? Thank you again for everything – Albert Stubbins.' Other messages on it included: 'Tom – What a truly magnificent football occasion – thank you for the idea. No wonder you are an MP – Bobby Robson.'

The first time I actually met my hero was when I was asked to collect him from his hotel off the Edgware Road and take him to a BBC studio where Jeremy Paxman interviewed us both and screened some of the great goals Albert had scored over the years. We then went back to the Commons for this very special occasion. Greeting Albert were shoals of letters congratulating him, including a telegram from The Beatles, who were big fans of Albert and also Liverpool supporters. Indeed, they were such fans that Albert appeared on the sleeve cover of their album *Sgt Pepper's Lonely Hearts Club Band*.

Going back to my youth, my own footballing career was cut short after being considered a pretty useful player. At St Augustine's, Ramsgate, I had scored six goals for my school in one game that we won 11–0 against a Margate school, with me playing inside right. I stayed in that position as a Kent schoolboy player. Later, as a teenager, I sustained an injury that stopped me in my tracks and which was the result of a sheath knife thrown into the ground by one of our players after finishing practising at dusk. He was just showing off, not intending harm, but unfortunately my right football boot was off at the time. The blade knife went into my right instep and has affected circulation in that leg ever since. Certainly, it was instrumental in me not pursuing football at a higher level and also not to a standard necessary for inclusion in an RAF side when I did my national service alongside many budding internationals. I knew I couldn't compete with them between the age of eighteen and twenty-one. However, that was in the future, and on the day in question, I was carted off to Ramsgate hospital, just about conscious enough to recognise that I was on a newspaper boy's bicycle, slumped in the basket on the front. The young doctor, who I would have thought had barely qualified, was less than sympathetic – obviously believing I had been involved in some knife warfare. The person that threw the knife became a very good footballer on the books of Fulham FC, but I confess I didn't follow his career. However, years later I spoke to another former teammate and told him that I would like to find the boy who threw the knife so I could ring his neck – only to be told that it would be impossible as he had died the previous week.

My uncle Tom was an effective boxer in his day who was spotted as a youngster by a boxing scout. At the time, the scout pleaded with Tom's mother, my grandmother, for him to go into serious training as he was convinced that young Tom would make it big in the sport and be a potential champion. My uncle loved boxing and longed to take it up seriously but he ran up against his mother. She adamantly believed that 'no son of mine is going to earn a living being knocked around in a boxing ring', and when she said 'no' that was it. Had my grandmother lived, she would have no doubt attempted to say the same to me. However, she would have encountered strong opposition from her daughter, my mother, who encouraged both my eldest brother Jack, who became a handy boxer in the British Army during the Second World War, and me to take up the noble art!

In the First World War, Uncle Tom had joined the Durham Light

Infantry and fought in Gallipoli in 1915 and the Dardanelles. I have a photograph of him at a camp in Gallipoli with a rifle in his hand. He told his family how on Christmas Day in 1914 he heard his German opponents singing 'Silent Night' from their trenches. He also remembered how after that rendering the German troops started walking towards his trench with a small Christmas tree glowing with some lights. They also wrote a message that said 'Merry Christmas – we will not shoot if you do not shoot'. My uncle and other British soldiers climbed out of their trenches and met the Germans in no-man's land. They all shook hands, lit each other's cigarettes and sang carols before playing football – kicking empty Bully Beef cans and using their helmets as goal posts. He added that none seemed to want war.

Being my favourite uncle, I am sure that when the 1945 election results were announced, Uncle Tom was happy on two fronts. First, it meant that Labour was in power. Second, it meant rubbing Winston Churchill's nose in the mud. He hated Churchill. In the Dardanelles, many of his comrades were gunned down and slaughtered by the waiting Turks as they got off their landing craft. Uncle Tom felt that Churchill deployed those troops as a tactic to keep the Turks active while the Prime Minister tried to invade another part of the occupied territory. He felt that he'd sacrificed our soldiers for his gain.

Another reason why he could never forgive Churchill was because he turned guns on the miners on the outskirts of London. The miners had marched from Northumberland and Durham to protest against poor wages that left their children starving and in bad health. To their minds, the miners were underpaid so that the mine owners could become richer still. Although Churchill's guns did not fire at the miners, the threat was nevertheless present. Uncle Tom had to turn back, convinced that if he and his comrades had not done so, Churchill would have ordered the police and troops to turn on the helpless protesters. So my Uncle Tom was ecstatic when he saw those banner headlines in the *Daily Herald* the morning the 1945 election victory was declared.

It was those memories of my uncle, coupled with my own experiences when evacuated to the north-east and hearing similar tales from the Durham miners, that turned my thoughts to becoming active in the Labour movement. I was sad to hear of my uncle's death in January 1970 – five months before I became a Labour MP. I knew he would have been proud to know that I had achieved the ambition that he had helped to foster.

My academic school career was disrupted by the evacuations of myself and my siblings, and by the death of our young Brian, and for that reason I missed out on the 11-plus. It was a pretty dismal time for academic achievements, but I concentrated on my sporting passions and, increasingly, my commitment to the Labour Party.

At school I devoted much of my time to spelling out the success of the Attlee government in classroom debates. My interest in politics was very much alive at that time, thanks to my mother who had been a member of the Labour Party since its birth. She encouraged me to join it at the age of fifteen and soon after I was elected chairman of the Isle of Thanet Labour League of Youth. I should not have been allowed to join at that time as the age threshold limit was sixteen. Believing passionately that it should be lower, I went to the Labour League of Youth conference at the Filey holiday camp (Butlin's) armed with a resolution I initiated from my branch that it should be reduced to fifteen. On arriving at the camp, I took fright and went to a certain Alf Morris, later to become an MP for Manchester Wythenshawe and a Lord who famously authored the Chronically Sick and Disabled Persons Act 1970. He was then a student at St Catherine's, Oxford. I went to him, shaking with fright, and admitted that I was only fifteen and shouldn't be there. Alf responded: 'I wanted to join the Labour Party when I was fifteen, but wasn't allowed to do so. So I will be calling on you with your motion tomorrow – but keep your age to yourself.' The next day it was moved and duly passed and happily the age limit has been fifteen ever since. So, in a way, at a young age I made a little bit of Labour Party history – albeit illicitly.

In the same year, 1950, the Labour Party annual conference took place in Margate, the first since Labour had won a second general election that February with a small majority. My mother was one of the voluntary stewards and she introduced me to the much-loved and rotund Bessie Braddock, the MP for Liverpool Exchange. Nicknamed 'Battling Bessie', throughout her long political career, she and her husband Jack dominated Liverpool politics in the 1950s and '60s. At her funeral in 1970, Harold Wilson said: 'She was born to fight for the people of the docks, of the slums, of the factories and in every part of the city where people needed help.' People still quote her famous exchange with Winston Churchill:

Braddock: 'Winston, you are drunk, and what's more you are disgustingly drunk.'

Churchill: 'Bessie, my dear, you are ugly, and what's more, you are disgustingly ugly. But tomorrow I shall be sober and you will still be disgustingly ugly.'

Not very gallant of Churchill, especially against a very fine woman.

My mother introduced me to her as someone who was intent on being a Labour agent. In those days, agents were paid quite well, especially in the Isle of Thanet where they had a very successful lottery. Bessie Braddock gave one piece of advice that shaped the rest of my life. She said to my mother, 'A young bright boy like your son should raise his sights. Forget being an agent. He should become an MP like me.' I remember thinking, 'God, if Bessie Braddock thinks I should be an MP...' It stuck with me from then on. That was to be my ambition. I was all geared to become an MP and everything I did after that was aimed in that direction.

The year 1950 was a difficult time for Labour. We had won only a tiny majority earlier that year, and in April the death of Ernest Bevin saw the fracturing of party unity. A few days later Aneurin Bevan resigned from the Cabinet together with John Freeman and Harold Wilson. But Clem Attlee told us at the Margate conference: 'We have accepted the responsibility of carrying on government under difficult conditions. There can be no question of a coalition in peacetime.' More recent events have proved him right.

The next Labour Party conference that I attended after Margate was at Scarborough in 1951 – a short three-day conference as the next general election was upon us. Attlee called it for 25 October 1951; as he only had a meagre majority of five, he gambled on an election in the hope of ensuring a victory and a more stable government. No doubt part of the gamble was that the Tory opinion poll lead was narrowing at a fast rate and after a three-week campaign, it would hopefully be reversed.

We sped away to the hustings with the words of William Blake ringing in our ears: 'I will not cease from mental fight, / Nor shall my sword sleep in my hand / Till we have built Jerusalem / In England's green and pleasant land.' Buoyed by those sentiments expressed by Attlee, we thought we were heading for another Labour victory. Alas, it was not to be, although Labour polled more votes than the Tories. Fourteen million votes were cast for Labour in that election, a record number in any election to that date, but Labour lost due to the configuration of the boundaries. We had to face up to a succession of Conservative governments, with Churchill followed by Sir Anthony Eden, Harold Macmillan and Sir Alec Douglas-Home before we had success with Harold Wilson's first government in 1964.

Nevertheless, I remained enthused and determined to be an MP one day – so much so that I left school at sixteen, instead of eighteen, believing that the best way to get into Parliament was through the trade union route. I decided to become an electrical engineer and I was apprenticed with a firm based at Westminster called Barlow & Young. My family were more inclined, to ask others in my family to mend a fuse (in jest I hope), rather than calling on me, such was their faith in my electrical engineering prowess. Notwithstanding that, with my membership to the Electrical Trade Union, I became active in both the union and Labour Party, and indeed I made union history by becoming a shop steward on my twenty-first birthday. At that time one could not be a steward at that age until one became a member in the skilled section, so on the same day I obtained my 'skilled ticket'.

After my apprenticeship, I was conscripted into the Royal Air Force for my national service, and I was destined to train extensively in what was known as 'signals intelligence'. I did so not far from Birmingham and upon completion there were only two places I could be sent – either Germany or Hong Kong. I didn't want to go to either, largely because at the time I was courting the local Ramsgate beauty queen and didn't want to leave her, knowing that the competition to woo her would be strong if I left. I was determined to find a way out. With China being a communist country, I devised a wicked plan and got some of my friends to send me the *Daily Worker*, the communist newspaper, thinking, 'That will certainly get me out of a signal intelligence unit on the Hong Kong border.' However, they had obviously seen this kind of trick from others before, as they ignored my ham-fisted attempt to dodge my relocation to Hong Kong and I travelled there in 1956.

One day, on the parade ground in Hong Kong, the physical education officer barked out, 'Are there any boxers present?' Immediately I realised how important sport was in all the forces, and that this was the best way to have a good time away from the hard chores endured by the average recruit. Having boxed at school and for Ramsgate Boxing Club, I put my hand up, and it was probably the most useful thing I did in the RAF. I was in a tracksuit from then on and soon won a Technical Training Championship. Evidently, the decision to take up boxing was a godsend. The military were sports-crazy and there was intense competition between the different armed forces. There was even fierce competition within the commands in the RAF itself. It was very fortuitous for me when it was discovered that I could box. I was treated very well, to the displeasure of my many colleagues. I was allowed to have steak and milk and dine in the NAAFI – not in the canteen with the rest of the boys. Boxing did me no harm whatsoever, although some of my so-called friends may argue that it did do some damage in my case. The RAF was so keen in those days to beat the army, the navy and, later, the American Navy and Australian Air Force boxers stationed in Hong Kong and surrounding areas. I ended up having a whale of a time; eventually winning not only a Far East Air Force Boxing title in Kuala Lumpur, but also becoming the Colonial Middleweight Champion of Hong Kong. Although I didn't forget my lovely Ramsgate beauty queen, I occupied my time with many other activities. So I found it surprising that she was still around when I returned eighteen months later – though that relationship wasn't to last. Years later I went to her wedding and she came to mine and we have remained good friends ever since.

Hong Kong in the 1950s was a fascinating place for a young man, even if I was mainly interested in boxing and other sports.

The Japanese occupation had left many scars, while the civil war in mainland China saw a large influx of refugees from the mainland, which the government struggled to accommodate. The fear of a Chinese communist invasion was ever-present. The British garrison was reinforced and plans of emergency evacuation to Australia were made.

However, Hong Kong remained a British colony.

I experienced the uprising in Hong Kong in 1956, which began with a small incident – the tearing down of some Nationalist flags. Tensions erupted into massive looting and destruction to property. Fifty-nine people were killed with 500 more seriously injured. In the aftermath, four people were convicted and given the death penalty.

My RAF Camp, Little Sai Wan, was situated at the bottom of a steep hill in the suburb of Shau Kei Wan. On the first night of the riots, all the lights were put out. We were well-armed, fearing the worst. We stared up into the pitch-black town above us and took turns on watch. Luckily, after a week or so, the problem ended. The 1956 riots went some way to awaken the Hong Kong government to the dangers of low wages, long working hours and over-crowded conditions.

As part of my national service, I took a part-time course on Moral Philosophy at Hong Kong University. It was there that a notice caught my eye offering an opportunity to study at Oxbridge as a mature student. I enquired to find out if I qualified as I was only temporarily in the Colony and was told that I was eligible to submit a paper for examination. I certainly did not kid myself that I would aspire to become an academic, but my purpose would be to equip myself for a seat in Parliament one day. I was lucky enough to receive the help of a Father Patrick McGovern, a Jesuit priest who managed a retreat house in Cheung Chau and who later became a legislative politician in Hong Kong. After I had completed a ten-day leadership training course at the retreat, he gave me a glowing testimonial, saying:

During the course he showed a marked interest in all the specialist subjects … and we laid considerable stress on them. He struck me as being a man who has 1) Enthusiasm for social justice, 2) Considerable knowledge of politics, ethics etc., gained from his reading, 3) The interest and initiative to have gained much from his own experience as a worker, 4) Judging from the solid work which he put in during the course, he has both the application and the brains to derive great benefit from any opportunity of further study which would be offered him. I may add that it was refreshing for me to meet someone like Mr Pendry. Sociology is my own special subject and among those who come here for retreats and leadership courses, I seldom meet anything but apathy and profound ignorance. Mr Pendry was a marked contrast to this attitude, and I am confident that with his character, application and interest, he would derive great good from further study and is capable of developing into a person who would amply repay any expense or effort spent on him.

Father McGovern was an astonishing man who fitted no stereotype of a typical Jesuit priest. I had been educated for a long period of my school life by Benedictine priests and monks, and such was the rivalry between the two orders that it wasn't until I met Father McGovern that I realised that they were on the same side, so to speak. He was born in Dublin and at the end of his secondary schooldays felt himself internally called to the priesthood and religious life. The call was not altogether welcome. He was enjoying the freedoms of early manhood to the full and had no wish to exchange them for the restraints of religiously scholastic life. After a severe struggle with his conscience, he listened to God's call and entered the Irish Jesuit novitiate in 1938. He need not have worried. He accepted the foreseen restraints and duties of Jesuit life, but, within these limits, he was to enjoy life to the full to the end of his days. He went to Hong Kong in 1947, then, instead of doing the customary period of teaching after language study, he received permission to go to North America for social studies – strong aspirations were already stirring. He was ordained priest in Ireland in 1953, and returned to Hong Kong in 1955. The following decade was devoted to school work, with a few years of pastoral work and army chaplaincy in Malaysia. His interest in social work, however, remained keen. Long after I left Hong Kong, in 1968, with the help of a group of workers, he founded the Industrial Relations Institute (IRI) to train workers 'for participation in free, strong responsible trade unionism' and to help them to recognise the dignity of their work.

He remained director of the IRI for only a few years. As soon as the workers themselves were ready to take over, he resigned the directorship. Father McGovern made minor history by arriving on a motor bicycle for his first attendance as a legislative councillor. He died suddenly after a heart attack in Wah Yan College, Hong Kong, on Sunday 30 September 1984, aged just sixty-four. One of his obituaries recalled the time I knew him:

> The happiness of a consecrated life is founded ultimately on love of God, trust in Him and zeal for His glory. There can, however, be supplementary helps. Father McGovern's supplementary help was an ability to like very deeply the people he worked with or for. He liked the young men who came to him for temporary help and remained his friends for life. He made many lasting friends in his few years in Malaysia. He liked the soldiers he met as an acting chaplain in Malaysia. He liked, quite exceptionally, the young men with whose aid he founded the Industrial Relations Institute. When he was appointed to the Legislative Council he expected to be a fish out of water, but he soon found himself in the swim; he valued the immediate and continuing friendliness of his reception and he soon came to have a high regard for the hard work done by his fellow members and their devotion to the welfare of Hong Kong.

CHAPTER 2

EARLY BEGINNINGS

OXFORD UNIVERSITY

Thanks to Father McGovern's endorsement, and my own efforts, the University of Hong Kong informed me that, if successful, Kent County Council would be notified that I had passed the Oxford test with a view to funding my studies. I duly passed and went to Oxford University after some initial difficulties with the Kent Education Committee. I eventually received a grant, which came through after I had begun my course.

In hindsight, I think I took too much notice of the purser's advice on my first day that 'swotting for exams was one thing, but Oxford was more than that'. Students that strove for a good honours degree often ignored the overall benefits of an Oxford education. After all, Oxford was very much 'town *and* gown', he said, and there was a 'life both in and out of the spiral towers'. He went on to say: 'Don't feel you have to attend every lecture, as many of your lecturers have written books which are often the basis of their lectures.' In summary, his advice was to attend lectures to sample their teaching methods, but then possibly head off for the Bodleian Library to read the books they had written before retiring with friends to a local coffee house. Indeed, I often found it could often be more fulfilling to swap ideas over coffee with like-minded friends than to attend lectures.

In my view, his advice was partially right, but I probably overdid it by pursuing rather too many extracurricular activities to the detriment of my studies. I was commercial editor of the Labour Club's magazine, the *Clarion*, for which I generated a good deal of funding. I also sat on the executive committee of the Oxford University Labour Club, which was 1,000 strong at the time, with such luminaries as Dennis Potter, Brian Walden and Austin Mitchell. Dennis later became a famous playwright and author of great renown; Brian was a successful MP before becoming a presenter of TV programmes; and Austin Mitchell became MP for Great Grimsby when Anthony Crosland died. There were many more Labourites that made their mark in the years that followed and our meetings were addressed by such top politicians as Harold Wilson, Hugh Gaitskell and Aneurin Bevan. I also attended debates in the Oxford Union where I heard speakers like Fr Joseph Christie, one of the best speakers I have ever heard. I also remember a debate that was broadcast on the radio between Peter Jay and Pierre Mendès France, president of the Council of Ministers in France between 1954 and 1955, on the question of European Unity.

One of my memorable experiences at Oxford was having the great fortune to attend a number of seminars at All Souls by Sir Isaiah Berlin, mainly discussing his philosophical work, *Two Concepts of Liberty*. This remarkable man always proceeded his seminars by opening a packet of Piccadilly Cigarettes and offering them around to the twelve or so students present. As I was in strict training and had never – and indeed to this day – smoked a cigarette, I declined. With hindsight, I wish I had accepted one to keep as a memento of those special hours spent in the company of Sir Isaiah Berlin.

I attended another fascinating debate in November 1957 on the Wolfenden Report, about whether homosexuality should be legalised. The late Anthony Howard, a former president of the Union, was given special leave from national service with orders to 'kick the ass' of the proposer. The university magazine *Isis*, in its report of the event, described the anti-legislation proposer Kenneth Baker, an undergraduate at Magdalen, as 'looking and talking like a fossilised Edwardian Home Secretary, [who] adumbrated about offences against "Nature and Almighty God". These the law must restrain.' Baker proposed sending sexual deviationist to institutions, where they would learn not to be 'social' misfits. It is amazing that one can uncover things of this kind fifty years on. It goes to show that the chickens really can come home to roost. Imagine what I could have done with Ken's maiden speech at the Oxford Union when he was not a 'fossilised Home Secretary' but a real Home Secretary in 1990. Some years later, I wrote to Kenneth enclosing a copy of the *Isis* report of his speech and he replied: 'Many thanks for your letter and for sending me the cutting from *Isis* about a 1957 Union debate. You will not be surprised to know that I have totally changed my views. On many matters I have never thought consistency was a great virtue.'

OXFORD BOXING

The most important distraction from my studies was my love of boxing and keeping as fit as possible. A trainer called Alf Gallie, on discovering I had been in the RAF boxing team and had won a Far East boxing title in Kuala Lumpur and the Colonial Middleweight title of Hong

Kong in 1957, steered me in the direction of two Oxford boxers: Keith Fitton and Bob Atkinson – both were to become captains of the team during my time there. Both Keith and Bob, students from St Paul's in London, happily welcomed me into their ranks and cheered me on at my first fight for Oxford University against Glasgow University, which I won.

The Oxford University Amateur Boxing Club (OUABC), founded in 1881 is the second-oldest active amateur boxing club in the UK, so boxing for the Dark Blues was not only a great thrill for me, but also for my eldest brother Jack, who had first introduced me to the sport.

I went on to have a number of fights for Oxford. Although not all were up to the standard I had been accustomed to in the RAF, I met many interesting boxers who were still very skilled and had great personalities. Boxing often brings out the best in young people. In my current capacity as vice-president of the Schools Amateur Boxing Association (SABA), I am determined to get more boxing into schools because of all the healthy benefits it brings in youngsters. It ensures they pursue activities that are healthier not just for them but society as a whole. One doesn't often hear of schoolboy boxers getting into anti-social activities.

One of the most interesting characters that boxed at Oxford with me became the well-known actor and musician Kris Kristofferson. He was a Rhodes Scholar from America whose family origins were in Sweden. He was a useful guitar player, singer and a very handsome lad to boot. We went to one or two jazz clubs together. On one occasion, after leaving our training ground, he asked me for some advice about a *Daily Mirror* talent contest in which, if successful, the applicant would be given an opportunity to make a record. My advice to Kris was:

'You've got a good voice and you strum a good guitar, so go for it.' He replied: 'Should I really? OK, I'll do it.' He won the competition and cut his very first record. I'm certain that he most likely doesn't want anyone to know about it, as it was probably the worst record he ever made, but it was indeed the beginning of a very successful career. I was reminded of this story while thumbing through a glossy history of the Oxford University Boxing Club. An entry read:

> We also shared with other sports the contributions of some very tough and occasionally skilled South Africans ... and the occasional American, such as the durable Kris Kristofferson, whose tough-guy image was no film fantasy in those days! Others, like Tom Pendry, have since proved as fast with words as with fists in Parliament.

To be mentioned in the same paragraph as a superstar is indeed an honour.

Kris, of course, went on to find worldwide fame as an American country music singer, songwriter, musician and film actor. He has stated that he was greatly influenced at Oxford by the poetry of William Blake, who had proclaimed that if one has a God-given creative talent then one should use it or else reap sorrow and despair. More recently he said that he would like the first three lines of Leonard Cohen's 'Bird on a Wire' on his tombstone: 'Like a bird on a wire / Like a drunk in a midnight choir / I have tried in my way to be free.'

The club had as a trainer the great Percy Lewis. He was always escorted into the ring by undergraduates with gowns and mortar-boards to boot. On 1 April 1957, the 'Oxford Milkman' as they liked to call him on account of his day job, fought Hogan 'Kid' Bassey for the Empire title at Nottingham. After fifteen rounds of intense boxing, the soft-spoken Percy lost on a much-disputed decision and objects were thrown into the ring in protest.

Of course, even for me, Oxford was not just about boxing and sport! These were exciting times for our culture, politics, literature and the arts. At the Student Union I witnessed a famous bust-up between two iconic characters who would go on to do great things in different fields. The event was a tempestuous row involving Brian Walden, the then president of the Oxford Union, who became a politician and one of the best interviewers on TV, and Dennis Potter, who would go on to be one of Britain's best playwrights. Potter, in an unpublished article for *Isis*, accused Walden of trying to influence the upcoming elections to choose his successor, claiming that Walden had rubbished front-runner Rudolf D'Mella. Potter alleged that Walden had summoned him and spread various slurs about D'Mella's age, sex life and morals. When pressed on the allegations at a turbulent session of the Student Union, Walden went berserk, claiming they were a 'gross and grave libel'. All hell broke loose, which I witnessed with some amazement. When Walden tried to assert his authority, there was uproar. There were shouts of 'Inquisition!' The Commons Chamber often gets flak about unruly behaviour, but the Oxford elite in those days could show them a thing or two. Three former presidents of the Union were to adjudicate: Jeremy Lever, Jeremy Thorpe and Jeremy Isaacs.

Potter was found guilty of journalistic malpractice, but within a few years he began to contribute to the BBC's *Wednesday Play* TV series and then produced such acclaimed works as *The Singing Detective*, *Pennies From Heaven* and the semi-autobiographical *Stand Up, Nigel Barton*, which recounted the experience of a miner's son going to Oxford University, where he finds himself torn between two worlds. I bought his first book *The Glittering Coffin*, in which he wrote that his ambition was to be a competent Labour MP. That chimed with my own!

Walden, the son of a glass-worker, became an MP before I did, being elected for a Birmingham seat in 1964 and holding it until 1977 when he resigned to work full-time as a journalist and broadcaster. He was one of the best orators I ever saw in the House. And as a TV presenter he could be equally ferocious. In 1989, when her own party was beginning to turn against her, he famously interviewed the then-Premier Margaret Thatcher:

Brian Walden: You come over as being someone who one of your backbenchers said is slightly off her trolley, authoritarian, domineering, refusing to listen to anybody else – why? Why cannot you publicly project what you have just told me is your private character?

Margaret Thatcher: Brian, if anyone's coming over as domineering in this interview, it's you.

1959 GENERAL ELECTION

With the 1959 general election looming, I stupidly believed that I had learnt enough about economics, philosophy and politics to equip myself for a parliamentary career. I now know better, with hindsight. I regrettably decided at the end of Trinity term to try my hand at securing a hopeless Labour seat and fight the general election for the experience. Still believing the advice of Bessie Braddock all those years before, I continued to harbour my ambition and began the process of becoming a MP.

At that time, I had a good friend in Laura Woodcock, the wife of George Woodcock, the brilliant General Secretary of the Trade Union

Congress. Laura had high hopes for me, just as I had high hopes of marrying her daughter Vilja, who was a student at Lady Margaret Hall. In my attempts to court Vilja, I rang her and asked if she would accompany me to my college dance. She readily agreed, but before the dance I was playing football in a team that included a fellow student and friend, a Mexican called Ricardo Villa Escarlara. After the game I went to his room and asked if he was going to the dance that evening. He told me he was too shattered from the football match and would rather stay in and write an essay he had to complete by the following day. So I left him to it and met Vilja from her bus. After a dance or two I informed her that I had to make a quick telephone call to my sister and that I wouldn't be more than a few minutes. When I returned after about ten minutes or so, Vilja was not at the side of the room where I had left her. A quick glance at the dance floor and, to my complete and utter surprise, I found her dancing with Ricardo. He didn't look too shattered to me – he was dancing like Fred Astaire. When they finished, he escorted her back to the side of the dance floor where I was waiting. I took him to one side and confronted him: 'What are you up to? That is my date.' Being the perfect gentleman, he said how sorry he was and that he had had no idea, adding: 'I didn't realise that and I won't dance or see her again.' Relenting somewhat, I recognised that there seemed to be some healthy rapport between the two of them and, not wanting to get in the way, I wished Ricardo well and left him and Vilja to carry on. I went off to do the very thing Ricardo was supposed to do – bury myself in a book. The things one does for friendship. Without planning to do so, that night I became a marriage broker and I finished up being the best man at their wedding in Esher, Surrey, some two years later. They have lived in Mexico since then and

I have visited them there. They have a lovely collection of children and seem very happy – we still exchange messages from time to time and Christmas cards every year.

Notwithstanding my bad luck, I continued being a friend of the Woodcocks. Knowing of my ambition to become an MP, Laura managed to get me shortlisted for a hopeless Labour seat, Sutton and Cheam. She sent me the local paper where my name appeared along with the other candidates. However, to my puzzlement, there was a mystery candidate with no name attached. A note said he had to remain anonymous as it might affect his career prospects. On the day of the selection conference, I travelled from Ramsgate to Sutton where the mystery candidate was revealed to be Frank Judd, an RAF flying officer whose mother had fought the seat twice before. The reason for the secrecy was that no commissioned Officer of the Crown could offer themselves for a parliamentary election before being selected, although if successful they were allowed to resign their commission and then stand for Parliament.

At the selection conference, I was one of the first candidates to speak. I felt that I was doing quite well until I was asked, 'What do you think of the Radcliffe Report on monetary policy and debt management?' I had read something about the report in question in *The Guardian* that day, the day after it was published, en route from Ramsgate to the selection conference. However, I was not completely familiar with the particulars of the report and so my answer was very much in line with how I thought an academic would answer it, by saying honestly that I didn't know the details. I added: 'If the questioner would like to ask me any particular question on monetary policy and debt management, I will only be too happy to state my view.' There was utter silence in the room. Clearly no one else understood what the report was about, including, I suspect, the questioner himself. Those in the audience, I am sure, expected a more forthright political answer from me. I later found out that George Woodcock, knowing I had read economics at Oxford, thought it would be a doddle for me to answer. Another big mistake, and when I returned to where the other candidates were assembled, I told Frank Judd that I was asked about the Radcliffe Report. The next thing I knew, Frank went in to do his bit and I heard thunderous applause. He was subsequently duly selected.

Afterwards, a triumphant Frank offered to take me to the Woodcocks' home, where I was staying in nearby Ewell, and on the journey I asked him how he responded to the question on the Radcliffe Report. He began by thanking me for giving him advanced warning on the question, and described the great applause he received for his answer. When I asked him what his actual answer was, he replied, 'What can one expect? A committee set up by a Tory government. It's hardly surprising that it came out with Tory polices, but we will alter that after the next election.' Surprised as I was at that response, I invited Frank to come in and meet George as we approached the Woodcock house. He respectfully declined, stating that he had to go back to thank his supporters who had selected him. However, I had an inkling that he didn't want to come in because on the journey I had let it slip that George was a member of the Radcliffe Report and, as it turned out, the report was more aligned with Labour, rather than Conservative policy. It basically undermined the Tory monetarist agenda, which Mrs Thatcher later resurrected so enthusiastically, and with tragic results.

As Frank is now in the House of Lords, after being an MP and a minister, I still do not hesitate to remind him of the Sutton and Cheam

selection conference, but I do decline to remind him of the answer he
gave to the Radcliffe Report question. It was to my detriment, but
certainly to his advantage. That incident reminded me of the advice of
one of my tutors: 'Pendry, answer the question you've been asked and
not the one you wished I'd asked.' However wrong the answer, speaking with conviction to a question that people in their own ignorance
do not know the answer to will invariably get the result they desired
and receive applause, as it certainly did in Frank's case.

After that humbling experience, I was approached by the Southern
Regional Organiser of the Labour Party, Ron Hayward, who eventually became General Secretary of the party, and he asked if I would
fight another impossible seat in Eastbourne as the election was almost
upon us and there would be no time for a normal selection conference. I would be shoehorned in. Thinking it would again be part of my
learning curve, I agreed only to get an urgent call the next day from the
same Ron Hayward, saying:

> Forget what I said yesterday. We have just heard that Harry Grierson,
> the local agent for your Isle of Thanet constituency, has broken his
> leg and will not be able to do the agent's job at the election. As
> you know more about the constituency than almost any other able-
> bodied person, and as we can find another person to fight Eastbourne,
> I would like you to be the agent for the Isle of Thanet.

Clearly, I could hardly refuse, and for the 1959 election I was the parliamentary agent for Labour in my home area. The candidate they chose
for Eastbourne was later to be my leader on Paddington Council, Tony
Dumont, who of course didn't get elected at Eastbourne.

In many ways, being the agent in Thanet was a wise move. During that election campaign I met the General Secretary of the National Union of Public Employees, Bryn Roberts, who was a great orator and who only lost by one vote to Aneurin Bevan in the selection for the Ebbw Vale seat before the 1945 election. We got on well and, aware of my ambition, he said: 'If your heart is not in going back to college then come and join me at NUPE. Never mind being an MP, you will be able to take my job one day.' On my first day working for NUPE I discovered that he said that to all of the officers that he wanted for his union.

Held on 8 October 1959, the election marked a third successive win for the Conservatives, now led by Harold Macmillan, who increased their overall majority to 100 seats over Labour under Hugh Gaitskell. At first, Labour enjoyed large opinion poll leads, and it looked as if we could win. It was not to be. The Tories saw an upturn in fortunes as the economy improved. They fought under the slogan 'Life is better with the Conservatives, don't let Labour ruin it.' Macmillan very effectively summed up the mood of the majority of the British public when he said that most of the people had 'never had it so good'. Labour fought a competent campaign with a manifesto entitled 'Britain belongs to you', which accused the Tories of complacency over the growing gap between the rich and poor. Gaitskell made a key mistake by promising not to raise taxes despite manifesto pledges to increase spending. Early on election night it became clear that the Conservative government had been returned with an increased majority, which was hugely disappointing for us.

So, after the election in Thanet, which the Tories won, despite my Trojan efforts with a majority of 11,898 votes, I began my journey into

Parliament via the trade union world. I did have one break and left NUPE for another union post, which, as it turned out, didn't suit either that union or me. I re-joined NUPE and had a successful ten years there before I finally secured a seat.

SEAT SELECTION – WHITEHAVEN AND HULL EAST

As a NUPE area officer, I was dispatched to the union's divisional office in Birmingham. Within a few days, the Divisional Officer Bill Griffiths informed me that Derby Borough did not have one NUPE member because the Transport and General Workers' Union and the General Municipal Workers' Union had it all sewn up. Many of their members were concerned that as the two full-time officials of those general unions were both on Derby Borough Council, they were re-garded as their employers. They were looking for an alternative and NUPE was the obvious union to represent them. A strict NUPE rule was that none of their officials could become members of a council. Bill Griffiths sent me to Derby and there I began recruiting with gusto.

I was uninhibited by any baggage and I wanted to make a mark in the union with the ultimate aim of eventually securing a sponsor-ship to enter Parliament. During my decade with NUPE in the East Midlands, I was able to organise a great number of members into the union ranks, particularly in Derby itself. From having no NUPE members in Derby when I started, I can proudly state that when I left to enter Parliament in 1970, the union had grown to the largest membership of any in the town. It was also the largest affiliated union to the Labour Party, and to the Trades Council – the very body that refused our initial membership when I first arrived because of my clash with the general unions.

During that era, I was a bit of a firebrand, particularly on international issues – given my Hong Kong experiences, that was no great surprise – and on disarmament. I was an active member of the Campaign for Nuclear Disarmament and while at Oxford I had joined the Aldermaston marches and protests in Trafalgar Square. That was when I started dealing with the late, great Philip John Noel-Baker, later Lord Noel-Baker, a giant of the Labour movement who was the Labour MP for Derby South after winning a by-election in 1936. I forged a close relationship with him in Derby. On top of our interests on the disarmament question, we were also both sportsmen, and these two subjects alone brought us together. He had been an outstanding former Olympic athlete before he was renowned as a campaigner for world disarmament. He had been British track leader and had won an Olympic silver medal at the 1920 Olympics in Antwerp. He was the only person, when we met, to have won an Olympic medal and a Nobel Prize (for peace in 1959 at the height of the Cold War).

Years later, in November 1980, he wrote:

Tom Pendry first came into my life when, as leader of the regional administration of NUPE, he settled in Derby … Derby had been my constituency for almost thirty years – I was first returned to Parliament for the County Borough on 9 July 1936. That famous by-election had been fought on the issue of Abyssinia … I had always greatly enjoyed what MPs call their 'constituency work' – trying to help with the personal problems of citizens who were in difficulties of various kinds; keeping in touch with trade unions, Co-op Societies and branches; attending meetings of the party executive and its sub-committees. In almost no time at all after Tom Pendry's arrival, I began to find the party and constituency work much easier and more enjoyable. He was such an outstanding person, so well versed in public affairs of every kind, so knowledgeable on international as [well as] national policy, that I found I was always seeking his advice, always asking him to deal with this or that electoral problem, finding my ideas altered, verified or confirmed by what he said.

He had not been born when Abyssinia had been sacrificed to Mussolini by the Tory government. But he knew all about that grim betrayal, and the catastrophic sequel – the Second World War – to which it led. Indeed, his knowledge went further back – he knew how the Tories had sabotaged the World Disarmament Conference of 1932; he knew what individual Tory ministers had been to blame for rejecting and destroying the great plan of World Disarmament by President Herbert Hoover of the United States – a plan accepted by Weimar Germany, by Russia, by Fascist Italy; a plan that would certainly have succeeded if Britain had given it support. It was natural, therefore, that Tom took a lively interest, as I did, in the United Nations and its work.

Nor was that our only common interest. Tom had boxed for Oxford University; he had a warm and vigorous concern for every kind of sport. We were both ardent followers of the Rams – that Derby County team who, under Brian Clough, were twice Champions of the First Division in those years. We were both deeply committed to the Olympic Movement; we both thought it a noble institution and a most powerful [one] in the struggle for good international understanding and enduring peace.

It was only natural that from the day we first met, Tom and I should work together on the problem of armaments. We were, in particular, deeply concerned about the ghastly danger of nuclear war. We shared Lord Mountbatten's view that the nuclear arms race 'serves no military purpose'. We were concerned that all too often the West appeared to be setting the pace in the arms race, both in the production of new weapons and in the increase in military expenditure from year to year. The proposal to deploy great numbers of Cruise and Pershing missiles in Britain and Western Europe seemed to be a big step towards what Mountbatten called 'the brink of the abyss'. We believed, and still believe, that it should be possible to negotiate a treaty on multilateral world disarmament, conventional and nuclear, in the three years before these Cruise and Pershing missiles can be deployed. This is the path of sanity. It will make Britain no longer the aircraft carrier of a hundred targets which an enemy might attack. It is the path to the salvation of the British people and of the world.

It didn't happen the way that he and I feared, thank the Lord, or in the way we had hoped then, more's the pity. Times changed, the world changed. But Noel-Baker was a great man, and a great influence on me. And vice versa, according to his kind words above. He was made a life peer in 1977, as Baron Noel-Baker of the City of Derby, and continued to be an active supporter of disarmament. He was also president of the International Council of Sport Science and Physical Education. He died at the age of ninety-two – a sad moment in my life and those of the people he represented in Derby so diligently.

One of the benefits of organising for my union in Derby was that I recruited members from within local schools – ancillary workers such as caretakers, school meal ladies and other staff. On one visit to a Catholic school, I was introduced by the headmaster to his teaching staff. Later that evening, on visiting my local club, the Knights of St Columba, I mentioned to one of the teachers I had met earlier that a charming young teacher had caught my eye in his school earlier that day. 'Ah, that will be Moira Smith,' he said, and in an effort to help me meet her again, he added: 'She is very keen on the theatre. Why don't you get tickets for the Brendan Behan play *The Hostage*, which is playing at the Nottingham Playhouse?' This I duly did and on my return to the school a day or two later to deliver membership cards to those ancillary workers I had recruited, I was once more invited into the staff room armed with my tickets for the play. However, I found out that the young teacher I had my sights on was not Moira Smith, but another young lady who I was told later became a nun. The die was cast, however, and so I invited Moira Smith to the play and some years later she became my wife.

The first thing I discovered about Moira was that she was in the Young Conservatives – albeit she told me that the reason was because there were more party goings-on there than in the local Young Socialists group. However, she did not admire the Tory policies, especially in the field of education. During our courtship, at her request, I took her to a local ward meeting at which two local councillors were the guest speakers. On hearing them, she whispered to me: 'Are they really running our town? I could do better myself.' This she was to prove correct at a later date.

In 1966, NUPE decided to expand its number of sponsored MPs and embarked on a process of examination for those of its members who wished to be considered. I put my name forward together with three other union members who were already in Parliament. The results were announced at the Russell Hotel in London; all three of the sitting MPs passed the examination and I took the fourth place. When, shortly afterwards, the 1966 election took place, I was without a seat to fight unlike the other three, who were duly re-elected. So I continued with my work at my union post. To my horror, after the election, the General Secretary, Sydney Hill, asked if I wished to put my name forward again for the examination for the one remaining place. I had naturally thought that I should have been automatically placed on the list of sponsored candidates as I had successfully passed their test only months before. I thought it unreasonable for me to go through the examination process a second time and was so angry that I told him that I did not wish to be considered for a re-run. Therefore, it was with some delight that I received another letter from the General Secretary stating that his executive committee saw the logic of my position and placed me back on the sponsored list. As I was the only one now on that list, I had great hopes that I might find a winnable seat for the next general election.

Although I was extremely happy to be a union official conducting what I thought was quite valuable work for its members, I felt that by then I had earned my corn. I also became chairman of the Derby Labour Party and helped steer my wife to win a seat on Derby Council, which Labour had never held. At the tender age of twenty-six, Moira Pendry became the youngest alderman ever in the country, yet ironically Labour lost control after those many years of dominance. Happily for Labour and Moira, Labour regained control in the following year and Alderman Mrs Pendry became chairman of Derby Education Committee and vice-chairman of Derbyshire Education Committee.

With such experiences behind me, I felt I had done the union proud and looked forward to the prospect of representing its members in Parliament. My union's workers were always at the bottom end of the wage scales, and I knew they deserved a better deal. I intended to fight their cause if elected. In my quest for a parliamentary seat before the 1966 contest, I attended two selection conferences. One was at Mansfield, where I was trounced by Don Concannon, who later became a ministerial colleague in Northern Ireland. The second was at Rushcliffe in Nottinghamshire, where I was narrowly beaten by Arthur Latham, who in 1970 became the MP for Paddington North. After the 1966 election, I tilted my lance at two safe Labour seats. One was at Whitehaven in Cumbria, which had a Labour majority of 8,791, and the other was at Hull East in Yorkshire, where the Labour majority was 23,072.

My chances at Whitehaven seemed promising. There was already a local man in place who was considered to be the obvious choice by most party members, but his union, the General Municipal Workers, thought otherwise. Its regional office had placed a Dr Jack Cunningham, then known as John, as the union candidate for the seat. This was to the disgruntlement of many; especially that one person who had expected to receive the nomination. On my arrival to observe the feeling among the faithful, it became clear that my prospects looked pretty good as I was greeted warmly by not only friends of my union but others, including, surprisingly, those of the GMW. The Fire Brigade Union and other unions and ward branches also supported me. Jack Cunningham, it emerged, was the son of the regional organiser, Andy Cunningham, and many of their members felt aggrieved with their regional office on his selection, believing it a clear case of nepotism.

While campaigning for the candidature at Whitehaven, I also

discovered that the Hull East MP, Harry Pursey, was to retire at the next election. I was asked by the NUPE General Secretary to put my hat in the ring there with the full support of the union and its members in that constituency. So I headed for Hull and met the NUPE union members and others in the Fire Brigade Union and the Transport and General. I found quite a lot of support, which encouraged me to further pursue the opportunity. After that visit, I returned to the East Midlands and within a day or so, when in my Nottingham office, I received a phone call from a young man who said, 'You don't know who I am – my name is John Prescott.' I interrupted him, saying, 'Of course I know who you are, you're one of those National Union of Seamen who Prime Minister Harold Wilson described as "a tightly knit group of politically motivated men who were determined to create strikes to bring down the government and paralyse the country."' He in turn interrupted me and said, 'Enough of all that, why are you attempting to stand in my seat?' I quickly corrected him and said: 'Well, as I understand it, you're not a Member of Parliament.' He quickly replied in typical Prescott fashion: 'Not yet but I've got it sewn up and you're wasting your time.' He went on to say, 'However, I think I can do a deal with you nevertheless. I hear you are in for the Whitehaven seat.' 'That's true,' I said. 'I'm looking into this one also.'

John replied:

In that case, I can do you a favour. We have a very strong sponsored union candidate in the NUS and he's got a good chance of being the candidate in Whitehaven. If you stand down from Hull, I will make sure that he stands down from Whitehaven, and he will give you his full support and that of his comrades.

I told him that I would seek the views of my supporters in Hull. To that end, I visited Hull to meet members of NUPE, the Fire Brigade Union and others to explain the situation following my conversation with John. The general response was that Prescott had a following, especially among the younger members, having been a student himself at Hull University. However, there were also those who took the same view of the Prime Minister, that John was a bit of a tearaway and would not necessarily get a great deal of support from the older members. The leader of my supporters summed up the overall view for me: 'If it is in the best interest of the union that you go for Whitehaven, where you might have a better chance, then we will certainly understand and wish you well.' The rest is history. John went on to become the candidate and won the seat in the June 1970 general election with a very large majority of 22,123. In Tony Blair's government he rose to be deputy premier, running massive ministries and becoming a very effective politician. I had the pleasure of being his deputy as shadow Minister for Regional Affairs and Devolution from 1982 to 1984 and found him the hardest-working MP that I have ever encountered. I was only too happy to take some of the physical strain off him.

With Hull East out of the picture, I turned my sights back on Whitehaven. Even though it was a very long four-hour commute from Derby, it seemed worthwhile as I felt I had a pretty good chance. I discovered that the man who John Prescott told me would withdraw from the contest did not do so, nor did he make the shortlist. However, I accept it was not John's fault. When I met his union colleague in Whitehaven, he told me that he was not bound to adhere to any agreement that he was not a party to. No one had seen the principal candidate against me, Jack Cunningham of the General

Municipal Workers. I was greeted by all kinds of people, including the local party chairman, John Boyden, who was also a member of the GMW. He too was unhappy at that time with the way in which Jack had been selected by his union.

With tea and scones in place, John Boyden invited my wife and I over to his house and these invitations continued whenever we arrived in the constituency to discuss ways in which I could make inroads for the nomination. I made many visits to gather support in Whitehaven and on one memorable trip I visited the small town of Millom to see a union official in the attempt to obtain the support of his union. On meeting this earnest young man he listened to me attentively and when I gave him hundreds of good reasons why I should be his MP he turned to me and said very politely: 'You seem to be a very nice young man, Mr Pendry, but I don't think you are left-wing enough for our members and therefore we shall be nominating that left-winger from Preston, John Horam.' I often wonder whether that young man followed the fortunes of that great 'left-winger' John Horam, if so he might have been somewhat surprised to learn of his political career following that time.

Of course we now know that John Horam didn't get the nomination in Whitehaven, but he did get one in Gateshead in the north-east and became a Labour Member of Parliament in the 1970 intake of MPs, and, indeed, later a Minister of Transport in the Labour Administration of Jim Callaghan. But then he joined the Social Democrats and later the Tories, then became the Minister for the Cabinet Office, and later the Department of Health before becoming a Tory peer – so much for his left-wing credentials!

Everything seemed to be rolling along smoothly until one weekend

I went as usual to the Boyden home, but this time there was no invitation for tea and scones. I was kept on the doorstep with the words:

> You know, Tom, I think one needs to be loyal to the union and I just met Jack Cunningham and his delightful wife Maureen. I'm afraid that as much as we enjoyed you coming up here, and we hope you find a seat soon, it seems that the right thing for us to do is to back young Jack.

At that moment, I knew that I wouldn't get the candidature. That feeling was reinforced when selection day came around and I was on a shortlist with five other members. I thought I'd made a good speech but as Jack walked in when the vote was about to be delivered, there were a number of people nudging him as he walked through to hear the verdict. When it was announced that he had won the selection, I quickly got on my feet, congratulated him and wished him well. I told the delegates that if I didn't get a seat before the next election, then I would willingly come up and support him as I had met so many nice people here and I knew that it would be a joy to campaign in this area for their well-chosen candidate.

After the meeting, I was told that Jack and his supporters were in a nearby hotel celebrating his win! I decided to go and tell the wider audience there how much I approved of the chosen one. However, as I walked in with my wife, all their faces dropped, probably thinking 'what is he doing here?' I proceeded to say all the same kind things that I said about Jack earlier. We shook hands and have remained friends ever since entering the Commons on the same day in June 1970. In fact, Jack told me that when he went back to his home in Chester-le-Street two days later, the first letter he opened was from me congratulating him. I told him in the letter to come back to me if he had any problems with any of my supporters who were unhappy with the selection and I would willingly return to dampen any unrest. Luckily, there were none and his party always gave him 100 per cent support.

Since then, Jack and I have often talked about that selection and he insisted that he did me a favour. Since I was a member of the CND then, and as the nuclear industry was the biggest employer in that constituency, I could never have matched his scientific approach to the nuclear industry. He supported the industry throughout, and the constituency probably would have been a no-win for Labour in the 1970 election if I had stood there. So he was certainly right, especially since I got a seat shortly afterwards in Stalybridge and Hyde – which was marginally a better seat than Whitehaven and without nuclear industrial issues to concern me. So it all turned out well in the end.

STALYBRIDGE AND HYDE

On 6 April 1968, I received a letter from the acting secretary of the Stalybridge Borough Labour Party, Cllr John Porter, asking if I would like to be considered as their candidate, since their sitting MP, Fred Blackburn, was to retire. Before responding, I felt obliged to ring an old acquaintance of mine, John Roper, who lived in Hyde and who I knew wished to be the MP for that constituency. I had known him and his wife Hope as they had both been executive committee members of the Oxford University Labour Club in my days there. I told him of the letter, stating that surely this was the seat that *he* had his heart set on. 'Don't worry,' he said, 'I've got it all sewn up but it would be good experience for you as I know you are interested in another seat.' So, with that in mind, I headed for Stalybridge Borough Party (not the constituency party) and I secured their nomination. I then called John again and told him what had happened. He said, 'Don't worry, they in Stalybridge don't even turn up in Hyde,' which is where the selection conference was going to be held. On top of that, he had a number of nominations, he said, including one from my own union. So, reassured that it would be a good experience, and that it would not harm his ambitions, I went to the selection conference in Hyde. There were four other candidates on the shortlist and when John was the last to speak to the delegates I afterwards said to the others: 'I'm sure you will agree that John has got it.' They nodded in agreement, so I asked the panel if I might be allowed to congratulate him. They all agreed, thinking it would be a good idea.

We all trundled into the meeting to hear the chairman waffling on, saying how good we all were and how it was a pity that we all could not be the MP. To my surprise, he then announced: 'We have chosen Mr Pendry.' I found out later that I won by two votes. To John's credit, he rose and said all the kind things I would have said about him. When I was signing the necessary forms in front of the regional organiser, John said, 'Where is Moira?' 'She's just around the corner in her car,' I replied. He went out to get her and, as he approached the car, Moira jumped out and said, 'Congratulations, John.' She was, like me, convinced that he would win, but he said: 'No, your Tom has got it.' She was as shocked as I was.

John later secured a much safer seat and was duly elected to Parliament, along with me. Unfortunately, he later resigned from the Labour Party and joined the Social Democratic Party (SDP) along with founders David Owen, Roy Jenkins, Bill Rodgers and Shirley

Williams and later bat on the Liberal Democrats benches in the House of Lords. Since writing this, I am informed of his death and I was saddened to hear that news as he was highly respected by all who knew him.

I spent the next two years campaigning in earnest with Fred Blackburn's full support. I embarked on sponsored walks, sipped ales in every pub around and attended local football games, cricket matches and every other sporting event imaginable.

In 1968, I went on one of the Whit Walks organised by St Raphael's Roman Catholic Church in Millbrook, Stalybridge, with my sister Elizabeth. The priest, Father Fraser, asked if I would like to come back after the walk to go to a surprise eightieth birthday party for a nun called Sister Saint James. Elizabeth and I looked at each other, thinking 'could it be?';there was a Sister Saint James that had taught both of us at our infant school some 300 miles away in Ramsgate. On reflection, however, we thought there must have been many nuns of that name, so we dismissed any such idea. However, on return to the church we were pleasantly surprised to find standing there the very same nun we had known some thirty years earlier. We listened to speeches by the priest, other nuns and many of the parishioners heaping praise upon the eighty-year-old and then I spoke up. I was the new candidate at that time, so I was not known or recognised by anyone there. I asked: 'Were any of you taught by Sister Saint James?' There was silence. 'Well, my sister and I were,' and with a mischievous twinkle in my eye I added: 'And I still bear the scars from when she slapped my face and asked me to repeat after her "God is Love, Pendry, God is Love".' The look of shock on the faces of those around us vanished immediately after Sister Saint James, on hearing the name Pendry, embraced my sister and I and explained to all what a wonderful family she thought ours was. Everyone then realised the reunion was a happy one. I recognised later how great a fan I had, as she was probably the most important and loved person in Stalybridge. She would go from door to door to visit the sick regardless of their religion and, after embracing them, she would mention that they should vote for 'her Tom' – she was probably instrumental in the election outcome.

On another occasion I joined forty-two members of the Tameside Olympic Gymnastic Club on an eighteen-mile 'marathon' over Coombes Rock, Hayfield, alongside budding athletes from eight years old upwards. I won further support during a savage winter weekend. Snow threatened a Stalybridge Celtic Cheshire League fixture with Winsford at Bower Road one Saturday morning. Club officials and supporters worked heroically to clear the pitch and, despite many cancellations across the region, a referee declared that the match was ON. The trouble was – how to inform the fans? Officials contacted me, and the word was spread via the loudspeaker on my election 'battle' van! Having embarked on such activities, and having enjoyed a fair amount of press coverage, I knew that I had a fair chance come the election, although the majority was a small one to defend.

These were difficult times, with the Wilson administration under constant attack. As a prospective parliamentary candidate my job was both to defend the Labour government and attack both the Tories and their friends in the media. After Labour's Frank Robertson defeated a Conservative in Hollingsworth in council elections, I told a Labour meeting: 'Although it would be idle to deny that we are going through a rather difficult period, there is no reason to lose our nerve. This government will never be blown off course by the scurrilous attacks made upon the Prime Minister in the Tory press.' Closer to polling day, I said: 'The party that will win the next general election will be the party that faces the realities of the '70s and does not try to bribe the electorate with sweet promises.' And I told delegates at the Pack Horse Hotel, Mottram, with some confidence, that that party would be Labour. With hindsight, I was wrong in the short term but right in the longer term. My view, at both a national and local level, was that creeping cynicism was a construct of the Tories, and at that meeting and many others I completely rejected the idea that there were 'no good causes left to fight for'. High on my list of priorities, then and always, was to narrow the gap between pensioners and low earners and those in the higher salary bracket. I urged the government to narrow the gap between rich and poor in the Chancellor's next Budget. That, I argued, would do much to heal the 'scars' of the last century. On education, I said at the time: 'We are moving far too slowly towards a fully integrated comprehensive system. If we are really going towards a society based on equality of opportunity, the present system must be speedily replaced.'

Although not yet an MP, I like to think I was in tune with my would-be constituents and used every opportunity to press their day-to-day concerns. For example, many families were caused great distress during a cold winter by the pilot lights on their heating being blown out. I took the matter up with the Gas Board and the North Western Gas Board, complaining of the 'lack of research on the vexed question of winds and cross-winds blowing out gas pilot lights'. I told gas bosses: 'People go out in the morning leaving a warm house and they return in the evening to find that the house is cold.' Such issues are hardly earth-shaking, but they affect a lot of people and my efforts to pressure gas bosses into sorting the problem was warmly received locally.

And then in late May 1970 we got into the proper election campaign. My view throughout the campaign was that, while it would be easy to fight the election simply by exposing Tory hypocrisy, we had to remain a party of challenge and purpose. In my selection speech, I said:

> Contrast our achievements with theirs, the achievements not only of this party, but of the people of this great country. Even when fighting against a background of economic difficulty, our government makes provision for vast increases in social security, benefits, housing and health and welfare and education. This represents the emergence of a new political climate. As a socialist, I am eager and anxious for the next five to ten years.

Of course, the Labour government fell to Ted Heath and the Tories, but I bucked the trend in my constituency. On the night of the 1970 election count, I knew I had won when I came across my Tory opponent being sick in the toilets of the town hall. I was very fortunate – my hard work had paid dividends. My joy at winning, however, was tempered by the knowledge that the Conservatives had won the overall election and that Ted Heath had become Prime Minister.

The reasons for that lost election are many and varied, and not all of them were clear at the time. Premier Harold Wilson may have underestimated Heath. Harold's tactics had been to take Heath by surprise because the Tories had been expecting an October election. Some say Harold wanted to go to the polls before the introduction of decimal coinage in early 1971, for which his government had been responsible and which he thought was hugely unpopular. Some commentators believe that the loss of national prestige after the England football team's demise in the World Cup against West Germany contributed to the Labour defeat.

Contrast that with the 1966 World Cup win by England in which many said Harold Wilson played the upbeat nationalist card – some might have thought Harold and not Geoff Hurst scored the winning goal! Still others believe that the early lead in the polls led to Labour complacency. I was certainly not complacent at Stalybridge and Hyde, and at my count it was very much touch and go. My brothers had to shield my dear mother away from the TV in Stalybridge Labour Club where the famous Bob McKenzie was listing a number of constituencies that were swinging away from Labour to the Conservatives. My constituency was included in his list. Instead, I won by some 2,000 votes and my boyhood dream came true. Although unhappy at the overall results in the country, I was certainly looking forward to entering the House of Commons as a Labour Member of Parliament – all thanks to my mum and Bessie Braddock.

I hope that before Bessie died in November 1970, she would have noticed that a certain fifteen-year-old she advised at the Margate Labour Party conference in 1950 had taken her advice to 'raise his sights and aim to become a Labour MP', had achieved just that. It is also ironic that I could have easily become the MP for her constituency in Liverpool Exchange. A certain Bob Parry, whom I had defended unsuccessfully when he was sacked from his union post with the National Union of Public Employees, rang me to tell me that Bessie was going to retire and asked if I would be interested in taking her place as his family dominated the General Council of the party and had the majority of the Constituency Party votes. He assured me that it would be a 'piece of cake' to shoehorn me in. Accepting that this was an attempt to repay me for sticking by him in his hour of need, I thanked him, accepted his gesture of goodwill and awaited developments. However, imagine my great shock when I read in a newspaper a few weeks later that Robert Parry had been selected as the Labour candidate for Liverpool Exchange. Robert was elected in June 1970, and he eventually made his maiden speech on 14 December 1970 after asking me if I would hold his hand, so to speak, as he was incredibly nervous. This I did, after all that is what comrades are supposed to do. He got through it – but only just!

CHAPTER 3

ENTERING THE HOUSE

MAIDEN SPEECH

On the day I was to enter the House of Commons, I travelled down from Derby with two other newly elected MPs, Tom Torney and Dennis Skinner, later and to this day known as the 'Beast of Bolsover', plus two sitting MPs, Tom Swain and Eric Varley. At Westminster, I found in the cloakroom a hook with my name on it along with a section to place my sword, if I had one, of course. In theory, there was also a place outside for my horse, again, if I had one. Regrettably, I didn't have a desk or a secretary, and there was a pile of mail that had built up in a pigeonhole since the election two weeks earlier. I couldn't help thinking somehow that this place had got its priorities all wrong.

As a newly elected MP, I had to first swear allegiance to Her Majesty and enrol in the House before even contemplating my maiden speech, or indeed asking any questions. My maiden speech was the first worry on my mind and, if they are honest, every new Member is always just as concerned. The other important issue for me was that the sooner a new MP got enrolled, the sooner they would get on the payroll and, incidentally, if they stayed the course long enough, then one day they could become Father of the House ahead of others in their intake. As I was one of the first to enrol in 1970, I could well have become Father of the House one day if I hadn't become a member of the House of Lords – a blessing indeed, as I should not have liked that particular honour!

Most MPs I know look back on their maiden speech and think that it was probably the worst speech they ever made, mainly due to the nervousness they felt upon addressing that forum for the first time. Conversely, I can say that my maiden speech was probably the best I have ever made. By convention, a maiden speaker first compliments the MP who spoke before him and also praises his predecessor; in my case it was Fred Blackburn, who had represented the constituency as a Labour MP for some twenty years. I said he was a very popular MP, with a terrific knowledge of the rules and procedures in the House. I added:

> It is not generally known in the House, perhaps, that he was a great-
> ly loved man in his constituency. In the Boroughs of Dukinfield,
> Stalybridge and Hyde and the urban districts of Longdendale and
> Tintwistle he was greatly loved because he cared about the problems
> of his constituents, and they regret very much that he had to retire. I
> hope they do not regret too much that I am here in his place.

Little did I know at the time that I would beat his record by representing the constituency for thirty-one years.

The other convention for a maiden speaker was generally not to be overly controversial. I could not resist breaking that rule. I had attended a function at the London School of Economics on the Saturday before my speech where the Solicitor-General, Geoffrey Howe MP, who I knew was going to respond to the debate at which I was to make my maiden speech, referred to the pending Industrial Relations Bill. He stated that in the Bill there would be a way to bring Queensberry Rules into our industrial relations. Those rules, of course, are the ones that govern boxing. On the specifics of the Bill, I accused the government of stubbornness and aiming to rush it through as quickly as possible. 'If the government think that they have a mandate on this, then that really is wishful thinking,' I said.

In June, not one in a thousand electors knew the likely contents of the Bill, and since this document has been published I am sure that the percentage has not altered in any way. The tragedy of this document is that it is a lawyer's document, written by lawyers for lawyers and without even a small element of practical application within it.

I pointed out that much of the Bill followed the 'crude and bigoted' assessment of the Inns of Court Conservative Association who believed that the unions had become too powerful for comfort. I added: 'The basic premise from which the government is operating is that, somehow or other, we are riddled with strikes. Again, the evidence is to the contrary.' I pointed to the evidence of a Professor Turner, of Cambridge University, who found that the UK had a lower strike incidence than any other major non-Communist country except Western Germany. And, bearing in mind the Solicitor-General's previous comments, I concluded my speech: 'As an ex-ABA boxing champion, I say to the Solicitor-General, who spoke on Saturday of injecting Queensberry Rules into our industrial relations, that even under Queensberry if one leads with one's chin one will get knocked out.' I sat back down to many shouting 'Hear! Hear!', especially from the sponsored group of trade union members on our side of the House led by Eric Heffer, Stan Orme and others in the Tribune group.

My maiden speech was followed by a Tory re-tread, East Surrey's William Clark, who generously said:

> I must congratulate the Hon. Gentleman the Member for Stalybridge and Hyde on a forthright speech, if not a fighting one. It was a speech he had given a lot of thought to, and I am sure both sides of the House look forward to hearing him in the future.

The next morning I went into the tearoom and found the Labour Chief Whip, Bob Mellish, reading my speech. He asked me to get a cup of tea and join him and, needless to say, I obeyed that diktat instantly. He said: 'I've been reading your maiden speech and, of those I've read so far, yours was by far the best.' Even after that compliment, I never thought what was to follow would cap it, which was an invitation to go on the front bench as an opposition whip. That meant I was the first promotion of the 1970 intake of Labour MPs, which included the late John Smith, Dr Jack Cunningham, Neil Kinnock, John Prescott, Gerald Kaufman and others who shot ahead of me in the years that followed.

The first time I sat on the front bench, Neil Kinnock approached me with the words 'What are you doing here, boyo?' I replied foolishly, and was later to regret it: 'Sheer talent, Neil. Sheer talent.' This was probably the worst thing I ever could have said; during my time in the Commons he was to be the only leader of the Labour Party who didn't put me on the front bench, unlike Harold Wilson, Jim Callaghan,

Michael Foot, John Smith and Tony Blair. I am not saying it was just because of that remark, but it did cross my mind from time to time. I raised this in jest with Neil later, and his explanation was hardly credible. He said he wanted backbenchers like me to remain there because of the great work we did from there – since 1970 I was never on the back benches until Neil sent me there in 1983 when he became the leader. I expressed my disappointment to my mother who was a Neil Kinnock supporter through and through. She retorted: 'There must be a really good reason.' I could have knocked down anyone else for that remark, but not my mum, although John Prescott and a Labour whip told me there were other reasons why Neil did not make me the Sports Minister. I think there must have been a bond between the two because on her ninety-fifth birthday, Neil sent her a beautiful card that is mounted on my wall in my office in the House of Lords. It stated: 'Dear Elizabeth, Sorry I missed you last week but you have a standing invitation to 10 Downing Street on your 100th and 110th birthdays. Love, Neil Kinnock.' Unfortunately my mother didn't reach the 100th mark as she died at the age of ninety-seven, and nor did she ever reach No. 10 – she didn't have the same bond with John Major.

I was immensely proud of winning the seat at Stalybridge and Hyde, and felt hugely privileged to be serving its people as their MP. The constituency had been created in 1918 and had been held by the Conservatives for thirty-four of the years since then. The MP Gordon Lang retired on health grounds in 1951, and his successor, Fred Blackburn, was returned in 1951 with a majority of 298 – the one after that was even smaller and was only picked up in subsequent elections.

The constituency is a lovely place on the lower slopes of the Pennines – and what a history it has! In the 1770s, Stalybridge emerged as one of the first centres of the textile industry and played an important part in the country's Industrial Revolution. The Huddersfield Narrow Canal was completed in 1811 and it too had a long and distinguished history. However, when I became the parliamentary candidate for Stalybridge and Hyde, I was horrified to find that successive councils of both political persuasions had over the years buried the canal. I pledged then that I would make it my business to do whatever I could to fight to restore it to its former glory. Happily, in 1999, I was able to persuade the Millennium Commission to give a grant of just under £30 million backed by money from English Partnership, Tameside Council and others. I was privileged to open it in May 2001 and a plaque is displayed on one of the bridges in the town centre. Now there are narrow boats and hundreds of wild birds descending on the canal.

But, originally, the introduction of such machinery was met with violent opposition from the Luddites and the doors of mills were kept locked day and night. A Scottish regiment under the Duke of Montrose was sent to the town. It was led by Captain Raines who made his headquarters at the Roe Cross Inn. In November 1811 gangs of armed men destroyed power looms and fired mills. The disturbances in Stalybridge culminated with a night of violent rioting on 20 April 1812. However, the Stalybridge textile industry continued to grow – by 1814 there were twelve factories and by 1818 the number had increased to sixteen. Irish families seeking better wages poured into the town and Stalybridge was among the first to establish a Mechanics' Institute to educate the growing number of workers. This was a time when working people were rising up to demand the right to vote, for men if not, then, for women. Stalybridge contributed 10,000 signatures to the second Chartist petition that was presented to Parliament in

April 1842. The petition was rejected and the first general strike spread across the land, eventually involving nearly half a million workers throughout Britain and representing the biggest single exercise of working class strength in nineteenth-century Britain. In August 1842, a strike at Bayley's Cotton Mill in Stalybridge spread to Manchester and the surrounding areas. In writing *The Condition of the Working Class in England* (1844), Friedrich Engels used Stalybridge as an example: '...multitudes of courts, back lanes, and remote nooks arise out of [the] confused way of building ... Add to this the shocking filth, and the repulsive effect of Stalybridge, in spite of its pretty surroundings, may be readily imagined.' The outbreak of the American Civil War in 1861 hit the Stalybridge cotton mills, which rapidly ran short of cotton, and thousands of operatives were laid off. The tragedy was repeated across the region and families starved in what became known as the Lancashire Cotton Famine. Contributions came from all over the world for the relief of the cotton operatives in Lancashire; and at one point three-quarters of Stalybridge workers were dependent on relief schemes. A thousand skilled men and women left the town, in what became known as 'The Panic'. The Stalybridge Borough Band, reputed to be the oldest brass band in the world, was formed in March 1871, holding its first rehearsals and meetings at the Moulder's Arms, Grasscroft Street, Castle Hall. The founder was Alexander Owen who conducted the band until at least 1907, and I am proud to be its president.

Perhaps the most important part played by the band, and indeed an important part of the early history of Stalybridge's industrial struggles, is that which relates to what is referred to as the 'Peterloo Massacre'. On 16 August 1819, a vast crowd assembled in the space of three acres in Peterloo to demand the reform of parliamentary representation. The magistrates in Manchester, who frowned upon the object of the protest, ordered the yeomanry to charge the crowd. As a consequence, many of the protesters were killed. Stalybridge Band was engaged to play at the assembled point in Peterloo for a Henry Hunt, known by the name of 'Orator Hunt'. For any band to be chosen by Hunt was considered an honour by bandsmen and women. Hunt was revered by the radicals but disliked by the Tories and on their way to the rally, the Band had to pass through crowds. Many were humorous and support-ive, but the Tories sneered remarks. On arriving close to the rally point, the Band were forced to retreat on the orders of those who feared the objectors of the Hunt meeting who were determined to smash the instruments of the Band. As a result they retreated to the chorus of crowds chanting 'There goes the gentlemen of the Stalybridge Band.'

At the beginning of the twentieth century, the population of the town peaked at 27,623, but as trade dwindled it declined. In 1955, new housing estates were built to replace the slums and, gradually, redun-dant textile mills were occupied by firms in the various light industries. The manufacture of rubber goods, plastics, chemicals and packaging materials were all introduced, as well as the addition of synthetic fibres to the textile trade, reducing unemployment.

Of course, that was to come later, and the effects of area unemploy-ment created by the decline of the mills in Stalybridge had an impact on the fortunes of Stalybridge Celtic FC, which had been a flourishing club in the early 1920s. They had reached the Third Division North in 1921 but they had to leave it voluntarily because of the decline in spectators. They are to this date the only club to have relinquished their position in the course of their season.

When Tameside Council was born in 1974, Roy Oldham, coming in from a rural district council, became chairman of the education committee, and he had no idea about comprehensive education, which was demanded by the incoming Labour government of 1974 for all councils. In his haste, he ill-advisedly adopted a comprehensive scheme that had been developed on the other side of the Tame. It was in Lancashire, which had been developing a process of comprehensive education over the years, whereas Stalybridge and Hyde was in Old Cheshire, which had had no such plans. I opposed the plans as tactfully as I could, but not tactfully enough for Roy Oldham. In conjunction with my wife, who was chairman of education in Derby, I helped to install a proper comprehensive system.

One day in the Commons, I was asked by Fred Mulley, Minister of State at the Department of Education, and an ardent Sheffield United fan, if I would like to go see Sheffield play the following Saturday. I wasn't sure I could make it, but on the Saturday morning in question, upon reading *The Guardian*, I found that there were millions of pounds going begging from the Department of Education under Shirley Williams, and only the best schemes could be submitted to her for a slice of that money. I immediately barged into Roy Oldham's house. He was surprised that I was even talking to him, but when I said, 'We are off to Sheffield United,' he was so flabbergasted that he got his coat, got into my car and immediately said, 'Who are they playing?' I said I couldn't care less, 'but I do know who is going to be there'. We arrived at Bramall Lane Ground and the game had already begun. However, I insisted they collect Fred Mulley from the directors' box and we pinned him up against the wall, poor man, and said: 'Look, this money that is going by the end of the financial year, we want a good slice of this because we have some adaptations for our comprehensive scheme which would be impossible as it stands without extra money.' Anxious to get back to his football, he promised to do everything he could to assist us. Roy and I left the ground with our fingers crossed. In the end, we got the largest slice of money from the department outside of London, which allowed us to have a workable comprehensive system of education, including the Copley Recreation Centre.

Stalybridge was extensively portrayed by the painter L. S. Lowry until his death in 1976. His house is marked with a blue plaque on Stalybridge Road, Mottram in Longdendale. There is also a statue of him, holding his sketch pad, on a bench near where he lived in Mottram in Longdendale. I had the privilege to take Lowry to the polling station in Mottram on a number of occasions, although he never let on to me who it was he was voting for. I was told by Roy Oldham – who did have a close relationship with him, being a nearby neighbour – that Lowry didn't always vote Labour. Roy did have it on good authority, however, that Lowry did vote for the both of us, for the work we put in locally – or at least I hope so, as I did take the trouble to take him to register his vote.

Another great painter living just a mile away from Lowry was my good friend and a firm Labour supporter, the late Harry Rutherford. Harry left the Hyde School of Art as a fourteen-year-old before attending Manchester School of Art under the French impressionist artist Pierre Adolphe Valette, where Lowry was also a fellow pupil. Rutherford was arguably more talented than Lowry and later went on to be taught by the famous Walter Sickert in 1925. Harry was the youngest pupil to enrol in Sickert's new art school in Manchester where Sickert considered Rutherford to be his 'intellectual heir'. Indeed, that rang true, as Harry moved to London in 1931 to join Sickert and had a very successful career performing for the BBC regularly. He also starred in his own programme called *Harry Rutherford's Sketchbook*. Harry eventually returned to Hyde where I met him on many occasions. He often frequented my house and I found him a most delightful companion. The painting Rutherford was most proud of was his *Northern Saturday*, painted in 1948,which is still displayed proudly in Hyde Town Hall.

It was generally thought that living about a mile from one another, Lowry was not as friendly to his rival Rutherford as one might have thought. I think, however, there was a possible jealous streak, as I was told Lowry was rather envious of Rutherford's success before Lowry made it big himself. Sadly, both of these great artists have now passed on.

INSPECTOR PETER GODBER

In August 1973, I was asked by my boss, Chief Whip Bob Mellish, if I would like to go on a seven-day parliamentary visit to Hong Kong along with a colleague of my choosing to accompany me. As Jack Cunningham was my closest friend in the House, I asked him and, as he had not been in the colony before, he readily accepted my invitation.

We arrived in Kai Tak airport only to face seemingly hundreds of reporters and photographers awaiting us. Vainly, I believed that my fame as a former colonial boxing champion of the colony had galvanised the press into taking action. I was very soon to be disabused of any such thoughts after being met by the acting Director of Protocol, Mr Pottinger, who arrived in a very smart white Rolls-Royce. Jack and I were politely shuffled by him into this handsome limousine and told by him, 'Ignore the press. I will tell you why they are here on our journey to your hotel, the Mandarin.' It was then revealed to us that, as we were flying into Hong Kong, Inspector Peter Godber of the Hong Kong Police had jumped bail and had arrived in Britain with about $600,000 he had allegedly amassed illegally.

Both Jack and I, at a subsequent press conference, made it clear that we were in the colony to look specifically at the areas of concern to the UK government's opposition party, and that we were particularly interested in the textile industry, industrial relations, housing and social welfare. Jack was on top of those concerns, being a scientist, and had wished to acquaint himself with the science-based industries in the colony. We told the eager press corps that we would refer, in some detail, at the end of our stay to the many expressions of anger relating to the Godber case.

We hoped to set out our mission plan unstintingly, but we first had to overcome the consequences of an unfortunate meal on the first night in the floating restaurant within Aberdeen Harbour. We were taken there courtesy of a sister company to one in my constituency in Hyde. I thought it would be to Jack's liking (he is a lover of good cuisine) as it was a prize venue and pollution-free. Unfortunately, it turned out to be the exact opposite – the floating fish we chose from the gigantic fish tank were, in our case, anything but pollution-free. After a few days of suffering from food poisoning we experienced some embarrassing moments. One of which was at our first meeting, where we must have been considered the dumbest MPs ever to hit the colony. When our hosts had finished their introduction and requested questions, we both declined to oblige, as we couldn't wait to get to our loos in our hotel!

Happily that didn't last long and we amassed many productive insights into the magic of Hong Kong. The colony was certainly a different place from my time there with the RAF in the 1950s.

By the mid-1950s, Hong Kong had increased its population to a staggering 2.2 million. To be fair, the Hong Kong government then did an incredible job building temporary housing. Thousands of makeshift shanty huts were built on the hills surrounding the centre of the island and the new territories. After the 1953 Shek Kip Mei fires left 53,000 homeless, massive multi-storey apartment blocks soared over the city, aping New York's skyscrapers.

Having been, as indeed Jack was also, a trade-union official before entering Parliament, a good part of our time was devoted to looking into labour relations. In view of this interest I visited Deputy Commissioner Ian Price, who agreed with me that labour relations were a field for obvious reforms in Hong Kong. I stressed the need for ILO (International Labour Organisation) conventions to be ratified in the British Colony and I was assured by Mr Price that it was his aim also. I also stressed the need for legislation to make it illegal for employers to discriminate and to give their workers the right to organise. I told the *South China Morning Post*:

It is absolutely essential that workers should be given the right to combine and organise. There ought to be legislation to make it an offence for employers to discriminate, but there also ought to be a code of industrial relations so that everyone can know their rights. The government must be seen to be independent of both employers and trade unions.

But I conceded: 'You can have many bits of legislation flying around, but you have to inch your way forward. If you go too fast it becomes counter-productive.' Mr Price stated by the end of the year that he was confident that legislation against union discrimination through LegCo (Legislative Council of Hong Kong) would bring Hong Kong in line with ILO convention 28 – the Right to Organise and Collective Bargaining Convention. Happily, I later discovered this was achieved in the timescale he outlined.

During our stay, there was a serious strike at a shipyard in Shau Kei Wan organised by a local communist-led union. The leaders, on hearing of my involvement in the colony, contacted Mr Price's office requesting that I meet with them. Price was reluctant at first to pass this news on to me, but he relented when the strike became more serious. I went to the yard on a very rainy day, and up a very rickety staircase into a very dingy room with a large picture of Chairman Mao on the wall. It soon became obvious that the leaders were frightened men. I got the impression that they had called the strike at the behest of their bosses on the mainland, and that they didn't know how to get out of the problems that had been forced upon them. I presented a compromise formula to Price, he accepted it, and the strike was called off. I thought then that the workers of Hong Kong needed a few TUC officers to teach them a thing or two about organising industrial strikes.

When Jack Cunningham concluded his bit on often different aspects of our visit, our official tour came to an end. Jack departed to the UK, but as I had promised to stay and take on very seriously the troubles surrounding the Peter Godber affair, my extended tour commenced.

His escape had sparked public outcry over the government's anti-corruption efforts. I stayed for another two weeks, during which time I found out in more detail the background to Godber, and his arrest. Godber had been a Chief Superintendent of the Royal Hong Kong

Police Force in Kowloon and had played a leading role in restoring order during the major disturbances of 1966–67 when communists fought to bring down the colonial administration. There were bomb attacks, riots and violence against those opposing re-unification with China. Several Hong Kong policemen were killed. Godber, during these tumultuous times, had put no fewer than 4.3 million Hong Kong Dollars (approximately US$600,000) in his overseas and local bank accounts. The police anti-corruption branch investigated his mysterious wealth and ordered him to explain his source of income. Godber immediately arranged for his wife to leave the colony, then dodged immigration and passport checks, and walked onto a plane at Kai Tak Airport bound for London.

Over forty years later, I discovered that Ian Hernon, now the deputy editor of *Tribune*, was one of the journalists who tracked down Godber to his ramshackle cottage a few miles outside Rye where he was hiding, unknown to the local constabulary. Ian told me:

> I was twenty and stringing for the *Daily Express*. I remember knocking on the door and a man with a big bushy beard answered, told me to eff off, and slammed the door. I was half-way back to the garden gate when I thought, 'Christ! It's him.' I told the local superintendent, but he was not very interested, saying that the Hong Kong warrant for his arrest was not recognised under UK law. It took you, Tom, to sort that out.

I recognised the need for swift action before proposed activities by various groups escalated into an explosive atmosphere in Hong Kong. That was something I knew about, given my experiences in 1956. I like to think that because of the favourable press coverage of my visit, I did help to keep a lid on any disruptive actions.

The young students in particular impressed me; they seemed ardent for change. But I said publically that I would be stressing to Foreign Secretary Sir Alec Douglas-Home that the new generation of Hong Kong Chinese were not accepting some of the conventions in Hong Kong that their forebears had done. I explained to the *South China Morning Post* that there could be no identity with the young until they had a real part in shaping the society in which they lived. I had a clear feeling that unless Britain could show that it recognised the need for a change, the tension was curdling below the surface and there could be problems ahead. However, the first test, and the most urgent current issue, was that of Peter Godber and the widespread demands for his return to face the judicial system of the colony. That was my promise to those I had met and that was what I intended to do. With my mission completed, I packed my bags and left the colony for the United Kingdom.

I found no difficulty in having my meeting with Sir Alec Douglas-Home. He understood precisely why I wanted to see him and was well-briefed; he clearly knew a great deal about the activities I had witnessed in the colony. Before outlining my feeling for urgent action in the Godber case, I stressed that even before Godber there was already the feeling of the existence of corruption and anti-social polic-ing. The Godber case could be the lighting of a fuse and something had to be done to ensure he was sent back to Hong Kong. After about half an hour I said to Sir Alec how much I appreciated the time he had taken but that I must allow him to get on with his important business. However, he insisted that I should stay longer to give him further examples of my visit. He informed me that the highly popular Governor of Hong Kong, Sir Murray MacLehose, was in London, and was next to meet him. When I left, I felt confident that he would act accordingly.

Godber was arrested in Rye in April 1974 but it took more than eight months of legal wrangling before he was extradited to Hong Kong. His February 1975 trial saw him convicted of corruption and sentenced to four years in prison plus confiscation of 25,000 HKD. His conviction led to the creation of the Independent Commission against Corruption in 1974. He later resided in Spain.

The Godber affair is still vividly remembered in the Far East. Kevin Sinclair of the *South China Morning Post* summed it up:

The saga of corrupt policeman Peter Godber exposed a police force that was on the take. Everybody seemed to know vaguely that corruption was universal in Hong Kong. But no one seemed quite aware of the extent of the problem. This was to change abruptly in 1973 when police commissioner Charles Sutcliffe demanded that chief superintendent Peter Godber explain the source of his wealth. What followed led to a social firestorm. Godber was allowed to remain at liberty. Using his police identity papers, he sneaked into the secure area at Kai Tak airport, boarded an aircraft and fled to the UK. When the news broke, Hong Kong erupted in righteous fury. Students demonstrated and community leaders demanded action.

That action, of course, took place following my promise to meet with Sir Alec Douglas-Home and the establishment of the Independent Commission against Corruption. The ICAC was headed by Sir Jack

Cater. Jack was a good friend of mine, a Stepney-born Cockney, and a former senior civil servant in Hong Kong before running Cable and Wireless in the colony. Cater recruited Sir John Prendergast, a wily Irish anti-espionage specialist and former director of the Special Branch, to head the graft-busting side of the commission. He was called back from retirement because Jack Cater had worked with him against rioters in 1967 and knew him to be an honest man.

After one of the most hectic and rewarding three weeks of my parliamentary life so far, it was gratifying to have so much sympathetic press for my endeavours. The most pleasing of all was the editorial in the *Hong Kong Star* which read in bold type 'Thank you, Tom Pendry!' I was hailed as 'the most sensible British Member of Parliament to visit Hong Kong for a long time' because I had understood how frustrations and resentments could explode into civil disorder, such as the 1956 riots in Hong Kong. The *Star* added that they were not all crooks in the Far East – some London papers were conveying that image to the British public since the Godber case hit the headlines. I thought that after these favourable press comments I would be embarrassed with many requests to return to Hong Kong and wondered how I could fit them all in. I shouldn't have worried, as in the forty years since I have only been to the colony twice – once invited, and the other time at my own expense. But, as Harold Wilson once said, 'A week is a long time in politics.' This couldn't have been more accurate when applied to my Hong Kong experiences.

NEW DEAL FOR SECRETARIES

The office of a busy MP cannot be maintained without the help of a good secretary. However, prior to 1973, the traditional idea was that an MP was more than capable of providing the secretarial support that they needed privately. Secretaries were not considered an essential part of the work-force, and so the allowance for secretarial help was capped at £1,000 a year – and even then, the whole allowance didn't have to be paid out to the secretary and could be split with other staff members, such as research assistants. Secretaries really had a rough deal, having to work for multiple MPs just to make ends meet, and even then were not likely to make more than £1,500 a year. Many of them did not receive holiday pay, nor have access to a pension scheme, and many paid for their own insurance stamps.

In 1973, I led the campaign for a better deal for secretaries after requesting a pay review. I put down an Early Day Motion, which was signed by 257 MPs and which was sent to James Prior, the Lord President of the Council. To the surprise of many MPs, especially Labour members, both Prime Minister Ted Heath and Prior advanced the cause we espoused. They together did more than any of their predecessors to enhance the wages and conditions for MPs and their secretaries in the Commons. That autumn, Heath adopted the inde-pendent review bodies' recommendation in full, while Prior gained major points by increasing secretarial allowances after receiving a dep-utation from Tory MP Christopher Brocklebank-Fowler and myself.

My concern for the need for proper pay for secretaries did not rest with those who only worked in the House of Commons, however, for after my parliamentary visit to Hong Kong I took up the problems ex-perienced by the colonial government secretaries that they had raised with me about their lack of adequate remuneration. A delegation from those secretaries visited the UK and I arranged for them to meet the Colonial Secretary, Goronwy Roberts, who actively endorsed their cause, which resulted in the Hong Kong government yielding to his edicts. As a consequence, the Hong Kong secretaries secured better remuneration and conditions and when I returned to Hong Kong some years later, they put on a nice little banquet as a thank you.

SIR JOHN BETJEMAN

In 1973, the country greatly celebrated the royal wedding of Princess Anne and Captain Mark Phillips. To mark the occasion, the Poet Laureate, Sir John Betjeman, wrote the following poem:

> Hundreds of birds in the air
> And millions of leaves on the pavement,
> Then the bells pealing on
> Over palace and people outside,
> All for the words 'I will'
> To love's most holy enslavement–
> What can we do but rejoice
> With a triumphing bridegroom and bride?

This was not Betjeman's best work. When asked for my comments on it in the Commons Press Bar, and not knowing then as I do now that I was talking to Chris Moncrieff – the ace Press Association journalist in the House – I responded tongue-in-cheek that the poem was the work of an idle scribbler and I believed that I could do better. Even Betjeman admitted to its shortcomings when he told *The Times* that the wedding poem was 'one of the most laborious things that I have ever written'. After my comments to Moncrieff attracted front-page attention, it wasn't long before supporters of Betjeman came to his defence, asking for the Labour Party to issue a public apology. Nigel Dempster, the *Daily Mail* diarist, took a different approach and challenged me to put my money where my mouth was and write a better poem. He added that if I accepted the challenge, then the *Mail* would give £100 to a charity of my choice. Dempster added that he would tell his readers that I had entered into the spirit of the challenge. Coincidently, I received a request from the Stalybridge taxi drivers asking if I would make a contribution to their fund, which gives the old-age pensioners of Stalybridge a visit to Blackpool for free every year. I told Dempster to send the £100 to the taxi drivers' fund and I would have a go.

I wrote the following:

Towering Gothic arches etch the curving skies,

Peering into the ribboned streets below

Masked and thronged by heaving crowds.

Calmly they survey.

Slowly, as at a distance grows

A murmur, then a roar,

One hundred thousand voices unleash their cheers hurling their

sound into the dark and dismal air.

Flags hysterically wave.

The Princess, gloriously arrayed, smiles and waves, a gracious bride

Golden and bedecked, on creaking wheels, the coach trundles

behind the tossing plumes of stirring steeds.

Aloof and proud.

The final moment comes among the hallowed splendour.

She, quiet, calm. He, nervous, proud – are joined together, man and

wife following in the custom of ancient times

Now, peace.

To be left alone.

I was rather pleased with my poem and it was published in the *Mail* with the headline 'MP waxes poetical over royal wedding'. On the day of that wedding, a letter came across my desk from Mary Wilson – now Lady Wilson of Rievaulx – the wife of the late Harold Wilson, then the Leader of the Opposition. Criticising neither Sir John Betjeman's poem, nor mine, Mary wrote how she had read my poem with great interest and outlined the credentials of a formal style over the free-style approach that Betjeman used on his poem. Mary concluded her letter by reiterating what Betjeman had also mentioned, how difficult it was to write to order.

Mary's letter wasn't the only one that I received. There were many others from all over the globe asking me to judge their own works of art or congratulating me on my efforts. The Oxford University Poetry Club, I'm sure with tongue firmly in cheek, asked me if I would put my name in for consideration to be the next Poet Laureate. Even Andrew Roth's biography of me described me as a poet, among other less flattering references.

CHAPTER 4

LORD COMMISSIONER

After the 1974 general election on 28 February, Labour returned to power. It was the first election since the Second World War not to produce an overall majority for the winning party. Many people had expected Ted Heath and his party to scrape through, but we won 301 seats against their 297. It had been a tight contest and we knew there would be difficult times ahead, but we were helped by a decision by the Ulster Unionists not to take the Conservative whip. And after years of three-day weeks, power cuts and strikes under Heath, the Tory slogan of 'Who Governs Britain?' backfired. In the Labour manifesto, Harold Wilson said:

The government called this election in panic. They are unable to govern, and dare not tell the people the truth. Our people face a series of interlocking crises. Prices are rocketing. The Tories have brought the country to the edge of bankruptcy and breakdown. More and more people are losing their jobs. Firms are going out of business. Housing costs are out of reach for so many families. The Common Market now threatens us with still higher food prices and with a further loss of Britain's control of its own affairs. We shall

restore to the British people the right to decide the final issue of
British membership of the Common Market.

However, the Liberals did not have enough seats to go into a viable
coalition, making the formation of a stable government in this parliament a practical impossibility. Harold Wilson was forced to call another election the following October, which we won more comfortably.

But, going back to our first narrow 1974 victory. When Wilson
selected his ministerial team, I was with other parliamentarians on a
delegation to America. Along with other potential ministerial candidates, like John Prescott, I had embarked with the hope that I would
be back in time to accept an offer from Wilson if I was fortunate
enough to be selected for his ministerial team.

The trip to Washington was going very well until I was handed
a telegram from the British ambassador at the embassy. The note
read: 'Return to Westminster to join the new government.' None of
the others on the delegation received such a telegram. Only then did
I realise that Charles Morris, the parliamentary secretary to Harold
Wilson, had clearly known more than I did. John Prescott, like me,
is a great lover of jazz, and the next city on our delegation tour after
Washington was New Orleans. It truly broke my heart that I had to
return to London and miss out on the city. John, who may well have
disapproved at not getting the call to join the government, didn't seem
to show it. His love of jazz seemed to transcend his desire for ministerial power at that time. Imagine my mixture of emotions on missing
my jazz in New Orleans and arriving at Heathrow to hear that it was
already announced in *The Times* that I had been appointed a Lords
Commissioner of the Treasury in Wilson's government. Nevertheless,

I was still hoping one day to make it to New Orleans. Alas, to this day it hasn't happened.

THE BAHAMAS AND JOHN STONEHOUSE

As a Lords Commissioner of the Treasury, I was asked to lead a delegation to Nassau to present a Mace to the House of Assembly in the Bahamian Parliament. It was a significant event, as it was a notable step in recognising the Bahamas as an independent Commonwealth country. The Mace is a symbol of the authority of the Speaker of the House in our Parliament and in their Assembly, but it was also an expression of goodwill and friendship and would hopefully reinforce the close ties between the Bahamian and British Parliaments. On arriving at Nassau airport on 2 November 1975, with my delegation comprising of William Shelton, MP for Streatham, and Michael Ryle, Deputy Principal Clerk of the House, I was greeted by the High Commissioner, Peter Mennen, who took me to one side and said he would like to discuss my delicate assignment in private. Imagine my sense of puzzlement when he asked if I had been made aware of the 'Mace situation' while in London. My reply was: 'Obviously not. I thought this was a "jolly" delegation, so you had better tell me now as the Mace was on the plane with us and I was looking forward to spending a few days in the Bahamas with the delegation in leisure time after the presentation.' The High Commissioner then explained why it was a difficult mission. It transpired that when premier Lynden Pindling was Leader of the Opposition, he became very incensed in a particular debate and got a hold of the Mace and threw it out the window, and it was not recovered. The event, which was known as 'Black Tuesday', occurred on 27 April 1965 and the debate was over the revision of constituency boundaries, which would have favoured the already governing United Bahamian Party in elections. The resulting election in 1967 was a win for the Progressive Liberal Party, with independence from Great Britain being granted in 1973. I now had the task of presenting the Mace to Parliament, with Pindling now as the Prime Minister – a difficult and delicate mission indeed.

Unfortunately, the trip was marred in my case by a severe case of food poisoning on the evening before the Mace ceremony itself. My duty, alongside the High Commissioner, was to greet the worthies of the island due to meet the visiting parliamentarians from the UK. As people began to arrive, I was feeling very hungry watching others enjoying their food. I pointed out to the High Commissioner that perhaps he had eaten but I hadn't and was feeling pretty peckish. I asked if there was any way I could join in and have a snack myself in-between greeting the guests. He ordered a waiter to bring a dish of conch fish, which I discreetly hid behind me and spiked one at a time between greeting guests. The unfortunate result did not manifest itself until after the presentation when I went down with serious food poisoning and was taken to the local hospital. There I had the unhappy experience of not only suffering intensely, but also seeing my colleagues through my hospital window enjoying life on the beach and on yachts.

On my return from the Bahamas, I was expected, as is the custom, to give a short speech to thank the House on behalf of the Bahamian Parliament for presenting them with the Mace. However, my speech was interrupted by John Stonehouse MP. I was very upset that my neat little speech was ruined but I should have realised the strange circumstances surrounding John at that time.

John Stonehouse was a man of many parts – handsome, debonair (he always wore a flower in his button hole), bright and highly popular in the two constituencies he represented – first in the West Midlands seat of Wednesbury, which he held from 1957; then the nearby seat of Walsall North in 1974 after the former constituency was abolished. His career seemed to be going up and up from the time he was first elected. Harold Wilson gave him his first ministerial job as a junior minister of aviation. He then moved to the Colonial Office before becoming minister of state for technology under Tony Benn. In March 1968 he negotiated an agreement providing a framework for the long-term development of technological co-operation between Britain and Czechoslovakia. It provided for the exchange of specialists and information, facilities for study and research in technology, and such other forms of industrial co-operation that might be agreed.

He was then appointed Postmaster-General before that position was abolished, and, as Minister of Posts and Telecommunications in 1970. And a glittering political career seemed guaranteed. That was held back by some curious fraudulent dealings in an attempt to secure a regular income. By 1974 most of his outside interests were in financial trouble, and he resorted to deceptive creative accounting. The Department of Trade and Industry started taking a close interest and he decided to flee the country. In November 1974 his clothing was found on the beach in Miami but there was no sign of his body. It later transpired that he had fled to Australia to be with his lover Sheila Buckley. He adopted a false identity of two deceased constituents. Joseph Markham was the name on his new Australian counterfeit passport, while Clive Mildoon was the name used when he masqueraded around town. Moreover, among his many shady financial dealings, John ran away with £600,000 from a charity fund he set up to allegedly help hurricane victims in Bangladesh. I remember how at a Labour Party conference he went out

of his way to request my support within the Bangladeshi Community.
He knew that I represented a large number of Bangladeshi constituents
in Hyde, and as a consequence, I knew some highly placed members of
the Bangladesh government. However, by then I had heard about some
of his shady dealings within the co-operative movement and I declined
to assist him. What struck me most in my talks with Stonehouse and
his wife Barbara was that she made a bigger impression on me than his
overtures did. She had incredible green eyes. I couldn't believe that he
could have left her in such a callous way. Mistaken for the notorious
Lord Lucan, a suspected murderer on the run, John was arrested in 1974
and later, in 1975, deported back to the UK. Until his trial in April 1976,
he still remained an MP. In hindsight, I suspect that his interruption
during the speech I made after the parliamentary delegation to the
Bahamas was to make it known to the general public that he was still
alive and kicking.

During that interruption he spoke with some concern about the fate
of the Christmas turkeys that had arrived in the House of Commons'
Post Office. He said:

On a point of order, Mr Speaker. A great deal of publicity has
been given to the subject of turkeys. Apparently, two have already
been delivered to hon. Members, and it is suggested that the 635
of us are due to receive them ... but if these turkeys should arrive,
hon. Members may not be here to receive them, and as the House's
deep freezes will be quite incapable of holding so many turkeys
during the recess, could we have an assurance that, if they do arrive,
they will immediately be delivered to the hospitals in the locality
and that hon. Members will not have to meet the awful problem of

dealing with turkeys which will have been here a fortnight when they return?

Mr Speaker George Thomas slapped him down, stating: 'I have many responsibilities, but I am not sure that acceptance or storing of turkeys is one of them. No doubt the point which the right hon. Gentleman has made will be noted and dealt with appropriately by whosoever ought to do so.' I was then allowed to continue my little speech.

John Stonehouse was hauled into the Old Bailey in 1976 on twenty-one charges of fraud, theft, forgery and conspiracy. The trial lasted sixty-eight days, after which he was sentenced to seven years in prison. Following his release, he worked as a volunteer fundraiser for an east London charity, and joined the SDP, which later merged with the Liberals to become the Lib Dems. He died on 14 April 1988. Secret documents not declassified until 2005 indicate that Stonehouse had spent months rehearsing his new identity. But there were even more revelations to come in this extraordinary story.

In 1969, Stonehouse had successfully defended himself against claims that he was a Czech secret service agent. But the allegation was later substantiated in the official history of MI5 by Cambridge historian Christopher Andrew, who revealed that Margaret Thatcher had agreed in 1980 to cover up revelations Stonehouse had been a traitor since the 1960s as there was insufficient evidence to bring him to trial.

JOHN SMITH

John Smith MP and I experienced a number of good times together. I remember well a parliamentary trip we took with others to the US Democratic Convention in 1972. It was designated as a delegation of young politicians, which also included Jack Cunningham and David Hunt, then chairman of the Young Conservatives. On a spare after-noon, the delegates went swimming in the hotel pool and I observed that, as John dived into the pool, his hotel room keys fell from his trunks. I watched him go to the side, put on his glasses, look into the water and further dive in without success. He repeated this a number of times – not realising I had already dived in and recovered his keys. After some fifteen minutes or so, I waved the keys and said, 'Is this what you have been looking for?' John exploded and charged at me and if caught I might have witnessed an aggressive side to John not seen before or since. I recognise now how stupid I was, as it could have had serious health consequences for him, not knowing then of his heart problem revealed in later life. John clearly forgave me when he was elected leader of the Labour Party – it was he who appointed me to be the Labour shadow Minister for Sport.

On 11 May 1994, I attended a gala dinner organised by the Labour Party at a Park Lane Hotel in Piccadilly in London. John Smith was the principal guest of honour and it was very much a splendid occasion. His speech went down very well, with spirits high and cash being heaped into the party's coffers during the auction. It was a jovial party atmos-phere and John Prescott was the most generous giver at auction time – although it later transpired that he was bidding on behalf of a generous benefactor of the party. I was so pleased with the leader's speech. He hit all the right notes and seemed on top of the world throughout the even-ing. John was always a special person in my political life. We were elected on the same day in June 1970, and he never seemed to change from being a humble backbencher even when at the height of being leader of the Labour Party. One of the celebrity acts at the gala was the famous mouth organist Larry Adler who, at the same event the year before, had played alongside the equally famous pianist Roy Budd, who had recently died and was sadly missed. I asked Larry if he knew Sylvia Budd's telephone number as I had not heard the news of Roy's passing, being abroad at the time. Larry took my number and said he would ring through to me the following morning. Midnight arrived and my last recollection of John Smith was when he waved me goodbye as I left the hotel. John stayed behind and went upstairs, probably for another dram of whisky.

The following morning, I was watching breakfast television when I observed the dramatic events taking place outside the Barbican flats where John lived. Sadly, the story was as grim; it was revealed that our beloved leader had been pronounced dead. John succumbed to a heart attack in his flat that morning and was rushed to St Bartholomew's Hospital where he died. At that very moment, my phone rang. It was Larry, about to give me the phone number I had requested the night before. Before he said much, I stopped him and conveyed the terrible news that I had just heard. It seemed like five minutes of sobbing before I could get any words from Larry. He had clearly heard enough and the phone went dead.

After a respectable pause from any election news of a successor, and after John's funeral in Edinburgh, which I, along with many of my parliamentary colleagues, attended, the parliamentary party battle for leadership commenced in earnest. There were two main contenders with John Prescott and Tony Blair both vying for the post.

BERT GREEN

Bert Green made history by being the very first civil servant to be included in a traditional photograph with the Prime Minister and his government whips at No. 10, with the famous Gainsborough picture in the background. It was a great honour to be included and I knew Bert was so chuffed at the opportunity. However, his good fortune evaporated as only his body can be seen in the photograph – his head was removed and replaced with mine. I was in Strasbourg on the Council of Europe at the time, and, amazingly, my absence was not noticed. At the next whips meeting the Deputy Chief Whip, Walter Harrison, told those assembled that 'the photographs with the Prime Minister and his whips are ready for collection'. When I showed my puzzlement of this, Walter gasped; he clearly had not realised that I was abroad doing whip's business – ironically, as the whip for the party on our delegation at the Council of Europe, he should have of all people been aware of my absence. That was when my head was put on his body. Bert, believing he was making history by being the only civil servant to appear in this special photograph, in fact made history for another reason – by being displayed as partly a civil servant and partly a government whip on the wall of No. 12 Downing Street. This photograph has been the subject of every tour around the Whips' Office in that famous street ever since.

CHIEF WHIP

When Harold Wilson retired and James Callaghan became Prime Minister, I and some of my colleagues in the Whips' Office were once again hoping for a leg up. We knew that the current Chief Whip, Bob Mellish, was retiring, and a new one would almost certainly want a number of new recruits. We clearly hoped that if we were replaced we would be given some advancement for our hard work!

The normal whips meeting took place at 2.15 p.m. in the Chief Whip's office. On the day in question, when Callaghan was assembling his team, we made our way to the office only to find no sign of Bob or his replacement. I thought I'd have a little fun and I sat in the Chief Whip's chair, brought the rest of the whips to order and began the meeting. Very solemnly I began by saying:

As you all know Bob is leaving and I'm fortunate enough to be here taking his place. I have enjoyed working alongside all of you and I recognise that the world doesn't stand still and there will have to be some changes. I recognise fully that we wouldn't be in government if it wasn't for the collective efforts of this team who has sustained the government against the backdrop of such a small majority – but you must, I'm sure, understand and appreciate they'll have to make some changes to bring one or two new members into the office and one or two unfortunately will be either recommended to go on and up or to return to the back benches.

I began to realise that those assembled were taking me seriously. I began to laugh and said, 'Well, that fooled you all, didn't it?' – only for Jack Dormand, the pairing whip, to blurt out: 'Tom, haven't you heard the one o'clock news? You were mentioned as a contender for the new Chief Whip.' At that very moment, luckily, Bob Mellish came in with the actual new Chief Whip, Michael Cocks, and I made a hasty retreat from the Chief Whip's chair with, I'm sure, a very red blush on my face.

However, that wasn't the end of the saga. After the meeting, on my way to my office in the Norman Shaw North building, I bumped into the well-known and highly respected Martyn Lewis of the BBC. He said: 'Tom, you caused us a lot of trouble today. We've had your photograph in and out of our files as we were told you were the new Chief Whip.' I told him that I was sure it was because Michael Cocks had the same hairstyle as myself – we were both a little short on top. Perhaps he was photographed from behind and he'd thought it was me? 'No,' said Martyn, 'at the briefing this morning at No. 10 your name was given as the new Chief Whip.' I was later shown the front page of the *Evening Standard* where I was listed along with some other big names as going up to 10 Downing Street on my way to a new job. Unfortunately, that seemed to be the story of my life and I remained in the Whips' Office until my resignation sometime afterwards for different reasons.

I always took pride in the work I did for individual constituents and their families – whether it was helping people get decently housed, helping them deal with unblocked drains, sorting out disputes, or ensuring people got a fair deal in terms of entitlements to benefits and justice. After all, you can't go around knocking on doors to get elected and then not deliver something in return. But sometimes people came to expect I could perform miracles. The following is a brief local news report from that time:

> Proceedings were interrupted at Dukinfield court today when the father of a man refused bail said to the magistrates: 'Tom Pendry is going to hear about this and something will be done.'
>
> Duncan C——, a nineteen-year-old unemployed labourer, of Stalybridge, was committed in custody to the Crown Court accused jointly with entering Copley Comprehensive School, Stalybridge, and stealing property worth £21.41.
>
> The father returned to the court room two minutes later and when told to leave by officials, shouted: 'I want their names and you cannot stop me. I shall tell Tom Pendry about you…'
>
> He was escorted from the court room still protesting.

CHAPTER 5

AIRCRAFT AND SHIPBUILDING BILL

On 27 May 1976, I found myself as a senior government whip caught up in a House of Commons drama which has been described as unique in British political history.

It all began when the two Labour governments of 1974 pledged to nationalise the troubled aircraft and shipbuilding industries. Set against a period of hardship and economic strife, and coupled with the fact that both governments had a wafer-thin majority, the government proceeded to push its legislative programme through the House. At the time, the country was still licking its wounds from a three-day week imposed by the previous Heath government in reaction to the dwindling supply of electricity. The political climate was also different to the previous year, with all three major parties being led by new incumbents. James Callaghan had taken over from Harold Wilson, who was forced to step aside after winning both the 1974 elections, while Ted Heath was defeated by his own parliamentary colleagues and found himself replaced by Margaret Thatcher in February 1975. Moreover, the resignation of Jeremy Thorpe forced the Liberals to choose Jo Grimond as interim leader before David Steel took the post some months later.

Within this context, I and my fellow whips had to marshal through a programme of governance that included pledges to create a new Charter for Women, action on the European Common Market and co-ordinated policies on transport and the environment to react to the energy crisis of 1973. It also included a strong commitment to nationalise the economically troubled aircraft and shipbuilding industries – a commitment enshrined in the Labour election manifestos.

The necessary Bill had been first introduced in 1973 when it met with immediate opposition from the leaders of those industries – notably from a former Labour Cabinet Minister Lord Alf Robens then the Labour MP for Blyth, but at that time chairman of Vickers. Nationalisation was proposed in July 1974 and the Bill had its first reading in April 1975, outlining the powers and responsibilities of two new public corporations to be known as the British Aerospace and the British Shipbuilders. The Bill, however, failed to reach its Second Reading stage in the Commons during the 1974–75 parliamentary session due to pressure of other legislation and was reintroduced in November 1975.

When that Bill eventually came to committee, I was given the task of being the government whip at that stage. It had fifty-eight sittings; the greatest number in the history of the House of Commons. It sat for 140 hours, and the curious thing was that, throughout that time, no opposition member ever raised the issue that was later to cause the parliamentary storm. However, after the committee proceedings had been concluded, the Bill made its way to the Commons Chamber and on that fateful day a Tory MP, Robin Maxwell-Hyslop, in his submission to Speaker George Thomas, argued that the Bill was in fact a 'Hybrid' Bill. That is a Bill with characteristics of both a Public Bill and a Private Bill, one which spans both public and private interest, and as such they are examined in Parliament by a combination of both Public Bill and Private Bill procedures. The Speaker, after much deliberation, held that in fact the Bill was *prima facie* 'hybrid' and the motion proposed by the government to proceed therefore began its passage for debate against that background. Realising the government's vulnerability, the Leader of the Opposition, Margaret Thatcher, instructed her whips to maximise their vote – and her demands were matched by their determination to carry out her wishes to the full. Ship repairing was removed from the Bill because of the legislation's hybrid nature. The Tories wanted at best to kill the Bill or, as eventually happened, to force the government to make concessions, including removal of the twelve ship repairing companies from the nationalisation plan.

So it seemed logical for me, having spent all those long hours in committee as the government whip in charge of the Bill, that when the Division bells rang at 10 p.m. that night I could confidently approach the Division Lobby to vote for the government motion. I was then told by the government pairing whip, Jack Dormand, in charge of arrangements that normally allowed an equal number of MPs from both sides to be away on other business, to stay out of the Lobby as we were going to win – having sorted out the arithmetic with his opposite number, John Stradling Thomas, in the opposition Whips' Office. He added: 'You know the score, Tom.' In response, I said: 'Jack, I'll do it, but kicking and screaming. As you know, I helped to pilot this Bill through committee and it would appear very odd if I didn't support it now.' Angry as I was, I stayed out only to find that my colleague's arithmetic was faulty. The vote was 303 to 303 and the Speaker, adhering to a precedent set in 1862, voted with the government. However, when a second vote was to take place, then the Speaker would be required to vote for the opposition's amendment, and the second had been tabled by Thatcher. The government's vote would be nullified and a vote of no confidence in Her Majesty's Government would almost certainly follow within days.

On hearing that, and with the help of the whips' manager, Bert Green, I set off to investigate what had gone wrong, despite being urged by many of my colleagues like Neil Kinnock, Stan Orme and Eric Heffer, among others, to vote. I refused. After all, it was not only the government's neck on the line, but also mine. If I had been found guilty of cheating, my days would have been numbered. With only a few minutes left before the next and vital vote, I discovered that one of our ministers, Fred Peart, who had been counted as eligible to vote that morning, had gone abroad on parliamentarian business believing he was paired. Armed with that news, I made it to the Aye Lobby just in time to vote as the doors slammed behind me. The result was 304 to 303, and the government won by my vote!

Although the outcome was satisfying, I knew that this was not the end of the story for me by a long way. There was bound to be anger and resentment on the opposition benches, which was made clear to me when I came out of the lobby after casting my vote, at which point I found John Stradling Thomas, the Tory pairing whip, standing in front of me. He was clearly both bemused and furious and pointedly asked me why I had voted. I didn't feel obliged to go into details with him, so I hurried off to my office, somewhat flustered. I did not wish to witness what I felt would surely be a stressful time in the Chamber when the result was announced. Instead, I began finishing off a speech I was to make to an old-age pensions meeting in my constituency in Hyde the following weekend – all the while keeping an eye on the annunciator.

It was a major victory. The subsequent Act nationalised twenty-seven major shipbuilding and marine engineering companies, and a further six ship repair companies. In total, it emerged that British Shipbuilders were to account for a staggering 97 per cent of the UK's merchant shipbuilding capacity, as well as all of its warship-building capacity, 100 per cent of slow speed diesel engine manufacturing and approximately half of ship-repair capacity. The Act also nationalised and merged the British Aircraft Corporation, the Hawker Siddeley Group and Scottish Aviation. It was a big deal at the time, which was why the bosses and the Tories had fought so hard to block it. But all that was in the future.

What I missed on leaving the Chamber that night were the incredible scenes that had taken place in my absence. After the vote was announced it showed that the government had survived the alleged 'cheat vote'. A massive celebration on the Labour benches erupted in the chambers with Labour MPs cheering and singing 'The Red Flag' in jubilation. However, the opposition's reaction was naturally quite different. This was clearly displayed by Michael Heseltine, who had led for the opposition on the Bill in committee in his capacity as shadow Industry Secretary. To display his anger, Michael picked up the Commons Mace and with both hands swung it in the direction of the government benches. He was only restrained by his ministerial colleague Jim Prior, who took it from him and replaced it, unfortunately the wrong way around, which prompted the Speaker to suspend the sitting until the following day – it is a cast-iron rule of the House that proceedings cannot continue when the Mace is absent or incorrectly placed. The next morning Michael Heseltine apologised unreservedly for his behaviour. Heseltine was thereafter depicted in political cartoons as Tarzan, complete with loin-cloth.

Although I was not present to see this dramatic event, it was not long before I was acquainted with it. After the annunciator displayed

'House Suspended', within minutes my door opened and a very anxious-looking Jack Cunningham, parliamentary private secretary (PPS) to the Prime Minister, entered, saying with an anxious voice: 'Tom, you better come to see the boss. And I warn you he is not well pleased.' Jack accompanied me into the Prime Minister's office behind the Speaker's Chair. Those present included the Leader of the House, Michael Foot, and our pairing whip Jack Dormand. I was greeted with a very stern, if not angry, Prime Minister. 'Sit down, Tom. Were you paired at tonight's vote?' I told him that I had not been paired and that it was a question of the arithmetic by the pairing whips. I got the clear impression that I was not believed completely, and so Jim Callaghan demanded that Cunningham find the PPS to Fred Peart, a certain George Grant, MP for Morpeth. Jack was dismissed to find the hapless PPS, which led him to the Strangers Bar where he found George the worse for wear. That was not an unusual sight. George was the exception to the sensible rule that a minister with a drink problem should have a very sober PPS. Cunningham steered him away in his intoxicated condition to the PM's office. When he arrived, George excitedly blurted out in his Geordie accent: 'Whey aye, Jim! What a great night. Come down to the Strangers, we're all singing "The Red Flag", "The Internationale"; they would love to see you there.' Jim was in no mood to celebrate at this stage and he still partially believed that a 'cheat vote' had been committed in order to keep the government afloat, which could well lose us the next general election, especially if a vote of confidence was called with his small majority; going to the electorate in those circumstances could be fatal. 'Pull yourself together,' snapped the Prime Minister. 'Was your minister paired for tonight's votes?' George replied: 'Whey aye, Jim, I think he would be paired, but come on, Jim, let's go down to the Strangers Bar, let's celebrate. What a great night it's been.' It has to be said that George had not fully recognised the severity of the situation. Recognising George's inebriated state, the PM let him leave, as it would have been fruitless to continue.

The PM then sought to find the telephone number of Fred Peart's private secretary (his 'Sir Humphrey', in other words). This poor man was woken up at some unearthly hour and probably, one might have assumed, leaped out of bed not knowing who would be at the other end. If he had not been fully awake, then he certainly would have been brought to his senses when he heard the recognisable voice of the Prime Minister. Jim's first words were: 'I know you are not responsible for what your minister's pairing arrangements are, but would you in any way know if he was paired for the votes tonight in the Commons?' The civil servant replied respectfully, agreeing with Jim that it was certainly not his business to know such things, but he did volunteer the name of the hotel in Copenhagen where Peart was staying. Not caring about the time of night or early morning, the PM rang Fred at his hotel and not surprisingly found him, even at that late hour, in the hotel bar, saying: 'This is the Prime Minister here, Fred ... No. I'm not Harold.' It was clear that Fred was in a similar state to his PPS and had mistaken Jim for Harold Wilson, who had recently retired. The PM said: 'Pull yourself together, man. Were you paired for tonight's votes?' The reply was a hesitant: 'Whey aye, Jim, I'm sure I was. I think I was.' Fred was another Geordie!

After those conversations, Callaghan for the first time appeared to be on my side in the ongoing row. Turning to Michael Foot, he said: 'Take Tom home and pick him up in the morning. I want him at 10 Downing Street at nine o'clock.' However, by that time, the ordure had already hit the fan. Every TV, radio and newspaper was referring to the 'cheat vote'. The headlines and broadcast leads shouted that the government had won by one vote and that I was the MP who 'broke the rules'. The *Daily Express* also included a photograph of me with a write-up, stating that it would have been unwise for the Tories to offer any 'fists' in my direction, citing my history of boxing.

LAUNCHING AN INQUIRY

On leaving the meeting with the Prime Minister and Michael Foot at No. 10 and entering the Commons, there was a plethora of photographers and journalists trying to get a statement from me, but I declined to comment at that stage. Moreover, Mrs Thatcher called off any cooperation with the government in the day-to-day handling of Commons business, forcing overworked ministers to attend votes they might otherwise have safely missed. Eventually, on 11 June, the PM wrote to Thatcher suggesting they resolve the dispute with a proper investigation. I was not the most popular Member in the House during that inquiry, which took over a month.

To every Labour Member's relief, and most certainly to mine, the inquiry concluded that I had not cheated on the vote. In Thatcher's statement on 22 June 1976 to the House, she stated: 'May I say that as a certain name has been mentioned, I should like to make it quite clear that the inquiry found no personal blame attached to the hon. Member for Stalybridge and Hyde.' In his statement, Callaghan said: 'The right hon. Lady the Leader of the Opposition and I met informally last week to consider how best to deal with this. We recognised that there was a sense of grievance about the vote on 27 May.'

Speaker Thomas, from the Chair, witnessed the Thatcher statement also and sent the following note to me: 'Tom, I was delighted to hear

Margaret Thatcher's reference to you today. The PM spoke for everyone when he welcomed the statement. So you see, 'righteousness always triumphs' – if you wait long enough. George.'

As the inquiry found that there were some misunderstandings about the pairing and voting arrangements on 27 May, Mrs Thatcher demanded a re-run of the votes, which was agreed by the PM. This was duly done and on the re-run the government had a comfortable majority.

Throughout the inquiry process, there were two exceptions to the ban on pairing. The first was that ministers, following a long standing convention, were expected to carry out their ministerial duties. The other exception could have related to me, as I was to take part in a Granada *World in Action* TV programme entitled *Run for your Life*. Its purpose was to gauge the fitness levels of MPs and I was one of the four chosen. They wanted to register the stress level of someone in the 'engine room', meaning the Whips' Office in the Commons, given that the gap between the major parties was very small and stress levels were very high. However, I was not aware at the time of my selection for the programme of the amount of stress that I would endure after the so-called 'cheat vote'. The other three were chosen because they had particular weight problems.

We all reported to a well-known London gym and of the four, I was considered to be the fittest, the right height and the proper weight, but the issue for me was whether I endured stress to the point where it was injurious to my health. Soon after the visit to that gym, the issue of the 'cheat vote' arose and I alone of those four was prohibited from going on a regular basis to the gym. As a consequence, I put on a pound or two. Thanks to the producer, when the film was shown to MPs in Westminster Hall there was hearty laughter when it was revealed that, although the others had made some progress, I had not made any weight progress at all. The film omitted to state that I was still the fittest of the four, nor did they care about the reason why my stress levels were through the roof. On a sad note, one of the participants in the programme died shortly after the filming. After the film, many of us went down to the terrace – me still smarting at the ridicule of the misrepresentation of the facts by my colleagues. My feeling of injustice was confirmed by the husband of the producer, Austin Mitchell MP, who said to me that it was obvious that I was the 'fall guy' in the programme. How right he was, and I had to live with that 'unfit' tag to my name for some time after.

THE PLAY

In 2013, a young playwright called James Graham wrote a play called *This House*, which was based in part on the events that took place on 27 May 1976 and was heralded as a great success. This very promising young playwright captured much of the atmosphere of that night, although it was not completely accurate. For instance, Ann Taylor, then an MP, now Baroness Taylor, was depicted as the heroine, when in reality she wasn't a whip at the time of the drama. She only became so after I resigned from the government and my whip's position for the northwest. She later went on to have a distinguished career as a Chief Whip in subsequent Labour governments. But at the time – January 1977 – she was an unexpected appointment as whip, having a record of rebelling against the front-bench line and causing me, as her whip at the time, quite a few headaches. That is demonstrated by a friendly exchange of notes when she took the post. She wrote to me: 'Can we have a word sometime about some of your ex-problems? I think it would be helpful to me if we could have a chat about what the job involves – perhaps I should have asked before accepting!' I replied: 'My biggest ex-problems was with those of my flock who didn't toe the line from time to time – and sometimes that included you. Once that is sorted out, it will be possible to make some progress with the north-west members.' But I went on: 'Seriously, I would like to do all I can to assist you and you will find that the north-west group are very little trouble and I am sure that you will be able to cope.' And cope she did, bearing in mind she was then one of only twenty-seven female MPs in the House.

Among other stage extravagancies in the play was the bad language used by some of the whips, which was not typical of my colleagues of that time, certainly not to the extent that was shown. Despite some of the discrepancies, I think that James Graham should nevertheless be congratulated for his play and indeed the actors on their performances.

The importance of that dramatic event on 27 May 1976 also found its way into many publications. Michael Heseltine did apologise after swinging the mace. However, after Thatcher announced the findings of the inquiry that I had not cheated, I found it amazing to see in Michael Heseltine's book *Life in the Jungle*, published in 2000, that he had written that 'a serious piece of legislation had secured its passage because the government of the day had cheated' and then mentioned me by name. On hearing this, I issued a libel case against Heseltine, after which Michael rang asking me what I wanted. 'Michael,' I said, 'I want my good name restored. I know you are not on the best of terms with your leader [Thatcher] but she spoke the truth, as did the two Chief Whips following the inquiry.' He didn't respond to my remarks. The result was that he was forced to rewrite that section of his book and pay me a sum of money. I have often wondered over the years whether Michael realised that when I was on vacation from Oxford in 1958, I was a night porter at the Regency Hotel in Ramsgate and had to polish his shoes when he left them outside his room at night. He was the personal friend of the two men who ran the hotel, who were also fellow students at Oxford with him. One of the two was a Conservative county councillor in Kent who despised Ted Heath so much that he changed his name by deed poll to fight him in a subsequent election in Bexley.

One would have thought that after my Heseltine experience, that would have been the end to my name being dragged in the mud, but subsequent to Heseltine's book, Sir Ivan Lawrence QC also followed suit with his book *My Life of Crime* – when he wrote his book, he would not have known how close he came to being judged a defendant himself. At the Tory conference in Birmingham in October 2012 I attended in my capacity as president of the Football Foundation as part of my duties to ensure political impartiality and to go to every length to demonstrate this to all parties. I therefore attended all the party conferences for a day or so to mingle with the sport-loving delegates and to show how accessible we are across the party divide. At that conference, on looking around the bookstall, I observed the former Tory MP for Burton upon Trent, who had lost his seat in the previous election, signing his book at the head of quite a long queue. On approaching Ivan, I jokingly said: 'I never knew you had so many friends, Ivan.'

'Yes,' he replied, 'and you feature in my book.' He fingered through the pages to find the appropriate page. Suddenly his fingers froze and, after a slight hesitation, he said: 'I think I had better continue signing these books.' I smelled a rat and proceeded to buy his book. To my complete surprise, I read on page 146 the following: 'When it became clear that the government was going to lose the vote [Aircraft and

Shipbuilding], it decided to cheat. It did this by counting Tom Pendry, a government whip as a voter, when he had agreed to pair with a Tory colleague not to vote.'

The Mail Online reported my reaction: '…at that his brow darkened like the skies over the Ryder Cup in Newport. There was a silence. A pause. And an eruption.' On returning to the bookstall, I confronted Ivan with the words: 'You are in all kinds of trouble. Heseltine made the same mistake of alleging me a cheat and he has had to pay as a consequence. You will be hearing from my solicitor.' A very worried Ivan rang me later. He was in quite a state, probably having taken some advice. He told me that he would be finished if I went ahead with a libel case. At this point, he had already lost his seat, he wasn't able to sell his house in Burton upon Trent, and he had to borrow money from his wife to write the book. Moreover, he pleaded that a case against him would jeopardise his position at the Bar. I sought legal counsel and was advised I could be a millionaire if I went ahead with a libel case. My counsel argued that because of the retraction and settlement with Heseltine, any defamation of my good name as it related to the 'cheat vote' incident could be legally considered as libel with malice. However, despite my many colleagues saying that I should throw the book at him, being the big softie that I am, I conveyed to Ivan through my solicitor that if he gave £2,000 to The Passage, a charity I supported that assisted homeless people in London, and also paid my legal costs, then I would leave it at that. I can say that I am still nowhere near being a millionaire, but the thing that upset me most was that I didn't even get a thank you from Ivan when clearly the consequences for him could have been dire if I had gone ahead. This didn't surprise many of my colleagues, but it did me, as, despite his faults on this occasion,

I remembered him being very kind and considerate to my daughter Fiona as a fourteen-year-old on a visit to Rome when we were on a parliamentary visit to meet the Pope. He escorted her around the hotel where we were staying and he was impressed with her fluency in French, stating that she was better than him when he was her age – she was suitably flattered. Another strange consequence of this story was that, when reading his book, I discovered that we were at the same RAF Compton Bassett in Wiltshire during our national service in the same year, 1955, doing the same course. It would be surprising in the extreme if we had not met at that time for one very good reason, specifically, that on the Sunday morning parade, and before marching off to the local Church of England church, the call went out from the officer in charge for 'Jews and Roman Catholics to fall-out', and since I was a Roman Catholic and he was a Jew, almost certainly the five or six of us who fell out would have included the pair of us – one later becoming a Tory and the other a Labour MP. Small world, isn't it?

It was surprising for me to discover that the foreword in Sir Ivan's book was written and endorsed by none other than Michael Howard QC, former leader of the Conservative Party. Michael wrote: 'This book is a gem … and the book is a brilliant account of the trials and tribulations of life as a back-bench MP.' One wonders who would allow such words to be written in the foreword when the book contained comments that were clearly defamatory. Surely Michael should have spotted it, after all he was one of Margaret Thatcher's biggest admirers, as was Ivan himself, and also a QC. It is worth noting that Sir Ivan has now published a larger volume of his book and there is no mention of me or of the Aircraft and Shipbuilding Bill – strange, eh?!

CHAPTER 6

MINISTER FOR
NORTHERN IRELAND

A s the situation for the Labour government became somewhat easier following an unofficial pact with the Liberals, I felt some of the pressure had been lifted off me, and I resigned as a whip. I thought my career was levelling out so I quit not over any policy difference, but to spend more time with my family, especially my first-born child Fiona. Moreover, I enjoyed the freedom to speak up and ask questions about issues affecting my constituents – something I couldn't do as a member of the government. This was particularly important because two of my colleagues with parliamentary seats within Tameside, Bob Sheldon MP and Ken Marks MP, were also members of the government and could not talk about constituency issues at the time.

Now back on the back benches, I enjoyed the luxury of not being obliged to work long hours in the Whips' Office. That did not last for long, however.

On 10 November 1978, with Moira and baby Fiona in London, I waited until the 10 p.m. vote had been cast before driving off to my constituency with my family. After a short distance up the M1 we encountered heavy fog and we were diverted around Watford for some time before returning to the motorway. The journey was tortuous enough and we eventually arrived at our village home of Broadbottom in my constituency at around 3 a.m. All three of us were exhausted and I struggled to bed at some unearthly hour. At about 9 a.m., I was awoken by a telephone call, which I was in no mood to answer, thinking it would be one of my constituents well able to come to one of my six surgeries that I held every month. Moira answered on my behalf and moments later she came to my bedside to tell me that it was No. 10 on the phone and that they wanted to talk to me. To this day, I don't know who it was on the phone. Believing it to be something I could deal with when I was fully awake, I told Moira to tell whoever it was to ask if they realised that I had come through the night after the 10 p.m. vote, and didn't get home until the early hours of the morning and would they ring back later? She returned a few moments later to say that the PM knew that I voted last night but he still wanted to see me at No. 10 at 3 p.m. that day. That certainly woke me up. What have I done wrong? I thought. It couldn't have been a promotion as to the best of my knowledge no minister had resigned or died, nor was there a reshuffle scheduled. So off I went by Manchester Piccadilly fearing the worst and preparing to meet my fate – whatever it was to be.

Arriving at No. 10, I was met by my old friend Bernard (now Lord) Donoughue, head of the PM's think tank. He was as bemused as I was, and informed me that John Smith was in the Cabinet Room with the PM, and that when he came out I was to go in. He wanted me to tell him afterwards what my meeting was all about. Moments later, John Smith came out smiling like a Cheshire cat but said nothing. It later transpired that he had been promoted to Secretary of State for Trade.

I was ushered into the Cabinet Room to face James Callaghan on his own. He asked me about my baby Fiona and reminded me of the occasion in the Commons tea room when I broke all the rules and thrust my little girl, of only a few weeks, into his arms. After a bit of such small talk he said: 'You must be wondering why you're here.' He proceeded to refer to the infamous night of 27 May 1977, the day of my alleged 'cheat vote'. He pulled out what appeared to be a pocket diary that told him that from that day on he saw me as ministerial material because of the way I had handled that incident. He then said that he wanted me to be the Under Secretary of State to Northern Ireland, under Roy Mason. At that time in the late 1970s the Northern Ireland portfolio was hardly one for which members with ministerial ambitions were queuing up to get. Indeed, it was not necessarily at the top of my list of ambitions, yet when Jim Callaghan offered it to me, I had no hesitation in taking on what I knew would be a challenging, yet equally fulfilling role. When I left the Cabinet Room, I didn't see Bernard Donoughue to tell him the good news. I then blissfully prepared the following day to meet my new boss, the late Roy Mason, a veteran of some thirty years in Parliament representing Barnsley. As a young man, and a former Yorkshire miner, he was elected MP in 1953. On entering his office that day, Roy greeted me warmly as we had previously served together on both the Council of Europe and on the Western European Union when I was the whip. I immediately felt at ease in his company and throughout my time as a member of his team I could hardly have wished for a better Secretary of State to work under. He remained a good friend and was certainly the best boss I have ever had and I very much regretted to hear of his passing in April 2015. So off I went to Northern Ireland where I enjoyed my stay despite the potential hazards over time to my personal safety, which worried my family and friends.

When I arrived in 1978 there was a sense of war-weariness in Northern Ireland after almost a decade of the Troubles had left over 2,000 dead and many times that number injured, crippled or exiled. The death toll had peaked in 1972 when nearly 500 people, just over half of them civilians, lost their lives, but there was still a steady stream of casualties and outrages on all sides of the Ulster Divide. In Belfast, Derry and other cities and towns, the bomb and the barricade, the sniper and the army checkpoint had become a way of life.

Harold Wilson had secretly met with the IRA in 1971 and ministers did so again in late 1974 and early 1975 in an attempt to negotiate a cease-fire. The failure of the Sunningdale Agreement saw Wilson consider, then abandon, a plan for a rapid British withdrawal. Garret Fitzgerald, the Taoiseach of the Republic of Ireland, concluded that the Irish government could do little to help counter the expected anarchy if Britain did withdraw. In December the IRA declared a ceasefire. Despite that, sectarian killings actually escalated in 1975, along with internal feuding between rival paramilitary groups. The violence continued through the rest of the 1970s. When the Provisional IRA's ceasefire ended in early 1976, it developed a strategy known as the 'Long War', which involved a less intense but more sustained campaign of violence that could continue indefinitely. This was the situation in which I found myself when appointed Under Secretary of State.

The Troubles had been sparked by civil rights protests in the late 1960s by the mainly Catholic community, denied political clout by the mainly Protestant Ulster Unionists who had all the power. It quickly turned into a murderous campaign in which both sides used terror tactics against each other, the police and the British Army, and civilian targets on both sides of the Irish Sea. Over almost thirty years, more than 3,500 people were to be killed in the conflict. And it was not until the Blair government steered through the Good Friday Agreement in 1998 that an imperfect peace was achieved. Despite other acts associated with Tony Blair that he subsequently has been accused of, one thing is certain – the peace that now exists in the province is largely down to him. He, together with his close associate Bill Clinton, was responsible, more than any other, for ensuring that the necessary political and religious divide was healed, if not completely, then enough to have a stable and workable administration in the province.

I would like to think that in the short time I was a junior minister, I made a very small impact, not least because of my sports background. Within a few days of my arrival at Stormont I had to meet a deputation that my predecessor James Dunn had arranged. It related to an order that would have moved the sports department away from the Sports Council and into the Department of Education. The meeting took place at a golf club in County Down and it consisted of a delegation of worthy sportsmen led by the highly respected chief executive, George Glasgow. With some forcible verbosity he said: 'Typical of English folk coming to the province with no knowledge of how we deal with sport here. We understand the people of the province and what they want – and they certainly would not get it from those lofty people in the Education Department.' It went on in that way and others joined in before I spoke. 'First of all,' I told them,

I have observed the sporting scene, admittedly from afar in Northern Ireland, but I did attend the Munich Olympics in 1972 where I

witnessed Mary Peters win her gold medal and I have admired the
sporting success of many of your athletes, in particular some of your
young boxers.

I could see that they were hardly impressed with my worldly knowledge until I held up the document in question and calmly stated that
this was the work of my predecessor, not myself. I then tore it up and
threw it in the bin. I concluded by telling the delegation that the
Sports Council in Northern Ireland would remain safe in our hands.
So pleased were they at this that after the general election of 1979 I was
invited to a special function in my honour. I attended the opening of
a new sports headquarters where I met some members of that delegation, together with my old friend Mary Peters. It could not have been
a better baptism for me, a sportsman myself, to win over the sportsmen
and women of Northern Ireland.

In addition to my involvement with the Sports Council, I was also
Minister of Agriculture for Northern Ireland. As duty minister, one
weekend I woke up to hear on the radio that there had been some
terrible flooding in the province, especially bad in the Newcastle area
of Enoch Powell's constituency in County Down. My immediate
reaction was to go to investigate the situation. I first ordered some
gum boots and informed Powell's office, as protocol demands, that I
would be visiting his constituency. When I arrived, there was absolute
chaos and it appeared that all the emergency services were no longer in
existence – phones were defunct and there were no safety officers.
I waded through areas of heavy flooding and climbed over fences
before eventually realising that it was an impossible situation and
that this should never happen again. I then went back to Stormont

around lunchtime, but not before I had ordered all those responsible offices of the appropriate departments to come in and face my music, which I am sure they anticipated would not be melodic to their ears. It was a Saturday afternoon so I was of course the least popular minister of all time, and when these people assembled, I began by saying that I had seen the flooding at Downside and was not well pleased. Their faces were already very well drawn, probably in annoyance that their Saturday had been disrupted, but I spelt out that I wanted a much better system as from Monday morning. News of my impromptu lunchtime meeting was also conveyed to Roy Mason, but he didn't complain, even when my activity hit the national news back home, with Angela Rippon's description on BBC News about the extent of the flooding and the hapless minister ploughing through the swamps in an attempt to comfort the stranded folk in that part of County Down.

One of the most controversial issues I dealt with when I was in Northern Ireland involved IRA members in HM Prison Maze. I did my best to defuse the dangerous tension.

I spoke to a representative from the IRA group, who made a request that the prisoners would welcome the opportunity to visit their immediate families at weddings, baptisms and funerals and in return guarantee that they would, if allowed this opportunity, adhere to any timetable agreed to, adding that a failure by anyone to do so would be dealt with by their fellow IRA inmates themselves. I knew precisely what that meant. So, on that basis, and recognising that most Catholics, and in particular those in the Maze, believed in the importance of attending religious events with their families, I telephoned the RUC's Chief Constable, Sir Kenneth Newman. He was clearly not well pleased with my phone call but had to accept my instruction. The Secretary of State on his return from London the following week did not in any way rebuke me for taking that action – or at least to the best of my knowledge that remained the case, although after Mo Mowlam became Secretary of State in 1997 she did claim the credit for that initiative in the Maze. In fact, the focus of her initiative – almost twenty years after mine – was on Ulster Loyalist prisoners, where she did indeed show great courage in meeting convicted murderers and terrorists face-to-face and unaccompanied.

One of the great delights of being in Northern Ireland was recognising that Cuan Oysters, part of Cuan Sea Fisheries Ltd, was part of my portfolio as the minister for agriculture. The department had been in league with the Guinness firm to bring Cuan Oysters to the province. It was a great success in the British Isles as one of the first commercial producers of Pacific oysters. What made Cuan Oysters special was that they were available and consumable the whole year round rather than only in the months ending with 'r', for oysters that were consumed by most in the UK were from oyster beds in Cornwall, Dorset, Devon and Kent, to name but a few. Established in 1974 in Strangford Lough, Cuan sadly no longer exists, but then was one of the UK's leading suppliers of live molluscs. Indeed, as one of the first commercial producers of Pacific oysters in the British Isles, the company had been at the forefront of oyster-marketing for twenty years, handling over 400 tonnes of oysters each year. The speed of the tidal movement and the huge nutrient richness of the water are what made them so good. The only accompaniment you needed was lemon juice and black pepper.

My ministerial job in Northern Ireland did not come without danger. During the troubled years the obvious form of transport for a minister going from place to place – sometimes in very delicate areas – was by helicopter. We were trying to keep one step ahead of IRA intelligence, which was surprisingly good. We had to make sure that we went in and out of areas as quickly as possible and there was only one time I ever had a problem. On this one occasion I was expected to be at Belfast City Hall for a function but I was delayed. However, when I got there it was surrounded by soldiers and police and, as it turned out, just before my arrival, an IRA terrorist had got inside the cordoned area of the centre of Belfast and shot a high-velocity bullet in the direction of City Hall. The IRA obviously felt they got some bad information as the minister wasn't there at the time expected, but they nevertheless demonstrated that they were still a serious menace in that regard.

It is said that the most bombed hotel in Europe was the Europa in the centre of Belfast. Many dignitaries and heads of state had stayed in this hotel over the years and so the building became a strategic target for the IRA. It suffered some thirty-three or so bomb attacks between 1970 and 1994. Immediately next door was the very lovely Grand Opera House, and in one bomb attack the IRA had damaged both buildings. As the appropriate minister, I set about restoring the Opera House to its original state by ensuring that adequate funding was found. After we lost the 1979 election and I became a shadow Minister for Northern Ireland, I was invited to its reopening by way of a thank you. It would appear that the IRA had problems within their ranks, as so many of them went to the Opera House on a regular basis that they were not at all happy about the damage that had been done to this historic building by their colleagues.

There were some dangers one had to consider that were not as explicit as others. One of the big problems facing the farmers in Northern

Ireland was the damage that stray dogs could do to livestock, especially to sheep. As the minister for agriculture I had to make a judgement as to whether farmers would be able to have gun licences. I remember vividly going through some cases when I came across an application that seemed to me straightforward and obvious, for consideration of an extra gun licence, as the applicant was a farmer who had some considerable damage to his flock of sheep by dogs. I was about ready to sign an agreement that the farmer should be given a licence when my civil servant said: 'Minister, I have to tell you that the farmer requesting this extra gun licence has a brother who is on the run from the authorities and he may well wish to pass that gun on to him.' That was the kind of dilemma I had to face all the time and it was very difficult to judge at times.

There were, however, moments among the danger that were humorous. Being a Roman Catholic in Northern Ireland could have had its problems because the Royal Ulster Constabulary (RUC) officers assigned to me were almost exclusively Protestants. However, whenever I went to Mass on a Sunday morning, two of my officers had to pretend to be Catholics to go into the church, and therefore also had to attempt to make the sign of the cross for authenticity's sake. Failure to do so would have signalled that they were fraudulent Catholics. While they were trying their best to appear as two normal parishioners, their fellow officers in the getaway car outside of the church would keel over with laughter because they knew that these two colleagues of theirs, after pretending to be good solid Catholics, would also have to put money into the collection plate.

I was popular with security and protection officers because I liked good restaurants with great food and wine. By contrast, the Secretary

LEFT As a Kent schoolboy soccer player
RIGHT On my twenty-first birthday, before heading for my national service in the Royal Air Force

A rare photograph of Aneurin Bevan MP speaking at a fringe meeting of the Labour League of Youth conference at Filey, 1950

LEFT Upon my selection as Labour candidate for Stalybridge and Hyde

BELOW Prime Minister Wilson wishing me well on the forthcoming election in 1970

The 1970 intake of Labour MPs

ABOVE In deep conversation with Laurie Pavitt MP, behind a star-studded front bench of Harold Wilson's Cabinet, 1974

© PRESS ASSOCIATION

RIGHT At my desk as a minister in Stormont in the Northern Ireland office

ABOVE With Gordon Taylor, chief executive of the PFA, and Bobby Barnes, deputy chief executive, holding the prestigious award given to me by the PFA for my services to football

BELOW Being fouled by Ed Stewart, playing for the All-Party Football Team at Dulwich Hamlets Ground

LEFT At a charity cricket event
signing autographs

BELOW My team of stars,
including Nobby Stiles,
Mike Summerbee, Dave
Mackay, John Prescott MP
and Bernard Donoughue MP,
playing a charity game for
one-parent families

With Ken Bates (centre), then chairman of Chelsea FC, putting the last brick on Chelsea's hotel

With Mr Mikhail Gorbachev at a dinner in his honour at the Guildhall, London, 8 December 1993

At the Atlanta Olympic Games, 1996, celebrating with Jonny Searle and Denise Lewis on winning their bronze medals

Launch of Labour's tourism policy in 1997, with Jack Cunningham MP and leader of the Labour Party Tony Blair

At the formation of the Football Foundation at 10 Downing Street, 2001

Launching the Football Foundation with Tony Blair on the lawn of No. 10 as its first chairman

LEFT With Brian Clough, then manager for Derby County, getting him out of trouble at a press conference in the Commons, denying his intention to run for Parliament
RIGHT Presenting Prime Minister Callaghan with an LP record of Stalybridge brass band – the oldest brass band in the world – of which I am president © PRESS ASSOCIATION

With the parliamentary jazz band, including colleagues Ken Clarke MP and Llin Golding MP

Gentleman giving money to a busker for the Musicians Union Welfare Fund – the busker being Johnny Dankworth, one of the finest saxophonists in the world!

of State Roy Mason and the Minister of State Don Concannon liked beer and the odd ploughman's lunch. So it was a nice change for my RUC officers to recommend good and safe restaurants in the province, knowing full well that whenever I ate out, I would always need to have my security with me. There was always a queue to be on my roster as it meant that they could enjoy great food at nearby tables with their wives or girlfriends, while keeping an eye on me. The RUC officers assigned to me were very grateful for the gourmet meals, so much so that I have in my office today a plaque from the RUC with the names of my four detectives that reads 'To a minister we were proud to serve.' However, I know exactly what they meant by that – the good food and the good life that I was able to afford them and their wives or partners!

I was always surrounded by security while in Northern Ireland, and back in London one would assume that my office in Whitehall, or anywhere for that matter, would also be a very secure place. So you can imagine my surprise when I arrived at my Whitehall office on a Monday morning to find that my cocktail cabinet and some of my cigars had been rifled. I realised that the culprits were probably some of my treasured civil servants who I didn't wish to get into trouble – otherwise I'm sure it would have raised some controversy if the press caught wind that the Northern Ireland's office was not immune from that sort of vandalism. I did get the department to recover my whiskies in the end and I wrote the incident off as a very unusual occurrence and certainly something that would never happen in Stormont where we had similar cocktails cupboards in our offices untouched by civil servants and only occasionally by ministers!

My time in Northern Ireland was also made enjoyable by my lovely daughter Fiona, who was just a few months old. She went down really well with everyone as they had never had a minister with such a young child, so she was well doted on and for the first time ever they had a baby cot installed in my office. Fiona was always entertained by my security escorts who were with me, too. However, when we travelled with two cars (the first for me, the second car packed with ammunition in case we were in any way stopped) unfortunately they also put my little Fiona in the dangerous car with them. She wasn't the least bit worried, though, and amused herself by communicating with her daddy in the first car by radio.

During my first Christmas as a minister I took my wife and young Fiona shopping. Fiona met Santa Claus for the first time in the Belfast Co-op, but her first reaction was to burst into a flood of tears at the sight of this bearded giant dressed in red and white. It took some time to console her by buying a small child's police car that she could sit in. The next day's press said it was a present from the Co-op – it was no such thing, as I bought it and then brought it back to Manchester on the Queen's flight. Fiona enjoyed her new toy enormously for some time before her young brother was born and took it over from her.

I also had the pleasure of meeting Gloria Hunniford, the Ulster TV star, at the beginning of her career. I was first introduced to Brum Henderson, who was the Managing Director and later chairman of Ulster TV. During my first week he told me that I should come and see the end of a special programme that was just brought in called *Good Evening Ulster*. Gloria, who used to work for him as a secretary, had pestered him constantly, saying that she could do a better job than others who were presenting programmes, so he gave her a chance on that show. She told me that although she lived in Hillsborough, she had never been to Hillsborough Castle – the royal residence whenever the Queen or Prince Philip are in the Province. I arranged for her and her then-husband and children to come as my guest one Sunday. They had a good look around the castle followed by some tea and I have been in contact with Gloria off and on ever since.

When the 1979 general election was announced, I was still expected to continue my ministerial job. I ran into a *Belfast Telegraph* newspaper vendor in the city centre who said: 'I hope Maggie wins but if only there was some way of keeping that wee man on the hill for us.' He was referring to Roy Mason and I conveyed this to him some time afterwards, although I didn't think he liked being referred to as that 'wee man'. Nevertheless, it was generally felt that Roy was a very popular Secretary of State and I thought that too as he was certainly a man of the people of Belfast and the rest of Northern Ireland regardless of the political or religious divide.

During that same general election period, I was in talks with the famous John DeLorean, who was bringing production of the revolutionary DeLorean DMC-12 motorcar (later featured in the 1985 film *Back to the Future*) to Northern Ireland. He prided himself on the fact that he had situated his factory in between a loyalist and a republican area and was employing a great number of people from both sides. Some years later, in 1982, when visiting New York, I thought I would look up DeLorean in his New York office to tell him how much we regretted the lack of success of his prize car. I was assured it was of his own making as the car was geared for the American market with a right-hand drive, where his particular designed car was in decline. Had he marketed his car in Europe, I don't think he would have been in the financial trouble he later found himself in. I didn't know until he told me that a British newspaper was gunning for him by hacking his Swiss bank accounts. He asked if I could give him a contact of a good PR company who could assist him in presenting him in a more favourable light. I duly gave him the name of a person known to me, and told him that I would, on my return to the UK, get him to ring DeLorean. The following day I heard that he had been arrested on charges of drug trafficking. Of course he was foolish, however he was besotted with his dream of a car that was a world beater and as I drove the car, together with the then Minister for Sport Hector Monro MP, on the Mary Peters track in County Antrim, I could vouch for both its design and performance.

The 1979 general election result saw the end of my ministerial career, but in opposition I was together with many of my parliamentary colleagues including Brynmor Jones, who was appointed together with me as shadow spokesman for the province, and I was able to continue my association with Northern Ireland for the next three years, during which the conflict there was still present.

My experiences in the province both in and out of the government were years I would never have swapped at that time with any other department of state other than sports. This was a delicate time in Northern Ireland and I am proud that I in some small ways contributed to the eventual peace accord. Otherwise the carnage would have continued unabated, and every casualty had a family, friends and workmates who grieved whatever the circumstances. As I've said many times, Tony Blair deserves a full share of the credit.

CHAPTER 7

LAUNCHING CAREERS

In May 1982 I received a phone call from a young barrister called Tony Blair. His father-in-law Tony Booth who was a constituent of mine, had suggested that he contact me. Tony Blair wished to be a Labour MP and Cherie had called her father and asked for help. Booth wrote later: 'I was thrilled to hear that our family tradition of political activity was about to be picked up by a new generation.' I subsequently received a call from a very subservient-sounding person who said: 'You don't know me but my name is Tony Blair and I am the son-in-law of Tony Booth, one of your constituents who thinks you can help me become a Labour MP.' My response was immediate: 'Have you ever been in the House of Commons?' He replied to the contrary, so I invited him to be my guest the following evening.

Tony's first visit to Parliament on 11 May 1982 was historic. In his book, *A Journey*, he recounted his very first experience of walking through Westminster Hall and the Central Lobby. He wrote:

I walked into the cavernous Central Lobby where the public wait to meet their MPs, and I stopped. I was thunderstruck. It just hit me. This was where I wanted to be. It was very odd. Odd because so unlike me, and odd because in later times I was never known as a 'House of Commons man'. But there and then, I had a complete presentiment: here I was going to be. This was my destiny. This was my political home. I was going to do whatever it took to enter it.

I remember Tony's description of me from his book, when he said I was 'a very shrewd, capable guy, committed of course, but he had seen enough to make himself pretty worldly wise'. He also later recounted: 'Tom thought me a pretty strange bird that evening. We had barely been introduced when I started plying him with questions. How do you get here? What can you do for me? Who do I see? What do I do? How shall I do it?' Bemused, I replied: 'I didn't realise you were in such a hurry.' He was a very eager young man, and I offered him valuable advice on the workings of Labour politics.

This was followed by visits to the Soho restaurant The Gay Hussar on Greek Street. On 15 June 1982, I received a call from Tony asking what my plans for lunch were that day as he desperately wanted to see me. After looking at my diary and seeing nothing remotely better than a free meal on this young lawyer, I accepted. I therefore met Tony at the restaurant, which was a famous haunt of many left-wing politicians, lawyers and political journalists. We had hardly sat down before he blurted out: 'Let's face it, Tom, all the good seats have gone for the next election,' which turned out to be in June the following year. He also pointed out that his wife Cherie was to contest Thanet North, near where I was born. He wanted to help her but he had read in that morning's paper that there was a by-election pending in Beaconsfield following the death of the sitting MP, Ronald Bell, at the end of February that year. I didn't even let him finish his sentence: 'Tony,' I said, if you are serious about wanting to be in our place then you have to get down there. It is twenty-five miles down the road. If you get the nomination, of course you will lose heavily but the eyes and ears of the political world will be looking on and if you do well you never know. It is unlikely that a good seat will come up before the next election and, to be realistic, you will have a good chance of securing a seat next time around if you contest a hopeless seat now.

I added that if he fought Beaconsfield, it would be well-covered by the media as a candidate from the newly formed SDP, Paul Tyler, was to stand and this would be big news in itself. I added: 'Tony, the icing on the cake for your chances in securing the candidacy in Beaconsfield is that the secretary of the local constituency party is an old girlfriend of mine from my Labour League of Youth days.' Betty Bell Smith and I were about fifteen when we met but we had kept in touch over the years and I consider her a very dear friend to this day.

I returned to the Commons and rang Betty to ask her if she had anyone in mind to be the candidate, to which she replied she had a local man in her sights. I asked her to 'hold fire' and would she first meet a young barrister called Tony Blair who would like to contest the by-election. Bless her heart, out of loyalty to me she agreed and I promptly phoned Tony in his chambers and told him to get himself down there. Betty liked him more than the other guy she had in mind and worked to ensure Tony was selected, which he duly was.

In her book *Speaking for Myself*, Cherie Blair stated: 'Tom Pendry was right. Beaconsfield was as high-profile as they come.' As I'd predicted, the SDP candidate received lots of attention, however, the media was also occupied with other events. The Friday before polling,

British troops landed in San Carlos Bay in the Falkland Islands and in the following days thirty-one British soldiers were detained. The Conservative candidate Tim Smith campaigned off the back of these events with a call to support Thatcher's response during the crisis.

Tony predictably lost his deposit, but was nonetheless given much praise from sections of the media. Thanks to an intervention from Michael Foot, leader of the party, to the agent of a constituency by the name of Sedgefield in the county of Durham, life for Tony took an unexpected turn. The Sedgefield constituency had been recently created as a result of boundary changes that merged two constituencies in the county of Durham and, because of the pending general election, they had to find a candidate quickly and hurriedly assembled a shortlist. It became clear that the favourite on that list was Les Huckfield – a former MP for Nuneaton. However, this prompted, as I understand it, Michael Foot ringing up the local Party stating that he had no intention of trying to tell the constituency who they should select, but would they at least consider this young man, Tony Blair, who had done so well in Beaconsfield? The net result of that intervention was that Tony was put on their shortlist and emerged as the candidate for this very safe Labour seat by beating Huckfield by a margin of one. That one vote was very important for a number of reasons, for in the 1983 general election, Gordon Brown won his seat in Kirkcaldy with a massive majority. Had Tony not got the Sedgefield selection and become its MP, then when John Smith died, the leadership of the Labour Party would have almost certainly gone to Gordon. Another interesting possibility was that Tony and Cherie reputedly had a pact that, since both had political aspirations, whichever one of them secured a safe Labour seat, the other would stay at the Bar. It is conceivable that Cherie, given the Labour Party's desire to encourage more women MPs and the advent of the all-women shortlist, could well have secured that safe Labour seat ahead of Tony and history would have been very different.

When John Smith died, I was approached by Tony Blair and he asked if I would support him. I told him I couldn't give an answer there and then because my old friend John Prescott was in the field and I had worked with him on the regions and devolution portfolio. I thought it right that I should first tell him before I committed myself to Tony. I wrote John a note outlining the reasons why I was supporting Tony and then later rang Tony at his home in Islington to tell him that I was fully behind him. Tony, of course, went on to secure the leadership of the Labour Party.

Labour, under Tony's leadership, ended eighteen years of Tory rule with a landslide majority at the 1997 general election, and went on to win an unprecedented two more in succession. The achievements during that period were impressive – the Good Friday Agreement, which brought peace, albeit an uneasy one, to Northern Ireland, after decades of bloodshed, which had claimed over 3,650 lives; the national minimum wage; an ambitious school-building programme; plummeting hospital waiting lists; better rights for part-time workers ... the list goes on and on. Of course there were also many contentious issues and controversial moves, most notably the Iraq and Afghanistan conflicts, but this is not the place to go over all that. Whatever the difficulties surrounding Tony's other wars, for sure in my view, having been a Northern Ireland minister, no one could have secured the agreement other than Tony. John Major did his bit initially but could not achieve the historical peace settlement that was Tony's achievement. I hope that history will be fair to his legacy.

But before such momentous events, Tony Booth wrote: 'On 19 January 1984 our family's first grandchild Euan was born. Tom Pendry made sure that the event was noted in Hansard when he congratulated Tony in the House of Commons.' Euan is now on his way towards keeping the political tradition alive for another generation.

And in an extraordinary twist, my cousin Pauline discovered a family connection with the Blairs. It transpired that one of Tony's grandmothers (on his father Leo's side), was a woman named Mary Augusta Ridgway Bridson (1888–1969), a colourful character known as 'Gussie' who was a star of the stage. The family tree shows that on the female side my cousin Pauline and her sister Rosemary are Tony's third cousins. When I was called in by Tony to discuss, I think, a sport-related issue, I took the family tree and I said to Tony, 'Did you know Aunt Gussie?' He looked at me in astonishment and said: 'No, I never met her but I've heard she was a great character.' I then showed him the family tree, which confirmed that there was a lineage between our families. Then he turned to Sally Morgan from his office in No. 10 (now Baroness Morgan of Huyton) and said, 'Not only did he get me here, but we are related!'

However tenuously related or not, I am proud to have played a part in launching Tony's career. In 2000, I received a special letter from Tony on the night of the thirtieth anniversary dinner that I organised to celebrate the 1970 intake of MPs. He thanked us all for the election victory successes during the '70s and for helping to rebuild the party during the opposition days of the '80s and '90s before we took government again in 1997. In Tony's own words: 'You all have been there, done that, got the T-shirt. Thank you all for all you have done. Have a great evening, you deserve it.'

He was not the only one I believe I helped along the way during my own political journey.

🐝

Sometime before the 1964 general election, I was contacted by Ted Eldred, who was then the agent for George Brown, MP for Belper in Derbyshire, later to become Deputy Prime Minister under Harold Wilson. At the time, I was a trade union official based in Birmingham covering a section of the workforce in both the East and West Midlands. Knowing this, Ted asked if I would meet a young friend of his who was working in the Blood Transfusion Service in Sheffield, Ted's home city. This young man was called Roy Hattersley and he was seeking support for the candidature of the Sparkbrook Constituency Labour Party in Birmingham. His mother, Enid, was a city councillor, while his father, Frederick, was a former Roman Catholic priest, who had renounced the priesthood to marry her. At university Roy had joined the Socialist Society and was one of those responsible for changing its name to the 'Labour Club' and affiliating it with the non-aligned International Union of Socialist Youth rather than the Soviet-backed International Union of Students. He was desperate to become an MP and had switched his course from English to economics because his mother told him that would look better on a political CV. Ted asked if I would help him, as he was a member of my union NUPE. I readily agreed. Our meeting took place in a Chinese restaurant off the Midlands Road, Derby, and I remember it well for two reasons. First, I was very impressed with this young man and I felt him worthy of my support. Second, as I was there at the behest of Ted

Eldred, who was also at the lunch, he took out the money to pay for his and Ted's meal, but not mine. Nevertheless, that was a minor matter.

My first move was to speak to Lil Stevens, the secretary of the largest women's branch of any union in the country, Birmingham School Meals. She was a redoubtable woman who later became the National President of NUPE. Lil responded positively, together with other branches that were in the division. Roy was duly selected. I was delighted until an angry Lil phoned me. They had all turned up to support Roy only to find out that he was a member of two other unions and not ours, though even so they dutifully voted for him on my recommendation. I'm sure her indignation didn't last long as Roy was one of the most promising of the new intakes in that 1964 election. He was elected by just 1,254 votes, but despite that small majority he went on to win every election until he was elevated to the House of Lords. During his years in the Commons he rose to great heights in both the Wilson and Callaghan governments, serving in the latter as his deputy leader. Following Labour's devastating defeat in 1983, Michael Foot decided to stand down as leader and Roy stood in the subsequent leadership election. John Smith was his campaign manager and a young Peter Mandelson also helped. Roy had the support of most of the shadow Cabinet, but the majority of the PLP, the constituency groups and the unions backed Neil Kinnock. In the final count, Kinnock secured around three times as many votes. As was standard practice at the time, Roy became deputy leader. Many saw them as a 'dream ticket', with Kinnock a representative of the left of the party and Hattersley of the right. Hattersley remained deputy for eight years and was also shadow Chancellor until 1987, when he moved back to shadow Home Affairs. Kinnock and Hattersley went on to rehabilitate Labour after the 1983 rout. Roy is now a fellow Baron.

After hearing on BBC Radio a series about Roy's life, I bumped into him when walking across Parliament Square. I congratulated him on the programme but said I was a little surprised at not hearing more about how he was selected for Sparkbrook with the help of NUPE branches in Birmingham. Sensing that I had a story to tell, Roy just kept on walking in silence.

JONATHAN POWELL

In 1991, I was on a parliamentary delegation to Washington that followed a visit made by party leader Neil Kinnock, and Denis Healey, his deputy. Both had been treated rather shabbily during a Washington meeting with Ronald Reagan. The President quite rudely asked Denis some inane questions like: 'What do you do in the UK?' At a delegation dinner in the British embassy, I was gently pulled to one side by a young man called Jonathan Powell who was the First Secretary in the British embassy and clearly a confidant of the ambassador. Jonathan asked how well I knew Neil Kinnock. I told him that I knew him quite well. On hearing this, he gave me his card and asked if I would pass on a message to Neil as he wanted him to know how much the ambassador and he thought Reagan's attitude to them was disgraceful. Jonathan said that the ambassador hoped that on their next visit to Washington he would ensure the red carpet treatment would be given to them.

On my return to London, I dutifully gave both the card and message to Neil. Not too long later, Jonathan joined the Labour Party's staff in the Commons and then 10 Downing Street under Prime Minister Blair. I hope that my message to Neil helped bring about this young man's rise in the echelons of the party.

Before our Washington meeting, Jonathan had been engaged in the negotiations on handing Hong Kong back to the Chinese in 1983–85. He was new to the British embassy when we met and was attached to Bill Clinton's presidential campaign. He later served as the first Downing Street Chief of Staff under Tony Blair from 1995 to 2007. He was the only senior adviser to last the whole period of Blair's leadership. During this period Powell was also the chief British negotiator on Northern Ireland. Powell continued to be a key right-hand man for Tony Blair. He was described by *The Guardian* as being 'at the heart of all his [Blair's] key foreign policy initiatives'.

CHAPTER 8

MOORS MURDERS

During my time as MP for Stalybridge and Hyde, my constituency postbag was always full to bursting. I feel proud that I did my best to help hundreds, perhaps thousands of decent people with their problems over a wide range of issues. It is one of the best things about being an MP – not that any praise is heaped on an MP by the press of this country. However, there were in my case three constituents who stood out as ones I wished had not passed my way. Namely, Ian Brady, Myra Hindley and Harold Shipman.

When I was first selected for Stalybridge and Hyde in April 1968, I was aware of the murders of several youngsters by Ian Brady and Myra Hindley. I was also aware that searches were concentrated on the Saddleworth Moors for the bodies of the victims who were suspected to have been buried there. The Moors were next to the boundaries of the constituency and it was clear to me when meeting the people at my selection conference that feelings were running high both in the area where the killers lived and also the areas adjacent to the Hattersley Estate in particular.

All these years later, one cannot forget the heinous acts of abduction, sexual assault and later the murder of five young children between 1963 and 1965 that were perpetuated by Brady and Hindley: Pauline

Reade, sixteen; John Kilbride, twelve; Keith Bennett, twelve; Lesley Ann Downey, ten; and Edward Evans, seventeen, were murdered and buried presumably on Saddleworth Moors. It was Hindley's brother-in-law David Smith who witnessed the murder of Edward Evans and eventually turned both her and Brady over to the police.

On 6 May 1966, Brady was convicted for the murders of John, Lesley Ann and Edward and was given three life sentences. Hindley was given two life sentences and charged for the murders of Lesley Ann and Edward. At that point in time, neither Brady nor Hindley had yet confessed to the murders of Pauline Reade and Keith Bennett.

Brady and Hindley's evil criminality did not fully emerge until their confessions in 1985.

The start of their killing spree began on 12 July 1963 with their first victim, Pauline Reade, who was known to Hindley's family. As Reade made her way to a dance, she was spotted by Hindley and Brady who persuaded her to get into their van to drive up to Saddleworth Moor to find an expensive glove that Hindley claimed to have lost.

Twelve-year-old John Kilbride was the next to be abducted and murdered, followed by Keith Bennett, also twelve, who disappeared on his way to his grandmother's home. Others followed, including ten-year-old Lesley Ann Downey, whom Hindley and Brady spotted at a fairground on Boxing Day 1964. They persuaded her to go to their home where she was sexually abused by the couple.

However, it was the brutal attack on seventeen-year-old apprentice engineer Edward Evans that led to the eventual arrest of the couple. The attack on Edward Evans had been witnessed by David Smith, the brother in law of Hindley. The following morning, he went to Hyde police station and reported what he had witnessed.

This prompted the arrest of Brady on 7 October by Superintendent
Bob Talbot of Cheshire Police. Despite protestation by Hindley that
the death had been an accident, a police investigation in his home at
16 Wardle Brook Avenue revealed a harrowing truth. A large collection of photographs were uncovered, most of which had been taken
at Saddleworth Moor. This led 150 police officers to search the moor.

Nine days after Brady's arrest, an arm bone belonging to little Lesley
Ann Downey was found. A few days later, police located another site
on the opposite side of the A635 where John Kilbride's decomposed
body was found. With winter approaching and the police investigation on the ground becoming more difficult, the search was called off
in November.

The trial of Brady and Hindley began on 19 April 1966. The pair
pleaded not guilty to three murders, those of Evans, Downey, and
Kilbride. A tape recording of Lesley Anne Downey pleading for her
life shocked the nation, and those who heard it in court were haunted
for ever more. First they appeared at Hyde Town Hall, and then they
were committed for trial at Manchester.

Sentences were duly pronounced, with Mr Justice Atkinson giving
life imprisonment to both. In summing up the case, the judge described the murders as a 'truly horrible case' and found the pair to be
'two sadistic killers of the utmost depravity', adding that Brady was
'wicked beyond belief'.

After my election in 1970, I was determined to see what I could do
to allay the fears of those parents whose children were victims of Brady
and Hindley and whose bodies had not yet been discovered.

Several years after the convictions, I heard that the film-maker
and playwright Rainer Werner Fassbinder had written a play called

Pre-Paradise Sorry Now. Its subject was the Moors Murders and was scheduled to premiere in London on 2 February 1972 at London's Institute of Contemporary Arts. The producers of the play, Romilly Productions, were then going to tour the play at Stephen Joseph Hall in Manchester, and then at Maxwell Hall in Salford. Worried about the distress this play would have on my constituents, I released a statement to the press on the day of the performance that said:

> I know that the prospect of this play's appearance in Manchester and Salford has already caused some distress. I will see how harmful this is – and if it is as bad as I think it might be, I will take legal advice on how to stop it coming to Manchester, if possible even by a court injunction.

That evening I attended the London premiere with my secretary, who took notes, and I was horrified that anyone could write and perform such a play when the tragedy was still fresh in the minds of those affected, especially the mother of victim Lesley Ann Downey, whose body was found several years before on 16 October 1965. The play itself ran for one and three-quarter hours and used reconstructed dialogues between Brady and Hindley. It made me sick to my stomach when I heard the screams of Lesley Ann Downey, including her desperate cries for her mother in one scene, and I was determined to ensure that the parents of the young victims in my constituency would never have to read any reviews of that play or hear the reactions of those who had viewed it. I also wanted to ensure that it was the play's first and last night of performance. I enlisted the support of my colleague Alfred Morris, MP for Wythenshawe, and we wrote a joint letter to Romilly

Productions demanding that they stop the production from going ahead and touring in Manchester and Salford. I also sent copies of that letter to the vice-chancellors of Manchester and Salford University. The letter read:

> As Members of Parliament representing constituents who were closely associated with the Moors Murders trial of 1966, we wish to appeal to you to cancel your plans to stage the play 'Pre-Paradise Sorry Now' at Manchester and Salford on February 8th and 9th. We strongly feel that this play, which some of us have seen and which deals at close quarters with the whole subject of the murders committed by Ian Brady and Myra Hindley, would cause great mental suffering and cruelty to many of our constituents, especially the families of the three victims of Brady and Hindley. We feel that the case is too recent – and too horrific to be presented in the form of a play, especially in the area where the tragic events of six years ago occurred.

The letter also had the support of other MPs including Ken Marks (Gorton), Charles Morris (Openshaw), Jack McCann (Rochdale), Gerald Kaufman (Ardwick), Gordon Oakes (Widnes), Paul B. Rose (Blackley), Robert Sheldon (Ashton-under-Lyne), Arthur Davidson (Accrington) and James Lamond (Oldham).

We were successful in our endeavours, as both Manchester and Salford University refused to allow the play to be shown at their venues. This was a partial victory, but not the end of this sorry saga of those wishing to exploit the tragic events or celebrate the sadism of the perpetrators.

There were attempts by those who should have known better, including Lord Longford, to ensure that Myra Hindley be allowed parole.

In contrast, Ian Brady didn't seek out a campaign for parole. Instead he appeared to regret that he faced his whole life behind bars instead of the noose. Up until 1964, the death penalty by hanging was enforced by the United Kingdom. The Murder (Abolition of Death Penalty) Act 1965 enshrined in law the replacement of the noose with a mandatory sentence of life imprisonment. The Act was introduced to Parliament as a Private Member's Bill by Sydney Silverman MP.

Over the next several years, questions kept returning regarding the issue of parole for Brady and Hindley – which was of major concern within my constituency. I took the position that Brady and Hindley should not receive parole and that it was too early to even consider a date for the parole review process. I appeared on Brian Walden's breakfast television show *Weekend World* in 1985 to reinforce my position and as a result I received many letters of support from not only my constituents but also from the general public.

Then came another shocking revelation a few months later. In an interview with Fred Harrison from the *Sunday People*, Ian Brady admitted to the murders of Keith Bennett and Pauline Reade. After hearing this, I immediately wrote to the Home Secretary demanding an investigation into the matter. In a press release dated 2 June 1985, I stated that: 'In the light of this (*Sunday People*) article, I feel it to be incumbent upon the Home Secretary to ensure that Ian Brady along with the author of the article, be interviewed by appropriate police officers to ascertain the authenticity of his alleged comments.' Following this statement, the Chief Constable of Greater Manchester Police interviewed Ian Brady in prison as well as Fred Harrison. The investigation concluded that Brady's allegations were true, with the bodies of Keith and Pauline not yet recovered from the moors.

Several months later, I received a letter from Margaret Brady, Ian Brady's mother, on 4 December 1985 with an enclosed copy of a letter that was sent to the shadow Home Secretary Gerald Kaufman from Ian Brady. Her letter to me said:

Dear Sir, I have been advised by Mr Bob Litherland, MP for Manchester Central to forward to you two letters one from my son Ian Brady who was in Gartree Prison, Leicester relating to his case – he is now transferred to Park Lane Mental Hospital Liverpool (29-11-85). The other I sent to Mr Kaufmann now in Gorton Constituency, so he sent it to Mr Litherland, however, when he wrote to me on the 29-11-85 stating as the case was of long standing etc. you are the person to represent my son. Yours Sincerely, Margaret Brady

It would appear in Brady's original letter from 29 October 1985 that he was trying to seek the help of Gerald Kaufman to facilitate his transfer to psychiatric facilities at Park Lane Hospital in Liverpool, also known as Ashworth Hospital. As Margaret Brady's letter to me already mentioned, Brady was subsequently moved to Ashworth Hospital, and it was there where I would eventually meet the notorious killer.

When in the Commons post office in September 1987, I was told by the postmaster he had received a letter addressed to a 'Mr Dickenson MP, Member for Stalybridge'. Knowing I was the only MP for that constituency, I took the letter and to my surprise I discovered it was from Ian Brady, writing from Ashworth Hospital. On reading the letter, however, I at once realised that it was not intended for me, but Geoffrey

Dickens, the MP for Littleborough and Saddleworth, where the bodies of the Brady/Hindley victims were buried. In the letter he wrote:

I heard the media quotes re your interest in my case (the 'Moors' Case). I'll begin by stating verifiable facts. David Smith had already a record of violence before meeting Myra Hindley and I. He kept a personal notebook which contained such statements as: – 'Murder is a hobby', 'Rape is a state of mind', 'Religion is a cancer' etc. This notebook of Smith's was quoted in open court at the trial. While the authorities held Hindley and I at Risley Remand Centre, Smith attacked two people with a bicycle chain (again proved at the trial) but, as he was the chief prosecution witness against us, the police neither charged nor prosecuted. After the trial, Smith was charged with attacking a man and was given a small fine; he then attacked another man and was given a £50 fine: then he stabbed a man with a steak knife and was given a three-year sentence; he was given full re-mission and promptly killed his father; this was regarded as a 'mercy killing' at his trial, and he was released after two days.

Smith asked me on a previous occasion to kill his father for having put his dog, Peggy, down. I refused. He then asked me to kill a youth he hated, and offered to take front and profile photos of the intended victim with his Polaroid camera. After Myra and I were sentenced, he openly admitted to all these facts on an ITV programme – not only one programme but several. I have corresponded with Mrs. West, mother of one of the victims, Lesley Anny Downey. In one letter she has stated that Smith was heard boasting in pubs of his deep involve-ment in the Moors Murders. His wife divorced him and stated that she'd shielded him at the trial by making false statements. It should also be noted that Pauline Reade (the latest recovered body on the moors) lived next door to Smith. I've given only facts in this letter. If you wish to visit me, to cross examine, I am available.

Please excuse the patchy structure of this letter.

Yours sincerely, I. Brady.

It would appear that Brady had heard Geoffrey Dickens on a radio programme referring to the case of the missing young boy Keith Bennett, one of his victims whose body had never been found. However, Geoffrey Dickens was a sensationalist and whenever he spoke publicly about the Moors Murders, my constituents, especially those on the Hattersley Estate where Brady and Hindley lived and performed their evil acts, found it distasteful and upsetting.

With that in mind, and recognising the force of those views expressed to me when Dickens had uttered unhelpful and often sickening remarks, I decided on receipt of Brady's letter to write to him on 7 September 1987, but not before speaking to Dr MacCulloch, head of Ashworth Hospital. He welcomed my more helpful approach and in his own words he said 'it would be disastrous if Dickens came, as we would have TV cameras, radio and press reporters outside our gates and it would be unhelpful in the extreme'.

I then wrote to Brady and in my letter I put him straight as to who really was the MP for Stalybridge. I wrote that 'over the seventeen years of my representing the constituency (which includes the Hattersley estate) I have been involved in your case on a number of occasions, and I continue to take a close interest in the developments surrounding it'. I concluded by stating that 'I wish to take up your invitation to meet you and discuss the matters raised in your letter so I will be seeking the permission of the Prison authorities to do so in the next few days.' Brady sent me an acknowledgement letter on 20 September 1987 with a note that read: 'I'd appreciate you informing me as to the date you fix upon, as I wish to avoid a clash of visits.' I then rang the head of Ashworth Hospital to arrange a visit.

When I arrived at Ashworth I was escorted to a private room to await Brady. Eventually, I saw him glance in, weighing me up as he overpassed the room allocated for the interview. However, within minutes he came in, sat down and immediately asked if I had any Gauloises cigarettes. When I told him I didn't smoke cigarettes – I'm a cigar man - he frowned at me and I remember thinking that this was not a good start for what I was about to ask of him.

However, before I could get around to discussing the purpose of my business there, he went into a long ramble about his background and informed me of two other 'happenings', as he put it – his murders. One had taken place in Glasgow, and another around Manchester Piccadilly Station. He sounded bitter about Myra Hindley who clearly realised by then that she was no longer under his spell and her return to Roman Catholicism riled him greatly. The meeting took five hours and was often interrupted by him receiving medication as his speech began deteriorating. According to the Governor, I spent more time with him than anyone else and I did eventually persuade him to visit the moors to look for Keith Bennett's burial place. I wanted to give Keith's mother peace of mind. After Brady agreed to that, my first move was to seek a meeting with Inspector Topping of Manchester Police, the policeman in charge of searching for the unfound victims. At that meeting I did not feel Topping was overly pleased with my involvement and although he arranged for a helicopter to take Brady up to the moors, as a result of my intervention, he made no mention of my involvement in his book *Topping: The Autobiography of the Police Chief in the Moors Murder Case.*

As it turned out, Brady's boast that he could uncover the whereabouts of young Bennett's burial spot was unfounded. Previous attempts by Myra Hindley and David Smith to pinpoint the spot had also come to nothing. Nevertheless, I didn't give up, despite my disappointment, which I knew was shared keenly by the boy's mother. I decided not to mention to her or any newspaper my visit to see Brady, in case it would add to her grief. Brady visited Saddleworth Moors in July 1987 with a follow-up visit in December. Both high-profile visits received national press coverage, but were unsuccessful in recovering Bennett's body. He remains unfound.

I received a letter from Brady on 27 October 1987 after his first return visit to the Moors. It read:

Dear Mr Pendry,

I am writing to bring to your attention an article by the journalist Fred Harrison in the Mirror. Several of my friends pointed out another slip by the chief prosecution witness David Smith. Harrison took Smith to the exact spot where I took the police to on the moor. The spot is over a mile from the road. Harrison said to Smith that he thought I had been puzzled by the changes since twenty-two years ago. Smith replied that the police had blundered by bringing me in by the back road instead of the front and stated that 'We always used the front road'. He's speaking in the first person: 'We always', and shows his knowledge of the spot. Yet he never led the police there.

Hope to hear from you.

Sincerely, I. Brady

Brady's letter was shortly followed up by another on 31 October 1987 letting me know that he had met with Topping on two occasions and that they had studied videotapes and an RAF photo of the area from 10,000 feet above. He ended the letter with, 'Thank you for what you have already done. I'm racing against the snow.'

I received a letter on 7 January 1988 from Brady detailing why the visit to the Moors failed. He wrote:

Thank you for helping to get me the second opportunity of going up to the moors to help locate Keith Bennett. But I'm afraid the whole matter was badly handled. In early Dec. a Dr Strickland came to my room and, after talking about something else for five minutes, he asked me, hypothetically, if the police came the next morning would I go up to the moors. I replied no, and stated that December held the shortest day of the year; second, that the weather was uncertain; third, it was the worst time of the year psychologically for me, which the medical authorities know. I pointed out that I had been trying to get back up to the moor since last July, and that I needed the maximum daylight hours, not the shortest, for possible success.

The next morning the police came to take me at 5 a.m. I pointed out to them the conversation I'd had with the doctor the day previous, and reiterated it. The argument lasted two hours. Finally the Senior Welfare Officer, Bob Fitzpatrick, persuaded me to go. Two wasted hours. We spent nine hours on the moor in five degrees below zero weather...

Although I did not see Brady again after these failed visits to the moors, I did receive numerous letters from him over the next year, many asking if I was going to visit him again. In one letter dated 12 April 1988, an agitated Brady stated:

There is the body of a man on the opposite side of the Saddleworth Moor, but I refuse to co-operate with this as it would lead to a 'friend' who disposed of a danger to me in the river Ouse. Apart from this, my object is to clear everything up, so that the police can't come back to me at a future date. If they simply wish to let sleeping dogs lie, and cover up, that's fine with me – so long as a successor doesn't decide to re-open all these cases. I am willing to see you for deeper discussion re all these matters...

P.S. Re. today's inquest on Pauline Reade. I have heard Mr Topping and other people talking about solving the Keith Bennett case by having Myra Hindley hypnotised. This is cheap sensationalism. I have already given Mr Topping a perfect description of the site but he has failed to locate it, and so have I, in the adverse conditions of the search. But I have a clear picture of what I'm searching for ... I also had a doctor who wrote to me re hypnosis last year – the authorities blocked it. I didn't need hypnosis, nor does Myra Hindley. What is needed is time and opportunity to locate.

The letters continued to arrive in my office, as Brady was adamant about exposing David Smith and his admission on TV of conspiracy to murder. He referenced an episode of *Weekend World*, which aired on 2 April 1978 and was presented by Brian Walden. I replied to Brady and informed him that I was waiting for London Weekend to send over a transcript of the programme.

After some time, the letters from Brady stopped. His final missive was dated 16 June 1988 and read:

As I have not received a reply from you to my letter two months ago, I conclude you have no interest in the matters it contained. I'm not surprised. I've just seen you quoted as saying that my crimes surpassed the Nazi holocaust.

Thank you and goodbye.

I. S. Brady

P.S. This letter is simply for record purposes, and requires no reply.

The reference he made to 'the Nazi holocaust' was not accurate, but rather a misinterpretation of a discussion I had on the Jimmy Young radio show. At that time, I was on the M1 with traffic obscuring my hearing and I didn't quite get Jimmy's question about the Nuremberg Trials. Something came out of that conversation that clearly was a distorted version of what I said. Nevertheless, Brady's final words 'Thank you and goodbye' were a great relief.

In the subsequent years, the issue regarding parole for the Moors Murderers surfaced again and I continued to receive letters from constituents expressing their dismay. However, I have always wholly agreed with my constituents that the horrific crimes that Myra and Ian Brady committed 'were of an evil nature and I do not feel Hindley should be released under any circumstances. I will continue to do everything in my power to make your views and the views of others in my constituency known to the appropriate authority,' as I wrote in numerous replies.

Despite Brady's letter to me in 1988 bidding me farewell, which I had hoped would be the last, he began correspondence with me again in 2000 regarding his treatment in Ashworth hospital and his hunger strike, for which he was being force-fed by tube every day. Brady had admitted to his solicitors that all he wanted to do was die but the hospital prevented such an action from taking place.

Also in 2000, the BBC had filmed a documentary on the Moors Murders and was planning to air it on 1 March as part of the *Modern Times* series on BBC Two. I issued a press release calling on Greg Dyke, then Director-General of the BBC, to pull the plug on the documentary film, but it still went ahead.

Despite my earlier efforts to stop theatre productions of these horrific killings, they did go on, much to my regret, and indeed that of the people I represented. The case has been dramatised on television at least twice since: in *See No Evil: The Moors Murders* and *Longford*, both in 2006. The first was made to mark the fortieth anniversary of the trial with the full backing of the victims' families.

Brady spent nineteen years in mainstream prisons before being diagnosed as a psychopath in November 1985. He was sent to Ashworth Psychiatric Hospital and from then on made it clear that he never wants to be released. Successive Home Secretaries have agreed with the trial judge that his life sentence should mean life. In 1982, the Lord Chief Justice, Lord Lane, said of Brady: 'This is the case if ever there is to be one when a man should stay in prison till he dies.'

After a 1999 attack inside prison, Brady went on hunger strike, but was force-fed. In March 2000 he wrote: 'Myra gets the potentially fatal brain condition, while I have to fight simply to die. I have had enough. I want nothing, my objective is to die and release myself from this once and for all. So you see my death strike is rational and pragmatic. I'm only sorry I didn't do it decades ago, and I'm eager to leave this cesspit in a coffin.'

Winnie Johnson, the mother of Keith Bennett, received a letter from Brady at the end of 2005 in which, she said, he claimed that he could take police to within twenty yards (eighteen metres) of her son's body but the authorities would not allow it. In 2012, Brady once more told the prison authorities it was his desire to starve himself to death, and once more his application was rejected.

The wounds Brady left among the families, friends and neighbours of his victims have not completely healed. They never will. His crimes shocked a nation and damaged the community I was proud to represent. At the time of writing this book, Ian Brady was still alive and in a very frail condition. He continues to make headlines, which will always serve as a reminder to the relatives of the victims, and those living close to where these tragedies occurred, of his crimes. The sense of horror will never go away.

CHAPTER 9

DR HAROLD SHIPMAN

Some would say there must have been something in the water at Hyde that brought about the problems I faced with notorious killers like Ian Brady, Myra Hindley and later Dr Harold Shipman. With the latter, it was impossible to believe that I had a serial killer living among my constituents as their trusted local GP.

When I first came into contact with Shipman in the mid-1970s, my first impression was that he was a kind and caring doctor who was popular with my constituents and also with fellow doctors in Tameside. The relationship between Shipman and the community was on the face of it a very healthy one, and he stood out as a man who commanded an air of authority and leadership. He was a very active spokesperson for the local doctors and was also the honorary secretary of Tameside Local Medical Committee. As the unofficial 'shop steward' of the doctors in the area, he voiced their concerns about budget cuts, shortages in staff support and the lack of appropriate drug supply. As a respected member of the community, for example, in 1983, he was interviewed on Granada TV's *World in Action* on how the mentally ill should be treated in the community.

Shipman was part of Donneybrook House medical centre in Hyde along with four other doctors and I had a number of meetings there with him and his fellow doctors. It was largely Shipman who dominated the discussions regarding issues about Tameside health services. I like to think we both acted with the utmost professionalism, which is practised by most MPs I know, even though he was clearly no Labour supporter. He once refused to go to a social function organised by his fellow doctors because the Labour Mayor of Hyde was to be present. To be fair though, he was always courteous to me even to the point of appearing deferential – although I am sure he did not take that view into the polling booths. Up until the time of his arrest, I, like the vast majority of his patients, believed him to be a thoroughly good, caring and hard-working doctor. Almost everyone who came to my own constituency surgeries in Hyde – I had two of the six there every month – were his patients and they all spoke highly of him. I felt at that time it was a pleasure to hear that I had in my constituency such a highly regarded General Practitioner. In fact, he was once described as a GP with 'godlike awe'.

Over the course of twenty years or so, I received many letters from Shipman. The majority of them were complaints pitched against the local Health Authority on either the lack of drugs or the level of financial support he was receiving from them. I engaged in discussions with the West Pennine Health Authority about Shipman's demands for more drugs, for more vaccines for his immunisation programmes. I also remember one letter I wrote to Shipman on 7 January 1988 in response to one he had written to me about the problems expressed by the Cervical Cytology smears department at Tameside and other hospitals in the area. I went on to tell him that I had brought the issue to the attention of my colleagues on the front bench and they had assured me they would take up the points in his letter. I then asked him if he could arrange for me to meet other GPs in my constituency – recognising that he was considered to be the nearest they had to a shop steward. The meeting was so arranged on 29 January 1988 at Donneybrook House. A whole range of issues were discussed but it was clear none of the doctors present had anything like Shipman's knowledge of the local scene.

Over several years he continued to advocate issues for the local doctors even after he left Donneybrook to open his own surgery in 1993 at 21 Market Street, Hyde. In all his letters to me from then on, he spoke with great concern of the inadequacies of the West Pennine Health Authority and the lack of medical and administrative resources he was receiving. In a letter dated 28 April 1998 to me, Shipman spoke about a complaint he had raised with the pharmaceutical company Farillon about their supply of cheaper vaccines for children. He told me that Farillon were supplying a poorer version of the vaccine instead of the higher-quality vaccine that he had ordered. In his letter he said: 'Since we are trying to protect the children, they should get the best and since this also protects the Doctor/Nurse from accidental needle stick injury we should be giving the best presentation (Pasteur Merieux) of the vaccine.' I took this issue up with Tessa Jowell, then the Minister of State for Public Health, and received a negative response in July 1998.

In another letter, on 29 May 1998, Shipman claimed that, due to the authority's maladministration, he had been subsidising them since 1993 and had submitted an appeal. He added that he 'would be grateful for any help' I could afford him. My reply was to ask him to detail specifically what he thought I could do to assist him in the appeal situation, adding: 'I fear the answer may be very little, but if I can help of course I will.'

Shipman also sent me his annual reports and business plans, which were very revealing in light of his future activities. Throughout his report, Shipman routinely highlighted the level of funding needed to maintain his level of care at his surgery. In retrospect, some of the entries were very compassionate in tone given his later crimes:

The future looks stable, patients are living longer and the number of very old patients in the community is a worry. Patients now have a printed drug card that they can use each time they wish to request a repeat drug item. Increased screening for raised fats, diabetes, blood pressure etc., means more prescribing NOT less and although there will be a saving eventually, initially it costs more. The use of ACE inhibitors has revolutionised therapy, fewer side effects, better compliance, better quality of life – more cost. Expensive patients, such as those on growth hormones, anti-rejection drugs – cost money. The two on growth hormones cost £15,000 per year. At the moment if they are notified to the FHSA, extra funding is available but for how much longer?

At the end of that report, Shipman signed off by saying: 'My grateful thanks to my staff, my wife and family, the Bank and to all the patients for their kindness, understanding and loyalty. We hope to continue to provide an innovative practice, maintaining the very personal care we offer.'

Imagine my horror when the bombshell exploded – the accusations that were made that he had killed numerous people within his practice. Not only was I shocked, but like many of his patients and colleagues I felt complete disbelief. His very close friend Dr Wally Ashworth, also a political supporter of mine, believed the accusations against him were ill-founded and held that belief right up until the point his guilt became obvious as his trial progressed. Few seemed to be aware of his background at Todmorden, Yorkshire, where he was in practice before coming to Hyde. It did come to light later when his trial began that some doctors at Donneybrook House suspected there was something wrong but failed to inform the West Pennine Health Authority of the fact that at Halifax Magistrates Court in February 1976 he had pleaded guilty to eight offences and asked for sixty-seven more to be taken into consideration. Shipman had been charged with unlawful possession of drugs and forging pethidine prescriptions for his own use. He was fined £600, and briefly attended a drug rehabilitation clinic in York.

Other aspects of Shipman's background, with the benefit of hindsight, held clues to his murderous behaviour. He was born in Nottingham, the son of devout, working-class Methodists, and he witnessed the death of his mother, to whom he was exceptionally close. In the later stages of cancer, a doctor administered a fatal dose of morphine at home. That was later to become Shipman's own preferred modus operandi.

It also emerged at the trial that, in March 1998, Deborah Massey of the family-run undertakers Frank Massey & Sons approached Dr Linda Reynolds at the Brooke Surgery with concerns regarding Shipman. She spoke about the high number of Shipman's patients they attended to and how it was indicated on the cremation forms that Shipman had often seen the patient the day before they died. With Shipman held in such high regard within the community, the doctors at Brooke Surgery proceeded very cautiously, not having any hard incriminating evidence. However, when another doctor from a different surgery joined the Brooke practice she confirmed that the variations and discrepancies in death rates at Shipman's practice were highly unusual. With the support of the other doctors, Dr Reynolds approached John Pollard, the coroner for the South Manchester District, and called for an investigation. The police were brought in but abandoned their investigation, citing lack of sufficient evidence. The post-trial inquiry later blamed the police for assigning inexperienced officers to the case. Between 17 April 1998, when they dropped the investigation, and Shipman's eventual arrest on 7 September 1998, he killed three more people.

The last was the former Mayor of Hyde Kathleen Grundy, a Conservative councillor who was well regarded by everyone. Political friends and foes alike, including myself, considered her to be a lovely person who had a friendly disposition and who had friends across the party divide and beyond. She was found dead at her home on 24 June 1998. It transpired that Shipman was the last person to have seen her alive, and he would also later sign her death certificate stating the cause of death to be 'old age'. Her daughter, Angela Woodruff, a practising solicitor, did not believe that her mother was ill, and it came as a complete shock to her when it emerged that, in her mother's new will, her entire £380,000 estate went to Dr Shipman and nothing was left to her. Immediately sensing foul play, Angela contacted the police and another investigation began. After her mother's body was exhumed and found to contain traces of diamorphine, Shipman was arrested on 7 September 1998.

Following their investigation into other deaths that Shipman had certified, they found at least fifteen other cases to look into. A pattern emerged in all of the cases: Shipman administering lethal doses of diamorphine before altering the health records of the patients to suggest they had previously been in bad health.

Another person involved in the discovery was Father Denis Maher, a local Catholic priest. He also became suspicious after so many of his parishioners, who were also patients of Shipman, died of sudden causes that baffled their families. Trusting, as they did, the 'well-loved local doctor', they never questioned the cause of death whenever Shipman signed the death certificates or even when he urged the use of crematoriums. However, in the very strong Catholic tradition, many of Father Maher's parishioners wanted a 'proper burial' for their loved ones, despite objections from Shipman. After Dr Shipman was implicated, Father Maher was present at each exhumation site where the bodies were then taken to the Brooke surgery in Hyde for post-mortem examination. On that basis, there was enough incriminating evidence to charge Shipman with the murders of Kathleen Grundy and fourteen others. From very early on it was clear that there were more victims, with another twenty-three excluded from Coroner Pollard's list of suspicious cases.

The aftermath of Dr Shipman's arrest was devastating. So many of my constituents were affected and two police officers visited me in the Commons asking for my assistance. They argued that the Shipman trial would attract many aggrieved family members and relatives who would want to be included and they felt that the inquest should be limited to fifteen cases for the first trial so that the investigation could move forward. They argued that any more than fifteen cases could confuse the jury and Shipman might well get off due to the case being buried by the sheer volume of evidence to sift through and absorb. I did my best to explain to the twenty-three families that the investigation at the first trial stages would need to be limited but, quite naturally, they were very aggrieved. They wanted to know what had happened to their loved ones.

As I continued my surgeries in my constituency I found that many were still in disbelief and still saw Shipman as an upstanding citizen – this was the effect Shipman had on the community. However, I later wrote to Health Secretary Alan Milburn on 20 March 2000 highlighting my support for a public inquiry, and also the fact that I was given assurance from the police that if I co-operated with them and Harold Shipman was tried initially for only fifteen victims, then the other twenty-three cases would be tried afterwards. Unfortunately, David Calvert-Smith QC of the Crown Prosecution Service informed me that he did not realise this before making his decision about not proceeding with another trial.

Before Shipman's trial began I received several letters from him while he was in custody at Strangeways Prison in Manchester. In one letter, dated 11 April 1999, Shipman wrote to me from his prison cell Z-15 CJ8198 asking for me to enquire of the West Pennine Health Authority regarding the future of his surgery. He wrote, 'I have a problem with the Health Authority. They, with the police, applied for me to be suspended from the NHS. The National Executives board have done so ... as I read the rules, the HA [Health Authority] have to "run the practice in a way that when I get out, the practice is still there and viable"'. Shipman was concerned that his wife Primrose would not be able to maintain his practice without funding from the Health Authority and stated: 'How can my wife see how she can budget, not knowing how much money there is in the bank?' I did take the matter up with David Common, the chief executive of the West Pennine Health Authority at the time.

Letters of this sort continued for the next several months between Shipman, David Common and myself, culminating in a letter dated 19 August 1999 informing me of the possible closure of Market Street Surgery. Shipman wrote:

Dear Mr Pendry,

I'm sorry to have to write again. As you know I'm suspended from practising and Dr Lloyd is acting locum. The Medical Advisor for the West Pennine HA recently visited him and told him 'When Dr Shipman is found guilty we are breaking up this practice so you will only be employed up to then'. He also has been given a restricted list of drugs to use. None are modern, most have side effects and all can be challenged in their effectiveness. I know I was an expensive GP but few of my patients had side effects, few failed to be made better. The cry of cheap, cheapest and nasty is the approach of this HA – any of the annual reports hear me out.

The HA give the impression that they do not like single handed GPs. The removal leaves Hyde and area with four large group practices, where is the patients choice? Not that the HA have taken this into account. The suspension order says the practice has to be handed back in as good or better than when taken over. The loss of two surgeries per week, the lack of evening or weekend covers by the practice does not make me feel the practice is being run well. There has been a loss of 250 patients from Sept. No new patients can be taken on – HA wishes. By March 2000 will I have a practice to go back to?

I appreciate if I get the wrong decision, the patients need a doctor. Usually, it would be advertised and a successor appointed. Why do the HA feel it is in the public's good to allocate them to large groups from where they migrated to the only single handed practice? Any taint applies to me not Dr Lloyd. He has the backing of patients and staff, he would in any other HA be considered a prime candidate to run the practice. The not guilty verdict would result in him being a partner with my intention to retire.

The intensity of the presses search for a story is beyond belief. I would not like Dr Lloyd and the patients to read of 'HA disperses Killer Dr list'. What good does that do? As the area is not 'open' Dr Lloyd cannot stick up his name and wait for them to come in. If it was he could do that and most of the patients would stay with him. He needs HA approval, hardly likely with Dr Banks's statement.

As innocent, I worry that the practice if still existing would be barred to me by the HA above the law and order of the State! Will the GMC ask for a partner or early retirement? Aware that the HA work in secrecy I expect no communication from Mr Common. My solicitor advises that if I cannot practice [sic] because of the neglect or intention (good or bad) by the HA would mean work again with D. Commons name being known by everyone as the man who cost the NHS £x million.

You appreciate the invasiveness of the press and if this was made public, this could make the people of Hyde's lives a misery again. If you can get another result so quickly, by getting the HA to state their motives, needs and actions, I'd be again very grateful.

Harold Shipman

Shipman's trial at Preston Crown Court, presided over by Mr Justice Forbes, began on 5 October 1999. Shipman was charged with the murders of Marie West, Irene Turner, Lizzie Adams, Jean Lilley, Ivy Lomas, Muriel Grimshaw, Marie Quinn, Kathleen Wagstaff, Bianka Pomfret, Norah Nuttall, Pamela Hillier, Maureen Ward, Winifred Mellor, Joan Melia and Kathleen Grundy, all of whom had died between 1995 and 1998.

Shipman consistently denied his guilt, and never made any statements about his actions. His defence tried, but failed, to have the count of murder of Mrs Grundy, where a clear motive was alleged, tried separately from the others, where no obvious motive was apparent. On 31 January 2000, after six days of deliberation, the jury found Shipman guilty of killing fifteen patients by lethal injections of diamorphine, and forging the will of Kathleen Grundy. The trial judge sentenced him to fifteen consecutive life sentences and recommended that he never be released. The General Medical Council formally struck Shipman off its register following his conviction, although it was argued that there could have been many more cases brought to court. However, it was concluded that it would be more difficult to have a fair trial in view of the publicity the case had already attracted.

In the course of the Shipman Inquiry, it was revealed that he was probably responsible for many more deaths, possibly 250 in number.

That made him by far Britain's most prolific serial killer – the notorious Dr John Bodkin Adams was suspected of murdering up to 165 of his patients but was found not guilty at a trial in 1957. Medical academics have speculated that Adams possibly provided the role model for Shipman.

Shipman was incarcerated at Strangeways before being transferred to Frankland Prison in Durham in February 2000 and then Wakefield Prison in West Yorkshire in June 2003 where he lived out his final days.

On 1 February 2000, Alan Milburn announced that an independent inquiry was to take place led by Lord Laming, a well-respected man of integrity who had experience in dealing with difficult cases in the field of social care.

I initially supported a public inquiry as that was what the relatives of the deceased wanted. The primary aim of the inquiry was to investigate and make recommendations on how to safeguard patients in the future, in addition to thoroughly examining the different agencies involved in the case. Although I supported my constituents, I did understand the reasons why the Department of Health could see the merits of a private inquiry and tried to explain the Minister of Health's position in my many meetings with the relatives concerned and to provide context and justification for such an inquiry, but still holding to my belief that a public inquiry was the only way to satisfy the wishes of my constituents. A previous inquiry headed by Sir Cecil Clothier after the conviction of serial killer Beverley Allitt, a nurse charged with the murder of four children at Grantham and Kesteven Hospital in Lincolnshire, had been quick and effective. I offered as much help as I could to the independent Shipman Inquiry and I received from Lord Laming on 8 February 2000 a note requesting a meeting. From that meeting, it was determined that the Inquiry would take place in Manchester at my request in order for my constituents to have access. Notwithstanding the strength of the government's position on this and having done my best to explain it to those affected, I felt I owed my constituents like Joe Kitchen and Angela Woodruff a duty to raise with Lord Laming the importance of a public inquiry. This I did on a number of occasions. I also believed that a thorough inquiry that gave access to all of those relatives and friends affected by the actions of Dr Shipman should be carried out with speed. I expressed these views in one particular letter dated 14 March

2000, addressed to Kathleen Grundy's daughter Angela Woodruff. She had written to me earlier that month, and I responded stating that I had contacted Alan Milburn regarding whether his department would reconsider having a public inquiry instead of the independent one, notwithstanding the new, revised improvements in the structure of that inquiry agreed by Laming.

At that point, the Laming Inquiry into the later Victoria Climbié case was still to proceed with the aim to address the issues that arose from the Shipman case, namely those relating to accountability, roles and responsibility and major faults within the health system. At the outset, Lord Laming made it explicit that the inquiry would not be a criminal investigation into the deaths as this was for the Police and the Coroner to determine.

I continued to press Alan Milburn, as well as Home Secretary Jack Straw, on concerns brought to me by my constituents. When I wrote to Milburn on 20 March 2000, I asked for his and Jack Straw's assistance on three matters that were important to my constituents. First of all, they wanted a public inquiry, second they wanted the cause of death to be changed on the death certificates of Shipman's victims, and finally they wished for the inclusion of twenty-three other cases on Coroner Pollard's list. I then met with Jack Straw, and swiftly got a letter back from him stating that he would allow for the twenty-three other alleged victims to be included on Coroner Pollard's list, as well as making the appropriate changes to death certificates based on the inquests into these deaths. However, still unsatisfied with the decision to hold an independent inquiry, the Tameside Families Support Group, along with members of the British media, went to the High Court and fought for a judicial review, which they won on 20 July 2000. This amounted to a successful campaign by the Tameside Families Support Group, which I supported.

In the minutes in one of their meetings in Dukinfield on 16 March 2000, however, it was reported that a person who was a well-known political opponent of mine stated that I was sitting 'on the fence' regarding wanting a public inquiry, which was blatantly untrue. When the High Court ruled in favour of the Tameside Families Support Group, I went back to the minister and told him that he should reconsider his position on a public inquiry. In a letter to Alan Milburn dated 20 July 2000, the very day I heard of the outcome of the judicial review, I wrote:

Dear Alan,

As you know when I met you to discuss an Inquiry into the Shipman case, I requested that a Public Inquiry should be held as this was the view of the relatives and friends of those who were the victims of Shipman. As you were adamant that an 'Allitt type' Inquiry would be the best way forward, and recognising that this was your determined view, I then, as you know, requested that the Inquiry under Lord Laming be held as close to my constituents' homes as possible and you agreed to that request, for which I was grateful. I also saw Lord Laming on a number of occasions and was satisfied that his Inquiry would be a fair and thorough one, and I related this to my constituents involved.

However, in view of the Judicial Review announcement today, I urge you now to reconsider your position and grant a Public Inquiry. Anything less than that now, I think, would be considered, not only by my constituents, but also by the wider public, to be seen as flying in the face of the wishes of those constituents, who have suffered

terribly at the hands of Shipman, and who desire a more open type
of Inquiry. Yours sincerely, Tom.

In my meeting with Laming, he did say that he met Milburn the very
morning that my letter of 20 July was on his desk. Laming told me
that he agreed with the concerns of my letter and so did Milburn,
which culminated in Milburn eventually announcing in September
2000 that the Shipman Inquiry would be wrapped up, and a public
inquiry would be held with Baroness Janet Smith at the helm.

I received many letters giving me support for the stand I took and
my position was acknowledged by the Prime Minister and the Minister
of Health, which was documented in Hansard. When the Minister of
State, John Hutton, announced that a public inquiry would be set up
and chaired by the Dame Janet Smith, he went on to say:

I would like to acknowledge the strong contribution made by my
right honourable friend the Member for Stalybridge and Hyde (Mr
Pendry) in getting an inquiry set up into these terrible crimes. He
has been in regular contact with my right honourable friend the
Secretary of State Alan Milburn about the case and has, in particular, been tireless in his support for the relatives of the many victims
of Harold Shipman.

Premier Tony Blair also said: 'I pay tribute to the work that my honourable friend has been doing to help his constituents to come to
terms with a terrible tragedy. I am sure that the whole House will join
me in sending our deepest sympathies to the relatives and friends of
those who died.'

As the inquest progressed, it was discovered that Shipman was an avid drug user. After he put his victims to sleep, he often took with him the leftover prescriptions for his personal use. In 2002, the first report on the Shipman Inquiry was published and concluded that he unlawfully killed at least 215 people with a further suspicion that he murdered forty-five more. Subsequently, five more reports were published, each deducing the checks and balances needed on death certificates, prescription drugs and reforms to the General Medical Council. Interestingly, the second report published in July 2003 concluded that the last three of Shipman's victims could have been saved had it not been for the inexperience and unsuitability of the two Greater Manchester Police detectives who investigated accusations made against Shipman in March 1998.

The second inquiry conducted by Dame Janet Smith found that the detectives, during interviews with Dr Reynolds, 'failed to ask many important questions' regarding the disparity between the death rates of Shipman's practice and her own, nor did they ask to see the records from which the rates had been derived. They 'did not ask why the features of the deaths gave rise to concern' nor did they 'seek to find out more about the circumstances of the individual deaths'. The senior investigating officer, an experienced policeman unused to working without supervision, visited the Dukinfield crematorium but 'he asked no questions about the system of cremation certification'. Astonishingly, during the course of the investigation, he made no check on the Police National Computer to ascertain whether or not Shipman had any previous charges.

Dame Janet's report said:

By the end of 1998, the Greater Manchester Police had good reason to suspect Shipman of being a serial killer, whom the first police investigation had failed to detect. The potential for criticism of the Force was recognised. Nevertheless … senior officers in the GMP concluded that the March 1998 investigation had been 'appropriate at that time'.

She concluded that had senior officers 'put the investigation in the hands of a more senior detective officer, one who had experience of devising and supervising a criminal investigation, and if that officer had acted with reasonable expedition, the whole course of the investigation would, in my view, have been very different'.

But we can all be judgemental after the event. On the failings of the 1998 police inquiry, Dame Janet added:

I must and do feel sympathy for those few who have been found responsible for the failure of this investigation. They must live with that responsibility for the rest of their lives. Although their predicament was of their own making, it should be recognised that it was their misfortune ever to be caught up in the consequences of Shipman's criminality. There must be many others who would also have failed if put in the position in which these men found themselves. My final word must be for the families of Shipman's last three victims. For them, these hearings and the reading of this Report will have been profoundly distressing. Once again, I can only offer them my deepest sympathy.

Through this process I continued to receive letters from Shipman as his MP, highlighting his concern for Primrose, his wife, making a plea that she should be treated fairly and implying that she had done nothing wrong. Even in his last letter to me a few days before his suicide, he never did confess to his guilt or display any sympathy for his victims. But dark forces were clearly at play inside his head. Shipman was found hanging in his cell, in D wing of Wakefield Prison, on Tuesday 13 January 2004. Prior to his transfer to Wakefield Prison, Shipman was on suicide watch at both Strangeways Prison and Frankland Prison. Wakefield deemed the suicide watch unnecessary. Clearly that was not the case as the tone of his last letter, which I remember clearly but which I have mislaid since, was of a man who had clearly decided to end it all.

Shipman's story did not end with his death in 2004. The topic stirred much interest in the nation and I was approached by several media outlets wishing to make a documentary of the case. In December 1999, I was first approached by the BBC to be a part of their *Panorama* programme that was to be broadcast on the night of Shipman's verdict. They approached me to get my view on how the Shipman trial had affected my constituents and how I had dealt with their concerns. I didn't feel that the programme was in their interests, so I declined.

A massive battle took place between Yorkshire Television, part of Granada Media Group, and my council. In early 2001, I was approached by the highly regarded leader of the Tameside Council, Roy Oldham, regarding concerns that Yorkshire TV wanted to film scenes in Hyde for their new drama-documentary called *Shipman*. Given the sensitive nature of the case, and the plain fact that the inquiry was still ongoing, many of my constituents were ardently against any form of documentary. Yorkshire Television contacted us to gain permission to film in Hyde, but I stood firmly behind Roy Oldham in saying no. The production of a documentary when wounds were still raw would have been too much for me or my constituents. Many letters and correspondence went back and forth between myself, Yorkshire Television, Granada Media Group and even the Independent Television Commission. In a press release from March 2001, I stated:

Tom Pendry, MP for Stalybridge and Hyde, deplores Yorkshire TV's plans to make a TV drama based on the tragedy of the Harold Shipman case. Tom Pendry said: 'I certainly feel that filming should not go ahead, especially at this time when the Public Inquiry is about to take place and I have been in touch with the Producer to urge him to reconsider his decision. I have also pointed out to him that Yorkshire-Tyne Tees may well be in breach of the Independent Television Commission's Programme Code, which says that producers should assess the likelihood of personal distress arising from the programme, taking into account how recently the event took place, the nature and the extent of the presentation of portrayal of any innocent part, and the extent to which the event continues to attract wider media attention.

Even at this late stage I urge Yorkshire TV to recognise the force of those who argue again for producing the drama, which will be seen by many as an affront to those who have suffered at the hands of Shipman! I am pleased also that Tameside Council are taking a strong stand against the plans to produce this drama and I hope they join with me in requesting that the Independent Television Commission urges Yorkshire TV to drop their plan in the interests of my constituents and the wider community.

Despite my opposition to the production, the film still went ahead and aired on ITV on 9 July 2002 with James Bolam playing the role of Harold Shipman. No filming was done in Hyde and the town was recreated in another part of the UK. There was a private screening that was held in Hyde, which I did not attend, and that left many of my constituents in tears.

A verbatim stage play called *Beyond Belief: Scenes from the Shipman Inquiry* was also produced in 2004 and performed at the Library Theatre in Manchester, next door to the city chambers where the Inquiry was held. The most recent production was in 2014 entitled *Harold Shipman*. It was a two-part Channel 5 documentary and involved the participation of several of my constituents. I took no part in it.

I would like to think that the press, tabloids and our TV channels in particular have learnt some lessons from the Shipman programmes and how much distress they caused by way of their actions. But somehow I doubt it – the phone-hacking cases and the Leveson Inquiry have since demonstrated that little has been learnt.

And the after-shocks of the Shipman case continue to blight the lives of the families of his victims. In November 2013, it emerged that police kept human remains of some victims for twelve years and then secretly destroyed them without informing bereaved relatives. As the *Manchester Evening News* reported, the organs of twelve were put in storage after post-mortem examinations had been conducted to establish how they had died. The problem of informing the relatives about the organs in storage was the one that Sir Peter Fahy, Great Manchester Police Chief Constable, had 'agonised' over. However, he concluded, together with his officers, to destroy them without consulting the families of the victims, believing it would spare them from further distress.

The remains were then incinerated and burned on 16 February

2011. In answer to criticism of this process, Fahy assured the victims' families that the process was done in a 'dignified manner'.

> I would hope that the public would understand that this was a very difficult decision for us to make but I want to assure people that we made this decision for the right reasons. It was never our intention to cause the families any pain or distress. These families had not only experienced the upset of losing a family member but had had to relive it in the glare of the media and the public time and time again – that is something that most people will thankfully never have to experience. A number of years had passed since the trial and Shipman's death and was it right for us to cause even more upset and distress by making the families relive this yet again? No part of any murder investigation is simple and every decision is made with the best of intentions. How much should we tell families? How much do they want to know? The facts of any such case are distressing enough but do we add to this with even more detail? These are questions that officers are faced with on a daily basis.

But, later, there were further allegations that the families had been 'seriously misled'.

In 2014 the Independent Police Complaints Commission launched an investigation into the body parts scandal and related complaints about the 'poor handling' by the force of an inquiry into a suspected sex offender. Following allegations from a whistle-blower, two senior officers were served with criminal and gross misconduct notices. For the families, like those of Brady and Hindley's victims, the nightmare will never go away.

CHAPTER 10

SHADOW MINISTER OF SPORT

MOSCOW OLYMPICS

The vexed question in both sporting and political circles over the years has always been 'could or should sports and politics coincide?' This certainly manifested itself during the late 1970s and early '80s, coming to a head at the time of the invasion by the Russians in Afghanistan in December 1979. As Russia was to host the 1980 Olympics in Moscow, the big debate on this issue took place not only in this country but also in other parts of the world, notably the USA.

In January 1980, the US declared that they would boycott the games if the Soviets would not withdraw their troops within a month. However, the US Olympic Committee (USOC), at a meeting on 24 April, stated they would reconsider sending a team to Moscow under the prerequisite that there would be 'a spectacular change in the international situation', which of course there was not.

Back in the UK, the situation in the Commons was of course quite different. Prime Minister Thatcher agreed 'hook, line and sinker' with the Carter approach and demanded a total boycott by our sports bodies in defiance of the declaration of the International Olympics Committee (IOC). After the US brought immense pressure on the

NATO countries to support the boycott, the IOC protested that 'such pressure was an inappropriate means to achieve a political end, and that the ultimate victims would be the athletes'.

So battle commenced, certainly at Westminster, and the most prominent opponent to the Thatcher line was by Denis Howell, Labour's former Minister for Sport during the 1964, 1966 and 1974 Labour administrations. He was by far the best person to lead the charge against what he and most sportspeople felt was a betrayal of the very meaning of the Olympic movement. It seemed that neither Carter nor Thatcher could accept the IOC's decision, nor would they understand that the IOC was an independent body that could not be dictated to by governments.

Denis Howell was my mentor, and not only the best Minister for Sport in my lifetime, but one who could probably never be bettered. He was an old Tammany Hall-type politician – hard-hitting and fearless, but generous in his ways with others who did not always agree with his views. He was, indeed, a very rare political animal. Denis was vain at times and stubborn to boot, but he was a passionate man – certainly as far as sport was concerned. He did baffle me on more than one occasion, though, as some of the political positions he took up seemed somewhat on the right politically. However, on sporting issues, there was very little difference between us, and certainly true of the proposed boycott of the Moscow Olympic Games of 1980. I was very pleased to follow Denis's lead on this issue, believing as we did in upholding the Olympic ideal. He stood firm in his opposition to the boycott, believing that sport should not be a tool with which to confront the Russians – that we should not be replacing diplomacy with international sport in an attempt to stop military action by one sovereign state against another. At the same time, Denis did adhere to the condemnation of the Russian invasion, but not the method chosen principally by Carter and Thatcher.

Other countries followed the lead of both Thatcher and Carter in a boycott, notably West Germany, China, Japan and Canada. The UK government, along with other countries like France and Australia, left the final decision about whether to take part up to the individual athletes, as long as it was acceptable to their respective National Olympic Committees. This allowed the UK to send a team of 170 to attend the games.

Richard Palmer, now executive vice-president of the British Olympic Association, succinctly set out his arguments at the time. After drawing parallels with the problems raised by apartheid in South Africa, he pointed to Rule 24c of the Olympic Charter, noting that National Olympic Committees 'must be autonomous and must resist pressures of any kind whatsoever, whether of a political, religious or economic nature'. He went on: 'From the moment that Detroit, in 1974, withdrew its bid to stage the 1980 Olympic Games and left the field clear for Moscow, the seeds of the problem were sown.' Numerous organisations bombarded National Olympic Committees with boycott demands and in September 1978 the BOA took the unusual step of discussing participation, something that would normally have been taken for granted. As a result it passed the resolution:

Throughout the history of the Olympic Games and in accordance with the established principles of the Olympic Movement, emphasis has always been placed on the participation of the individual competitor in the Games. The British Olympic Association therefore is of the opinion that subject to the views of each participating nation, and in accordance with the rules of the International Federation concerned, any competitor, if selected, should not be denied the privilege of participating in the Olympic Games.

That remained the 'cornerstone' of the BOA's attitude.

Denis Howell was joined by myself and other sport-loving MPs – notably those in the All-Party Parliamentary Sports Group, which Denis chaired himself. I know that he had by his side a very able researcher, Patrick Cheney, who worked tirelessly to foster good relations with others in what was to be a pretty bloody fight. At first there were some difficulties with some of the sport organisations, and even Sebastian Coe – later an Olympic winner in two events – was reluctant to join in Denis's campaign, although he eventually changed his mind and competed. In the case of the rowers, thanks to the efforts of some of the would-be competitors, notably Colin Moynihan, they also changed their minds and competed. In the case of Colin Moynihan, in 1980 I led a debate in the English Speaking Union at which, in the course of my speech, I observed a young athlete in a tracksuit enter the debating chamber. After I had sat down he rose to his feet and made a very competent speech in support of my argument. It was only later I discovered that the young man in question had hastily got to the meeting in Mayfair from Henley, where he was practising as a rower for the Moscow Olympics. He took a silver in those Games and later became a Conservative MP and eventually Minister for Sport.

It really was ironic that both Moynihan and Coe competed against the wishes of Margaret Thatcher yet finished up not only medallists, but Tory MPs. Colin later served as an Under Secretary of State and

Seb became the parliamentary private secretary to Roger Freeman, Nicholas Soames and William Hague, the Leader of the Opposition at the time.

Another irony of course was that both Coe and Moynihan had roles of responsibility in ensuring the London Olympic Games were a great success. Colin had been the chairman of the British Olympic Association (BOA) since 2005 and was also the director of the London Organising Committee of the Olympic Games (LOCOG). Seb Coe served as the chairman of LOCOG from 2005, and then succeeded Colin as the chairman of BOA in November 2012.

The issue of trade with the Soviet Union exacerbated the battle between Thatcher and Co. and the rest of the UK as the government was found to be quietly exercising double standards. I personally took issue with Thatcher, together with my Labour colleague Peter Snape MP.

I pressed Mrs Thatcher on the hypocrisy of focusing on the Games boycott while allowing trade to and from the Soviet Union to be untouched. I urged direct action, particularly over the import of Soviet greetings cards, which affected the employment of my constituents, while allowing British sportsmen and women to compete. Peter Snape had similar problems affecting his constituents and we jointly penned a letter to Thatcher. In a rather touchy reply to me from No. 10, she responded:

I must reject your assertions that we have been 'obsessed' by the issue of the Olympic Games and that we have ignored the use of economic diplomacy ... We have no intention of introducing a ban on imports from the Soviet Union, 90 per cent of which last year were diamonds, oil and timber and other raw materials.

She also rejected out of hand implementing legislation covering imported greetings cards. That showed her twisted priorities and her lack of understanding of the potential impact of her boycott on a generation of sporting stars.

The Olympic Flag was commonly found to be flying above many teams at the Games during the opening and closing ceremonies despite their national governments officially supporting the boycott.

When I arrived at the Moscow Games, to my surprise I was listed as a senior VIP. I had the use of an official saloon car with the Union Jack on it, I was given an interpreter/guide and I was put up in a brand spanking new hotel. I cannot prove it, but mine might have been the suite that was earmarked for Margaret Thatcher if she had decided to turn up. An added bonus was that I received a bunch of tickets that would have been liberally given to a British Official Delegation, and one of the beneficiaries of this was a star gold medallist swimmer Duncan Goodhew. Duncan came to me and said that his mother and brother would love to have tickets to see him in the men's 100m breaststroke final. I readily gave him the tickets – but on one condition: that if, as was expected, he won the gold medal, he would come to me in the balcony and let me take a photograph of him upon his triumph. Duncan did win and duly honoured his promise, visiting me at the side of the pool with a big smile on his face after the race. I took some photographs of him only to find the next day that I had no film in the camera!

Another benefit of staying in the hotel was that, on most mornings, I was able to enjoy breakfast with the great Dutch runner Fanny Blankers-Koen, who won four gold medals in athletics at the 1948 Olympics in London. Fanny was a thirty-year-old mother of two when she won her medals, earning her the nickname 'The Flying Housewife'. On a visit to the Kremlin, I also had the good fortune to bump into my former MP Philip Noel-Baker, himself a great Olympian of yesteryear.

My overall feeling was one of satisfaction, that I was able to see some of the great stars of British athletics – such as Allan Wells, Steve Ovett, Sebastian Coe, Colin Moynihan, Daley Thompson, Sharron Davies and many others who won Olympic medals – and while there I left Olympia before the flags came down. In many senses I could say I didn't boycott Thatcher and the Games, rather I upheld in my view the best of the Olympics and what the Olympic movement stood for.

The Olympic motto 'Citius, Altius, Fortius' (Faster, Higher, Stronger), proposed by Coubertin, generally considered the father of the Olympic Games, in 1894, is what we have all strived for.

However, that was not the end of the boycotts; the 1984 Olympics in Los Angeles saw a Soviet boycott in retaliation with the Soviet Union declaring the action was due to 'chauvinistic sentiments and an anti-Soviet hysteria being whipped up in the United States'.

SPORTS COUNCIL

In 1988, an experienced civil servant, David Pickup, was appointed Director-General of the Sports Council. His talents as an efficient administrator were soon apparent. Formed in 1972, the Sports Council took a different turn in 1994 when it was decided that funding would be directed to fewer sports, in particular, those in which the UK excelled.

That led to numerous problems, particularly over funding. As David reported in his memoirs, he inherited a 'sad landscape' of perpetual battles against different government departments for annual grants.

During his tenure, there was a switch of priorities from local facilities to school sport to prepare a generation of elite athletes at international level. David's campaigning for the introduction of the National Lottery also proved crucial.

At the time of his appointment, Denis Howell was still shadow Sports Minister, but his worsening heart condition made it increasingly unlikely that he could carry on beyond the next election. As David recorded, I was competing with Kate Hoey to succeed him. David wrote: 'For our part we sought to cultivate each in equal measure which was slightly tiresome (and expensive!) as their rivalry meant that neither greatly relished the company of the other.' I was told by David Pickup later that it was Kate who didn't wish to have a joint meeting with me. I must confess I didn't have any problem at all with sharing a meeting with her and the Sports Council, although she did not have any formal responsibilities for sport except her undoubted love for it and that she had won a junior high-jumping competition in Northern Ireland. However, I eventually built up a strong and productive relationship with David and the Sports Council, which they acknowledged on numerous occasions. They also largely endorsed my 'Charter for Sport', which I'll refer to later.

Then, in 1993, the government's Sports Minister, Iain Sproat, called yet another review. The consultation proved entirely bogus – the Sports Council pointed out it was the seventh review in five years, with each adding substantially to administration costs. David Pickup resigned in disgust. And I backed the Sports Council to the hilt.

In a statement I said:

After all these years of consultation and hard work, this represents a feeble and wasted effort on the part of this nebulous government.

All in all this seems to be a great opportunity lost for sport, served up no doubt by civil servants and incompetent ministers. It is typical of what we have come to expect from the government, going from one disaster to another, in such vital areas as health and education, and now sport. How long will we have to wait while 'other options' are being considered? How much money will be wasted during this costly exercise? Here we have a Sports Minister, who is known for his extreme dislike of waste and bureaucracy, riding roughshod over those who have genuinely attempted the much needed restructuring of British sport.

Much later, David Pickup gave me a copy of his book *Not Another Messiah – An Account of the Sports Council 1988–93* and inscribed in it: 'To Tom – ah, what might have been... David.'

GETTING THE JOB

When John Smith became Labour leader in July 1992, my good friend Jack Cunningham gave me what I thought was sound advice – namely, that if I had aspirations of serving in John's team, then I should not go too far from London when he was making his selection. I followed that advice and headed for London with my young son Dominic and spent some hours with him in my office, promising him that I would take him to the theatre that evening as a reward for all his patience. Looking out my office window, I observed a succession of smiling colleagues gathering for a celebratory drinking session on the floor below me. Doug Hoyle was there, spotted me and beckoned me to join the jovial lot, which I did with my son. I overheard a fellow happy soul ask why the list of the shadow team had not been announced, as surely by now it must be completed, and then Donald Dewar, a close friend of John Smith, said: 'I think they cannot get hold of a member who is abroad.' Already feeling as sick as a parrot, I nearly threw up as I certainly was *not* abroad, and if only one member was holding up the announcement of John's team, then it wasn't me. With that sinking feeling I went to the theatre with young Dominic, who enjoyed what I could not at the time – the production of Willy Russell's *Blood Brothers* at the Phoenix Theatre. On arriving at my flat that evening with Dominic I had a voice message waiting for me from John Smith's secretary, Ann Brown, in which she requested that I ring John in the morning. I thought it would be a message of regret from John (which is often the norm when one has been at the losing end of the selection process) with a 'there will be another day' kind of speech. Still, I went to bed an unhappy bunny.

On my arrival at my office the following morning, I rang John's number only to find his secretary saying, 'Oh, John is on the phone', quickly followed by: 'No, he is now free.' The next voice was John's, who said, 'Where the f*** have you been?!' When I told him that I had been in London all this time, he turned to his secretary and said: 'We must have had Tom's number down wrong.' Then, to my joy, he said: 'Do you want the Sports job?' 'Love too!' I said. He then replied: 'You deserve it. I have held back from announcing my team because I was waiting for you, but now I shall go ahead.' I could hardly wait to phone my family with news of my good fortune. I later went onto the terrace of the Commons to share a celebratory drink or two with my colleagues, only to find John was also there with some American visitors. He beckoned me over and introduced me to his visitors as his new Labour Sportsman. It was a very happy day after all!

SIMON TERRY

One of the earliest controversies I was involved in as shadow Sports Minister came within weeks of my appointment. It exposed a deep flaw in the Conservative government's attitude to sporting achievement and undermined John Major's commitment to the realities of those who aspired to Olympic success.

In August 1992, it emerged that Simon Terry, who had won Britain's first Olympic medal in archery in eighty-four years, returned home in triumph from the Barcelona Olympics – only to find that he had been stripped of social security benefits while he was away winning honour for his country. DSS officials had even telephoned the relevant Spanish authorities to make sure he was away. It transpired that eighteen-year-old Terry from Sleaford, Lincolnshire, had been on the dole while he was winning two bronze medals. He was a roofer and had trained for the Olympics while off work during the seasonal lay-offs that are a part of that trade. His father, Mike, explained: 'He doesn't get sponsored and it's been a struggle. If he was a runner who had won two medals, he would be worth a fortune.' A DSS spokeswoman confirmed that his benefits had been stopped because he was not available for work when he was abroad, but denied that he was a victim of yet another Tory clampdown on easy targets in the benefits system.

I was outraged. The reason he was abroad was because he had been winning medals for Britain. Here we had an Olympic hero returning home to discover this outrage. On the one hand, we had the Prime Minister and his administration basking in the reflected glory of our people winning medals in Barcelona, and on the other, this rigid, mean-minded, petty and vindictive action. So much for that government's sporting image – treating a young lad in that way while he was triumphantly flying the flag for Britain.

I fired off a salvo of a letter to ministers across the Whitehall departments in a bid to resolve the situation. I told Sports Minister David Mellor: 'It is bad enough that Olympic hopefuls must struggle financially in order to qualify for the Games, but when their own government fails to support them because of a technicality, it is a disgrace and a shame.' But, no matter who I raised it with, it bounced back to the technicalities of the social security system. Then-Social Security Minister Alistair Burt responded: 'Benefits are only paid abroad in limited circumstances where tightly prescribed conditions are satisfied. The Income Support scheme does not make special provision for those who go abroad to represent their country in sporting events like the Olympics and I think it is right that it does not.'

I was livid at that and other such responses. I had been bounced around government departments, at every turn being fobbed off with vague promises that it would be 'sorted'. It was not, and that was a kick in the teeth for the whole of the British Olympic movement. It was an insult not just to Simon Terry, but to all our athletes and fans.

LABOUR'S CHARTERS

Prior to the 1997 general election, I wrote the manifesto *Labour's Sporting Nation*, and both Jack Cunningham and I decided to dedicate the document to Lord Denis Howell of Aston Manor (Minister of Sport in 1964–70 and 1974–79) in recognition of his outstanding contribution to our sporting nation. As I have already said elsewhere, he was my mentor, and there couldn't possibly be another Minister of Sport as good as Denis. He was a tough politician who knew how to get his way in most cases – regarded unfairly by some as a typical Tammany Hall operator. To those not initiated with the term, it relates to vote-gathering in New York following the influx of millions of Irish immigrants fleeing the potato famine. In the case of Denis it related to his ability to legitimately galvanise people into political activity.

The launch of Labour's sports manifesto was the culmination of a great deal of effort on my part to push sports at all levels up the political agenda. As I constantly pointed out, Britain is a sporting nation – there are few, if any other, countries in which so many people participate, watch and debate so many sports so often – and Labour is the party of sport. Britain, too, has a rich sporting heritage – we invented many of the world's great sports, including football, cricket, tennis, rugby, golf and many more.

In this specific document, I said that Labour would 'implement a national strategy for sport dedicated to providing excellence at all levels. This would increase sporting opportunities and improve national sporting performances.' It would also 'tackle the decline in school sport by ending the sale of playing fields'. I raised this particular issue on a broadcast programme with then-Prime Minister John Major, in which I said that 5,000 playing fields had been sold off in the last few years under his stewardship. He declined to disagree with the figure and that was a very important plank in our programme. The drying-up of playing fields prevented our kids from exercise in a sporting way and decreased their propensity to reduce their weight levels.

Labour's policy on sport would develop, we argued, 'sporting opportunities for young people to help them foster a sense of their value to society'. We went on to say that we would 'provide a more strategic approach to sports funding through existing government grants, the lottery and local authority services'. We would also 'develop a British Academy of Sport to meet the need of elite athletes throughout Britain'. The document also outlined how we would set up a Task Force for Football to tackle the problems of the game; make the Football Trust a recipient of lottery money so that it could continue its essential work for football at all levels throughout the UK; local authorities would be encouraged to develop and publish a leisure and sports strategy; and sport would continue to be a permanent 'good cause' for the purpose of lottery funding. We had plenty of back-up from the sporting world: Olympic gold medallist and Commonwealth javelin champion Tessa Sanderson; International shot putter Judy Oakes; England rugby union international and British Lion Brian Moore; Great Britain international rugby league player Shaun Edwards; Brendan Foster, the Olympic medal winner, world record holder and commentator; British Olympic coach Tom McNab; the Paralympian medallist Elaine Barrett; and Chris Holmes, the most successful swimming Paralympian of all time – all of whom, along with many more, had been widely consulted ahead of publication of *Labour's Sporting Nation*. Our commitment, our involvement and our determination to raise the profile of sport in government was widely recognised. We promised to give sporting opportunities to the many, not just the few.

Such an exhaustive list of endorsements prompted Tony Blair to write to me, giving his congratulations and stating that we should develop this approach for other documents of the Labour manifesto.

The sporting manifesto recognised that the previous eighteen years of Tory rule had seen mixed fortunes for Britain's teams and individual sportsmen and women, and it was clear that other countries had left us behind in sporting achievement. We were not short of talent, so we examined the reasons for that sorry state of affairs.

Our main conclusion was that many of our leading athletes and our potential champions had been unable to find or afford the access to top-class coaches and facilities. That was due to the failure of the Tory government to nurture sporting achievement or even to understand the importance of sport to our national life. The evidence was all around us. While John Major talked up the importance of school sport, the Department for Education and Employment still encouraged the sale of playing fields. The development of plans for an Academy of Sport ignored the wishes of the very sportsmen and women it was intended to support. Then there was their failure to stamp out ticket touting, which so debases events and infuriates fans. The absence of a proper legal framework to eliminate racism in sport was also a concern. And, finally, we couldn't imagine that in any other country athletes had to rely on social security while they competed in the Olympic Games. Britain deserved better than this.

Labour's plans offered a fresh start. On top of setting up a Task Force on football, we used sports lottery cash to enable the Football Trust to continue its important work.

Furthermore, we would retain listed events on terrestrial television – national shared occasions that bind the nation together; strengthen the law to tackle drug abuse, racism and to stop ticket touting at all major sporting events. The overriding aim was to once again make Britain one of the top sporting nations of the world.

Tony Blair, in his introduction, wrote:

Whether you play, attend or view sport, it crosses the divisions in

our society. For young people in particular, it can provide an important link to a world from which they often feel excluded. A nation's
commitment to excellence is publicly measured through sport. The
Olympic Games in Atlanta revealed the extent to which we have
fallen behind other countries in providing a framework for international sporting events.

He went on:

At the centre of Labour's Sporting Nation is the belief that everyone
has the right to strive for excellence. That is why a short tennis coach
must be as dedicated to his or her achievement as the coach responsible for the national team. And if we are to make the most of the
wealth of talent we have in this country, we must strive to put Britain
back on the sporting map. That is why a Labour government will
provide full support for British bids to host international sporting
events. When it comes to sport, the great danger is not that we aim
too high and miss the target, but that we aim too low and reach it.

My point exactly.

CHARTER FOR ANGLERS

The overall sporting manifesto had been preceded by several others
pertaining to specific sports and sporting interests, which also reflected
the work I had put into my shadow ministerial responsibilities.

For example, Labour's *Charter for Anglers* is something that we
should all be very proud of, not least because it was the very first of
its kind from any political party. There are an estimated 5 to 6 million

anglers in this country – the largest distributed participatory sport of them all. The charter was so well received that, when I launched it during a press conference alongside Joan (now Dame) Ruddock MP and Elliot Morley MP, both front-bench spokespersons for Home Affairs and Agriculture respectively, I made sure that all the angling organisations were on the front bench, with the journalists sitting behind them. I first called on the journalists for questions and, as one can imagine, they were all virtually accusing us of courting the anglers simply because there were so many in this country and that we were just playing for the anglers vote. The journalists had their say – especially those from the *Daily Telegraph* and the *Daily Mail* – before I then said: 'Now, would you like to hear what the industry thinks?' I then went one by one along the front bench to each of the sea fishermen, salmon and trout fishermen, other fishing bodies and the *Angling Times*, whereupon they all positively endorsed the Charter. As I expressed later in the *Angling Times*: 'In my experience of politics, I cannot remember when a consultation has been responded to with such enthusiasm and positive ideas. That is a credit to anglers and the organisations who represent them.'

The charter recognised the importance of sea angling as a leisure activity, and we accepted that our policy in this area must inevitably reflect our policy towards the commercial fisheries. We accepted that the problems of fish stock management, over-fishing, enforcement and the Common Fisheries Policy inevitably impacted on the leisure fishing sector, and we pledged to seek a major renegotiation of the CFP, strengthening national control over fisheries management.

We also promised: to maintain our six-mile inshore limit and negotiate with the EU for the extension of the twelve-mile exclusive national limit; to strongly enforce existing restricted areas such as the south-west's 'mackerel box' with quota priority for selective methods of fishing and controls on discards; to provide better enforcement of landing of large quantities of sea bass under the guise of leisure fishing; a stronger role for the Sea Fisheries Committees in conservation policy; and a review of Minimum Landing Sizes (MLS) and a ban on roundfish landings.

Among the key proposals was our pledge to review the funding for the sport. The Labour government would order the Sports Council to examine the cash for angling, 'giving greater consideration to the numbers who participate in the sport'. One of the biggest issues for anglers, the lack of a national close season, would be addressed by Labour. We supported the National Rivers Authority plan to change by-laws and clarify regional anomalies. Under Labour, British Waterways, the government agency responsible for canals, would remain in state hands, 'to preserve the current access rights for all'. Fly fishing was not ignored – Labour said it would review the entire legislation for salmon management. And sea angling would be boosted by a 'major renegotiation of the Common Fisheries Policy, strengthening national control over fisheries management'. Closed areas would be introduced for fish breeding.

The *Angling Times* and other specialist publications covered the charter extensively – and positively. The angling community was very much in favour of our document and I'm sure we won many votes from people who might not otherwise have voted Labour, contributing towards our 1997 election landslide. The *Independent* newspaper reported on Friday 23 June 1995, the day after our launch, that we had 'made a calculated attempt to woo the working-class male voter by launching its Anglers' Charter, designed to bolster support from Britain's most popular participatory sport. [It was] intended to dispel any myths that Labour is opposed to angling.' The Charter for Anglers demonstrated our commitment to the sport. At the same time it reaffirmed our long-standing aim of protecting the aquatic environment. The charter did indeed address fears that Labour, which was and still is opposed to fox hunting and other game sports, may also be against angling – an impression that could cost it dear at the ballot box. My charter put those fears to rest. We admitted: 'Although the Labour Party has had a long-standing support for all codes of angling – coarse, game and sea – perhaps this support has not always been expressed as clearly as it could have been.'

Attempts were made by the fox-hunting bodies to gain support from anglers to create a united front, but they were resisted by the angling community who distanced themselves from such overtures, recognising that they had achieved their objectives through a future Labour government. We had nailed a myth and that would pay dividends in the subsequent general election.

BREAKING NEW GROUND

Another important policy commitment was outlined in our policy document *Breaking New Ground: Labour's Strategy for Tourism and Hospitality*, which was also enthusiastically endorsed by Tony Blair. We recognised that tourism – not least sporting tourism – was the world's largest industry and, indeed, in Britain, it was one of the largest economies – providing employment for more than 1.5 million people at that time. Our policy drew on ideas proposed by Blair at conferences, as well as intensive consultative discussions held over the past year by

Jack Cunningham and myself. As Blair rightly said in his foreword: 'This document sets out a strategy for a more successful industry: improving the country's transport infrastructure; expanding opportunities for training; raising quality standards and achieving more effective marketing promotion.'

So, under those headings, Labour recognised that tourism and hospitality should provide more major economic and social employment opportunities in Britain. We also talked about the importance of tourism and hospitality and the social and economic importance to Britain. Fast-growing areas of activity should not be underestimated – something that a succession of Tory ministers had overlooked. The one and only Act of Parliament on tourism up to that stage had been one introduced by Anthony Crosland, the then Secretary of State in charge of the tourism industry. The 1969 Development of Tourism Act created the British Tourist Authority and the tourist boards for England, Scotland and Wales. Labour was the first party to recognise that government support in marketing and back-up services to the tourism and hospitality industries was needed, and that the tourist boards were 'charged with the statutory duty of advising the government on all matters relating to tourism'.

Our new plan would 'implement a committed strategy to assist development of tourism and hospitality'. Central to the strategy would be the introduction of a new Development of Tourism Act, which would build on Labour's 1969 Act. The new act would, in particular, 'update tourism structures; enhance standards in service and provision; introduce a co-ordinating mechanism for overseas tourism marketing; encourage partnerships between local authorities, tourist boards and the private sector'. It was a strategy that was widely accepted in the tourism world. Those who endorsed it included: Adele Biss, chairman of the British Tourist Board; David Quarmby, chairman of the British Tourist Authority and English Tourist Board; Richard Branson of Virgin Group; Jeremy Logie, chief executive of the British Hospitality Association; Alison Cryer, managing director of Representation Plus; and Ken Robinson, the former chairman of the Tourism Society.

After we won the election, I went to a luncheon hosted by the Guild of Travel and Tourism. The guest speaker was Sir Rocco Forte, the well-known hotelier and a very big wig in the tourism and hospitality industries. He didn't know at first that I was there but before he got up to speak he did notice me, at which point he put his notes to one side. He then said to his audience: 'As you know, I am a committed Tory and I dreaded it when Labour won the last election – but I was comforted in the thought that at least we would have a minister that understood tourism and hospitality and would do his very best to enhance those industries – to our regret he didn't get the job.' I was grateful for Rocco's comment as it helped soften my disappointment at being overlooked for the position, and we have remained friends ever since.

A NEW FRAMEWORK FOR FOOTBALL

Possibly the most important document I produced during the run-up to the 1997 general election was *A New Framework for Football – Labour's Charter for Football*. It had a foreword by Tony Blair, in which he said: 'Pelé memorably dubbed football "the beautiful game"', but pointed out that its image at home had been tarnished as a result of years of neglect. The previous season, in particular, football had received plenty of publicity for all the wrong reasons. 'Government must play its role in reversing this trend,' Tony wrote. He went on to say that, as a football fan himself, he shared the concerns and aspirations of fellow supporters up and down the country and he firmly believed that our charter addressed the critical problems associated with the game. 'In doing so it builds a new framework in which football can flourish once more,' he said. Some of the issues that were highlighted included:

the re-emergence of hooliganism with the active involvement of far right extremist thugs; examples of appalling behaviour from supporters and players both on and off the field; evidence of financial irregularities, bungs and allegations of match fixing; the use of illegal social drugs by some players; escalating ticket prices and restrictive TV coverage, ensuring that the trend towards 'sport for the few' rather than 'sport for all' continues unabated; the precarious financial position of a number of small, lower league clubs.

In the manifesto, we pointed out that the gap between the leading clubs and the rest had continued to widen under the Tories. I wrote:

The present government has rarely seen beyond the top echelon of professional football. Labour, on the other hand, is alert to the fact that football exists at so many different levels, from the humblest local Sunday league match to the grandest Wembley occasion, all of which are part of the same heritage. Ideally football should take a lead in sorting out its own problems. However, government contributes over £50 million each year to the game, as well as carrying responsibility for the electorate's concerns. Society as a whole has a stake in the game and it is the duty of governments to assist in creating a framework within which football can prosper. Football is a sport we gave to the rest of the world and one which we ought to feel proud of. It is too important to be left to the ravages of the market or a few out-of-touch individuals.

We promised to establish a Task Force that would include representation from fans to examine all aspects of our national game. We promised to support the fans in seeking ways to ensure that troublemaking by the minority – particularly abroad – did not discriminate against genuine, law-abiding supporters. We were determined to take firm action against racism in football and intended to tighten the laws on racist abuse and anti-social behaviour at matches. Having always believed that a number of national sporting events should continue to be available on free-to-air television, Labour would review the size and scope of the list of events. We pointed out that the Conservative government has always failed to act in the best interest of football; Labour was the only political party that had a commitment to the whole future of the game. I quoted Lord Justice Taylor from his final report on the Hillsborough disaster: 'What is required is the vision and imagination to achieve a new ethos for football.' All those issues were addressed in our document, and I would like to think that it was in part my efforts, along with my working colleagues, that ensured such a strong commitment to sports in Labour's manifesto for the 1997 general election, which included the following promises:

A Labour government will take the lead in extending opportunities for participation in sports; and in identifying sporting excellence and supporting it. School sports must be the foundation. We will bring the government's policy of forcing schools to sell off playing fields to an end. We will provide full backing to the bid to host the 2006 football World Cup in England. A Labour government will also work to bring the Olympics and other major international sporting events to Britain.

That was to prove prophetic.

As shadow minister, I was heavily engaged in other football issues, along with boxing, both of which I will deal with in later chapters, as some issues carried on before and after my stint on the front bench.

NATIONAL LOTTERY

One of the most contentious issues I had to face as shadow Minister of Sport in 1993 was the need for a National Lottery. I was appointed opposition spokesperson when the proposed Bill was first debated, which raised a number of problems for the party. I found myself in quite a minefield, as the principles of the lottery were not of the kind that fell neatly along party lines. There were members on both sides of the House who held firm views on either side of the question of its morality. In particular, Margaret Thatcher had a strong objection to its purpose of allowing 'people with no worth becoming rich by luck'. On the Labour side, a strong anti-gambling, Methodist streak existed. Indeed, Harold Wilson, a devout Methodist, stated that the Labour movement 'owed more to Methodism than to Marxism'.

My problem, however, was much more difficult to square than the religious or moral objections raised. It was more a question of the number of people that would be affected by the Bill, especially in Liverpool where Football Pools was mainly based. The growth of a National Lottery, with its massive cash prizes to be won, would dwarf the benefits that the Pools had traditionally offered winners. By definition, the high pay-outs from the National Lottery could diminish the number of people taking part in the Pools, which employed thousands of people, and therefore create unemployment in what was one of Labour's strongest parliamentary regions. With that in mind, I initially had to combat Merseyside MPs, but, with the backing of my senior colleagues Mo Mowlam and later Ann Clwyd, I won them over. I argued that although I held strong views for sport to have a larger slice of National Lottery revenue, if it was administered fairly it could ensure that not only sports but also the arts, the Cinderella of the department, would benefit.

As the Bill progressed up to the end of April 1993, there were a lot of tough negotiations and hard bargaining at every stage, but the government proved receptive to most sensible amendments and made several key concessions, which I acknowledged as the Bill prepared to clear its last hurdle. I told the Commons:

On Second Reading I said that it was consistent to be committed to the idea of a national lottery but to retain some deeply held objections to parts of it. We thought that the Bill was flawed in many fundamental respects and we urged the committee to vote for our amendments and to reject the Bill as it stood. We said that, unless the Bill emerged on Report [Stage] in better shape, we reserved our position. Since the Committee Stage, there has been some hard bargaining. Following persuasive arguments advanced by my hon. friends and some free spirits on the Conservative benches, ministers did listen to the genuine concerns expressed. To their eternal credit, they promised to reflect on the many points that we had to put to them. That promise was kept. Since that time, there have been a number of meetings with ministers and some important changes, to the benefit of the charitable sector, the pools industry and the small lottery operators affiliated to the lotteries council.

I also praised Stan Orme for his work in highlighting the problems of small lotteries and added:

I had intended to make a number of points in the government's favour, but I judge that ministers do not want me to at this stage. I will therefore spare their blushes and content myself with pointing out that the government has made some important concessions. The Bill is still not as perfect as we would like it to be. As it travels to another place, meaning of course the House of Lords, I am sure that it will be further improved. The pools companies, for instance, would like more freedom to advertise on television and radio. In Committee Stage, the minister said that he would consider that, but nothing has been translated into legislative form. We hope that the Secretary of State will fight his corner with the Treasury, because the 12 per cent tax yield to the Treasury is far too high. I hope that, at the end of the first year of operation, that percentage will go down and not up. I trust that the Bill will be improved in the other place because we wish to see a better lottery. The opposition have always said that decisions on the Bill should be taken by a free vote. People who have fundamental objections to a lottery of any kind should be allowed to express them in the Lobby. However, if there is a division, we on this bench, who fought hard to improve the Bill, will vote for its Third Reading. We recognise the strength of feeling of those who feel that they still cannot support the Bill and, as they know, they are free to vote against it. I wish the Bill well as it goes to the other place. I hope that it leaves there an even better Bill than it is now.

And so it proved. The Bill went through and the first draw was seen by millions of TV viewers on 19 November 1994 – ten lucky jackpot winners shared almost £5.9 million. But it was sports, the arts and charities that proved, as we had intended, to be the real winners. Well over £20 billion has gone to 'good causes'. Currently 54 per cent is given to arts, sports and heritage via government agencies and the remaining 46 per cent is given to charitable, health, education and environment causes by the Big Lottery Fund. Since 1994, Heritage Lottery Fund has supported 39,000 projects across the UK with funding totalling £6.8 billion.

The National Lottery contributed up to £2.2 billion towards the cost of the Games, with Camelot achieving its target of raising £750 million towards this sum from sales of specially designed 'Go for Gold' lottery games ahead of schedule.

As shadow Sports Minister I knew full well the qualms many people sincerely held, but those figures speak for themselves.

Much praise is often heaped on John Major for introducing the Lottery and the subsequent funding that went towards the elite sports in this country – in particular to potential and indeed Olympic sportspeople. What seems to be forgotten, however, is that at the 1996 Olympic Games in Atlanta, from the British Olympic Association (BOA) headquarters in Wandsworth, Tony Blair relayed to those of us in Atlanta – Jack Cunningham, myself, together with many of the competitors at those games – Labour's manifesto commitment, which made it clear that once elected we would ensure that the Lottery was geared to helping the elite athletes of this country. It also bemoaned the fact that it should have been in place before the Atlanta Olympics. The government scheme was introduced after the 1995 Olympics and was therefore too late to help the athletes of those Games. However, it was Labour's proposal that would enable the Lottery to make a real difference to the quality of facilities and support available for those who enjoy sport in Britain. It was in our manifesto but it had been missed by many, even within our own ranks. John Major received all the credit when it was in fact our idea in the first place.

TESSA SANDERSON

I first met Tessa Sanderson, the Commonwealth and Olympic Games javelin gold medallist, prior to the 1997 general election.

Although born in Jamaica, Tessa did her serious training as an athlete in this country at the Wolverhampton and Bilston athletics club. As a heptathelete, she competed in javelin competitions in six consecutive Olympic Games – in 1976, 1980, 1984, 1998, 1992 and 1996 (winning gold in 1984) – and three Commonwealth Games – in 1978, 1986 and 1990 – as well as the European Championships in Prague in 1978. She had a serious rival during much of this time, with Fatima Whitbread, who herself had a distinguished athletic career.

However, when Tessa won the Olympic gold in 1984, the first for a British woman in that event, her victory was quite unexpected. In the end, her career outlasted Whitbread's, and she competed at senior international level until 1996. At our first meeting I expressed my surprise that she had been reported as being a supporter of Margaret

LEFT Not all work – on a parliamentary trip to the Brazilian rainforest
RIGHT With leader 'Boyo' Neil Kinnock

Michael Foot looking
confused with my gesture
– the cameraman
couldn't work out
my camera

With George Best and friend, having a sober drink

With my hero Albert Stubbins (left), alongside another devotee of Albert's, Bobby Robson, on the terrace of the House of Commons

The return match with Lennox Lewis, but why is he smiling? That's my best punch!

Lennox expressing his sadness at me not being made Minister for Sport

The Duke of York and Doug Ellis, then chairman of Aston Villa FC, at a charity function for the NSPCC

With Colin Moynihan, the then Tory Minister for Sport

Meeting with former President of South Africa F. W. de Klerk, when he acknowledged the effects the sporting boycotts had on apartheid

ABOVE With Nelson Mandela, alongside the late Charles Kennedy

RIGHT With my children, Fiona and Dominic

ABOVE Meeting Pope John
Paul II at the Vatican

LEFT A trendy Fiona with Papa
(Pope John Paul II) at the
Vatican

Three sporting kids

Michael Foot with my sister, brother and my mother on her ninetieth birthday at the House of Commons

My mum on the terrace of the Commons, discussing old times with Michael Foot

ABOVE With Jack Cunningham, celebrating twenty-five years of membership of the Commons

LEFT Entering the House of Lords, 11 July 2001

In front of the stand named after me in Stalybridge Celtic FC

Prince Philip presenting me with the Arthur Bell Trophy for my 'outstanding contribution to sport' at St James's Palace

Thatcher at the previous general election. I told her in no uncertain terms that Thatcher had no interest in sport whatsoever, as evidenced by her earlier attitudes toward the boycotting of the Moscow Olympic Games in 1982. I wondered if she, along with other athletes, refused to greet Thatcher when she attended the Edinburgh Commonwealth Games in 1986 because of her government's policies towards apartheid in South Africa. At that time, Thatcher's government refused to impose sanctions on South Africa, arguing that it would make the situation even worse. However, two weeks before they were to commence, Nigeria and Ghana were the first two countries to pull out and boycott the Games. Brian Oliver, former sports editor for *The Observer*, highlighted the news reports that came out of London:

> Two black African nations, Nigeria and Ghana, announced yesterday that they will boycott the 1986 Commonwealth Games later this month in protest of Britain's refusal to agree to major economic sanctions against South Africa. The boycott appeared to be an attempt to put pressure on Prime Minister Margaret Thatcher, who has long opposed economic sanctions. The Nigerian embassy in London conferred that the boycott was meant to 'dramatise to the British government how strongly we feel about the matter'.

Thirty-two of the fifty-nine Commonwealth countries boycotted the Games – mostly nations from Africa and the Caribbean. In one notable event, the Bermudian team travelled to Edinburgh under the pretence that they would be competing in the Games. However, the night before the opening ceremonies, word came to the athletes that the Bermudian team would not take part. With heavy hearts the following

day, a telephone conversation took place with the Bermudian leader
John Swan as the opening ceremonies were taking place in the background. In a last-minute switch, Swan threw his support behind the
athletes, leaving the team minutes to change into their Bermudian kit
and run out onto the stadium. Time was cut so short that Bermuda
missed their original slot and made it just in time to march into the
stadium just before the host nation. They waved their flags and revelled
in the thunderous cheer they received from the crowd. Unfortunately,
however, the celebration ended when the athletes awoke the next day
to news from the Bermuda Olympic Committee that they had indeed
been pulled out of the Games – this time for certain. Notwithstanding
a total of 1,662 athletes participated in the Games across ten different
sports – athletics, aquatics, badminton, boxing, cycling, lawn bowls,
rowing, shooting, weightlifting and wrestling.

Although the Games continued, it was not without its financial
woes. Edinburgh originally won its 1986 bid because no other nation
wanted to take the gamble and, having previously hosted many years
before, Edinburgh felt they had the infrastructure and finances to accommodate the Games. What the Games' Organising Committee
did not contemplate was the significant loss they would incur from a
lack of advertising and sponsorship revenue. With the debt running
more and more into the red, the owner of the *Daily Mirror*, Robert
Maxwell, stepped in with a promise to inject £2 million of his own funds
into the Games – an offer that he later reneged on as it was discovered
that he barely contributed any money at all. Maxwell also tried to sway
Thatcher's government into providing more funds but, not surprisingly, he was unsuccessful. In another instance, Maxwell held a media
conference to introduce a Japanese investor who offered to put up

1.3 million into the Games. Ryoichi Sasakawa, it was later discovered, had been tried but not convicted as a World War Two war criminal. In the end, the Games ran a massive deficit of £4.9 million, with the load of the financial burden resting on the shoulders of many small businesses. However, contracts were not honoured and many invoices went unpaid, leaving many of these businesses to go bust. The Games had the lowest turnout of athletes since 1950, which was compounded by the glaring absence of ethnic diversity among the competitors. However, Tessa Sanderson went on to compete in the 1986 Games where she won gold in javelin.

At a subsequent meeting with Tessa, I gave her a draft copy of *Labour's Sporting Nation*, the blueprint for our sports policy in the coming general election. I think it ticked the right boxes as far as she was concerned and she agreed to my request that she might assist in Tony Blair's campaign. I contacted Blair's campaign team who were absolutely delighted that she had agreed to take part. They recognised that she was a star act and during the campaign she was helicoptered to various sporting venues around the UK. She was well received by sports people and especially within the ethnic minority communities, where she had a strong personal following. We became pretty good friends during this period and she remained an enthusiastic supporter of sport-related Labour policy documents throughout the campaign.

The election (and our landslide victory) soon came and, on the following morning, Tessa appeared on GMTV with Eamonn Holmes. She was full of joy and hope for the new government and proud that she had done her bit to bring about its success. She went on to tell Eamonn how the sports world would be pleased with what was about to come to pass and added, to my embarrassment, that 'Tom Pendry is to be the new Sports Minister.' This was probably the worst thing that could have happened at that stage as Tony Blair, as with any previous Prime Minister, would not have taken too kindly to anyone pre-empting his official announcements. I have no evidence that this was the case here, but I winced nevertheless on hearing Tessa's words – no doubt said all in good faith. Of course, she was not alone in the world of sport in believing that, after five years as the shadow Minister of Sport, I should have been chosen for the job.

When the news broke that Tony Banks was given the nod, I had both Tessa and her agent on to me asking me what they could do to reverse that decision – her agent going so far as to say that he had many important friends in the sports world who could speak up against this outrage. I had to calm them both down by stating that that was not how things worked in the business of ministerial selection. I was nonetheless grateful for their loyalty and concern, so you could imagine my utter surprise when, a few evenings later on the terrace of the Commons, I observed from a discreet distance the lovely Tessa in the company of the new Minister of Sport, Tony Banks. It was, however, no surprise for me to learn the following week or so later that Tessa was made vice-chairman of the Sports Council, in which role she carried out her duties with gusto and some style. I have met Tessa on a number of occasions since, though we never discuss that period of our lives. These things happen of course not only in politics, but in life itself, so one just needs to accept them and move on.

THE ORATORY SCHOOL AND THE BLAIRS

One of the most pleasant aspects of being a shadow Minister for Sport is the number of invitations to various sporting functions one receives.

On one occasion I was invited to see the under-14's school rugby competition in Richmond, where I was to present the prizes afterwards. In the final game, the Oratory School was playing. I had not heard of it before, but I got on very well with the headmaster, John Macintosh, during the course of the game. He asked about my family and when I mentioned that I had a son, Dominic, who was a very sporting lad, he said: 'Well, my school would be ideal for someone like him.' The Oratory have won many trophies in sport, including, as it turned out, one for their success in the game I was watching. I did point out to John, however, that it would be very difficult for Dominic to attend the Oratory, as much as I am sure it merited my boy's attendance, because his mother was still based in our main home in Stalybridge, Cheshire. Nevertheless, John still invited me to lunch to visit and look around his school in the near future and I did point out that Dominic was coming down to London soon; I thought it would be a good idea for him to at least see the school.

A little while later, I received a very handsome prospectus from John – I doubt whether Eton would have a better one! Within a day or so, I received a phone call from Cherie Blair's father, the actor and constituent Tony Booth, asking if I knew of any good Catholic state schools in London as Cherie was looking for such a school for her son Euan. With the prospectus to hand, I told Tony Booth: 'I think I have found the very school for your grandson.' I shipped the prospectus off to Cherie. I did not get an acknowledgement that she had received it, but when I took up John's previous lunch invitation, I decided to take Dominic with me. We sat in his school's foyer and waited for the headmaster and, just moments after we'd arrived, John's secretary came out and said: 'I hope you don't mind, Mr Pendry, but he's tied up for a few minutes with some potential parents.' Lo and behold, who should come out of his office minutes later? None other than Tony and Cherie Blair having their first introduction to the Oratory School, which Euan subsequently attended along, later, with two of their other children.

John had asked Dominic to bring his scrapbook with him from home to talk about in the meeting. While Dominic was chatting away John winked at me – Dominic was getting so enthralled with his scrapbook, pointing out what had happened in the Algarve when he was on a family holiday, that he would have gone on for ages had we not curtailed his enthusiasm. John very much still wanted Dominic to go to the Oratory, but we had to face the fact that it was impractical with my hectic parliamentary schedule (I was living on my own in London during the week while my wife Moira was in Stalybridge). So the Oratory School fell through for Dominic, but I still became good friends with John. On the last occasion we met, I took John for lunch at the House of Lords and Dominic joined us – now a 34-year-old former Manchester grammar schoolboy and Managing Director of a PR company in London. Both John and he got on very well.

NOT GETTING THE JOB

We entered the 1997 general election with the firm belief that we would emerge victorious and form a new Labour government under Tony Blair, who had led the campaign with great style and purpose. Given my sporting background, I was looking forward to being the Minister for Sport – the position I most hankered after in government.

The result was a landslide for Labour with a win of 418 seats. I comfortably looked forward to that invaluable phone call from the master himself. Surely all the phone calls and messages from family, friends and the media congratulating me in advance couldn't be wrong, I thought.

On the Saturday evening after the election, I went to a boxing tournament in Manchester, as I was a steward of the British Boxing Board of Control. Before taking my ringside seat, I was greeted with alacrity by Frank Warren, the promoter of the event, with the words: 'Are you now the Minister for Sport?' Gripping my mobile phone, I told him that I had not yet heard. He then said: 'That's sad news because Sky want to announce it from the ring that not only did we have the Minister of Sport in our presence, but we have a former boxer as Minister for Sport.' Still clutching my mobile phone, I replied: 'Frank, unfortunately I can't help.'

The following day I travelled to Millwall football ground to watch the Women's Cup Final, and the FA Chiefs also asked whether I had heard if I was the new Minister for Sport, as virtually everybody in football expected the job to go to me. Still holding my mobile phone, I replied: 'I haven't heard,' much to their (and my) disappointment.

After another anxious and almost sleepless night in my London flat, I engaged myself in household chores while waiting for the call. In the early afternoon the phone rang and a voice said: 'This is the switchboard at 10 Downing Street, will you hold the line for the Prime Minister?' This was the moment I had been so desperately waiting for and I stood erect and straightened my tie. Tony's unmistakable voice – not at all like the nervous one in 1982 asking me if I could help him get in the parliamentary scene – came on the phone and I immediately said: 'Congratulations, Prime Minister.' He replied: 'It's been a long haul, Tom, but we made it in the end.' He added: 'I've got some sad news for you: I'm not going to give you the job.' Imagine the shock that hit me after having spent five years as the shadow Minister for Sport waiting to take on the ministerial position and working on our commitments on sport and tourism. When I asked him for his reasoning, he said: 'Time to move on.' I forgot about the niceties and told the new Prime Minister:

Tony, that is the most stupid thing you have ever said in your life. You only move on when you have arrived – for five years, first under John Smith and then you, I have done the job in opposition. I have been to Atlanta Olympics, Moscow and Lillehammer Paralympics, among others, and have written Labour's policy on sport, football, angling, tourism and many others endorsed by you and now you tell me to move on?

Tony, clearly shocked by my response, mumbled something, then said: 'I'll ring you later with another offer,' to which I replied: 'Don't bother', and put the phone down.

Later that evening I got another phone call, this time from Chief Whip Nick Brown, to say how upset Tony was. I responded: 'Not as upset as I am.' Nick did not offer me a position in government, as Tony had implied earlier on, but instead the Chair of any Select Committee I wished. As I had my sights on only one job, I retorted: 'Tell the Prime Minister that I am applying for the Chiltern Hundreds.' The Chiltern Hundreds is an ancient nominal paid office of the Crown that is used by MPs to resign, since they have no constitutional power to do so directly. It is a sinecure post and when an MP accepted the appointment, they would be disqualified from sitting in the House of Commons as it violated the principles of the separation of powers. 'No! Don't do that,' Nick immediately said. Of course, I had no intention of doing that whatsoever because I had nowhere to go, but I thought I would let Tony sweat a little thinking that he was going to have a by-election for the worst of all possible reasons before he'd even got his feet under the table at No. 10.

As is my nature – 'too soft for politics' my eldest brother Jack once told me – I wrote a handwritten note that I handed to Tony's PPS, Bruce Grocott, pledging support for him and the new government. I think that was very gracious on my part because, within minutes of learning my bad news, I heard on the TV that Tony Banks, a very genuine football supporter and of Chelsea in particular, had been appointed to the job instead of me. The next phone call was from my mentor Denis Howell. who conveyed his sincere condolences. He rang me every day for almost a week at one stage to offer me his place as chairman of the All-Party Sports Group, which I declined, saying truthfully that he was the inspirational leader in both Houses on sport. When Denis died, I decided to take the Chair if accepted by the Group and this duly took place. We had many great speakers pass through, such as Dame Kelly Holmes, Tom Daley, Duncan Goodhew, Karren Brady, Seb Coe, Colin Moynihan and Kate Hoey, to name just a few.

Tony Banks told me how he had been offered the post by Blair. He was in his garden having a barbecue when he was called to the phone and heard this voice asking him if he would like to be the Minister for Sport. Banks told me that he thought it was Rory Bremner imitating the Prime Minister and told him to 'piss off'. Obviously taken aback, Blair then made it clear it really was him on the phone. According to Banks, he then said: 'What about Tom Pendry?', to which Blair said: 'Do you want the job or not?' 'Yes, yes, yes!' was Banks's reply.

The reaction from the press was very favourable for me. Ian Wooldridge wrote a full page in the *Daily Mail* with a headline 'Just why did Pendry miss out on the job?' Ian wrote in lurid language, which had some degree of accuracy, of dining with three MPs who had lost the election:

The fourth had racked up a terrific victory for New Labour at Stalybridge and Hyde with a massive 14,806 majority, including a 9.34 vote of confidence on the swing-o-meter. Yet Tom Pendry, despite the Falstaffian bonhomie and French Riviera suit, was the sickest of them all. Deep down, he was sicker than soccer's sickest parrot.

The post of Minister of Sport had been awarded to Tony Banks, a chirpy Chelsea football fan whose immediate reaction was to say: 'I find myself in heaven.' The profundity of this remark was matched by the gravity of his first three public statements about the future of British sport. These were: 1. that Gazza has no brain; 2. that any foreign footballer currently earning a fortune here should be allowed to play for England; and 3. that he couldn't sit in the Royal Box at the Cup Final for fear of embarrassing all around him with involuntary expletives. We've had some terrible Tory Sports Ministers in the past, but none has made quite such a Neanderthal start as that. This is the argot of the 606 phone-in freak, the lingo of the lager bar, but there is a bit more to becoming Britain's Minister of Sport than being a demotic figure down the King's Road pubs.

Tom Pendry and I squat at opposite ends of the political spectrum but, like most of us whose lives are immersed in sport, I have enormous respect for a man dedicated to the Labour cause since he was fifteen and deeply into sport earlier than that: football and cricket in his native Kent, Commonwealth and RAF boxing champion during his national service, then an Oxford boxing Blue.

Astonishingly, only six days before the election he published a thoroughly sane, progressive and virtually non-party manifesto for the future of British sport. Neither left nor right could quarrel with its sound intentions and we anticipated, if Labour got in, a settled period of national sports strategy. Tom Pendry, to all sports insiders, was 1–10 in the betting. Kate Hoey was a cautious 8–1 saver in case the Prime Minister were intent on recruiting token women into his inner circle. Tony Banks was never even in the frame.

Eight days later the favourite was left in the paddock. Did Pendry fall or was he pushed? This is not a political broadcast on behalf of the Pendry party. It merely reflects the bewilderment of many who cannot believe that the best man for the job was jettisoned. In the meantime, we shall look at the performance of Tony Banks with considerable interest. Tom Pendry has pledged him his full support. Through gritted teeth.

Even though Westminster is a confrontational world, one letter bucked that trend. It was handwritten from my Tory opposite, Iain Sproat, Minister for Sport during the years leading up to the 1997 election. Sent from his Norfolk home – Snore Hall – and dated 18 May 1997, he wrote:

I am absolutely astonished to learn that you were not (for the moment, anyway) made Minister for Sport. You were, and are, supremely the best man for the job ... first, because you had done the work so well in opposition, but more importantly even than that, because you know and understand sport as a whole, not just one or two games, inside out, as a player and as a spectator; and have deep respect within the sporting community. The sporting community knows you, trusts you, respects you for your solid work and for your insights into sport; insights that spring from, not just mugging-up or shallowly gliding and skimming over a subject to make a speech in a glib, flashy way, but from your own wide love of sport and what it stands for and from your own experience as a serious sportsman.

Even more astonishingly, given that he was a political opponent, Iain went on to offer personal advice:

I have a serrated contempt for cynics and mere manipulators in politics, but I hope that over the next year, until the next reshuffle, you will box clever, wear the mask, never miss a vote, make eight-minute speeches in the Chamber once a month, be seen around constantly, but don't of the critical, intriguing group, volunteer to serve on a serious Standing Committee, and make short, strong, detailed contributions on that Committee, be cheerful and strong, bite your tongue, and make the whips say how loyal, useful, hard-working and reliable you are, and I am sure that at the reshuffle they will be desperate to put a man of your calibre and experience into the government. There are plenty of ministerial posts you could fill in a Premier Division, not just sport. Justice is the most important thing in public life, and it was not justice that a man of your quality, work-rate and experience should not be in the government. Anyway, that's what I think and that's what I'd do. Best of luck. Let me know if I can do anything to help.

I have been told by many of my fellow parliamentarians on both sides of the House that this letter was almost certainly unique. No one could ever recall a political opponent writing such a missive after an election defeat. He showed a generosity of spirit that all too rarely crosses the political divide, especially given that at the election he had not just lost his ministerial post, but his Harwich seat as well. I was greatly saddened to hear of his death in September 2011.

The letters of commiseration – reflecting the anger, disappointment and bemusement of the sports world – continued to pour in for months. Gordon Taylor, chief executive of the Professional Footballers Association, wrote how 'thoroughly disappointed' he was, adding:

> I am extremely sad and upset for you and hope that something better turns up around the corner ... I can assure you that you will continue to attract the admiration and respect of everybody in professional football in particular and sport in general for the hard work and care you have always shown in the past.

Boxing's Frank Warren, of the Sports Network, wrote to express his disappointment, as did Sir Rocco Forte and executives of innumerable sports colleges, universities, local authorities, and many, many more, who shared my belief that sport was a driving force for good. Howard Davies, the Deputy Governor of the Bank of England, wrote to me, recognising the 'huge work' I had done to establish Labour's credentials in sport, an issue of increasing importance in political terms. He added: 'But it looks as though your reward may be in the next world, rather than this.' Alan Hubbard, sports editor of *The Observer*, wrote: 'I think you would have done an excellent job – as you have while shadowing the post. It seems a shame all that hard work and experience has been to no avail.' Esteemed parliamentary colleagues, notably Alf Morris and Jack Dormand, also sent very touching personal notes.

And our new Prime Minister's postbag was also filled with expressions of regret from far and wide, many within the tourism industry. Terry Purslow of William Green & Sons, the famous shoe firm established in 1866, wrote to him from Northamptonshire, saying that, while he was delighted at Labour's victory, 'the only reservation occurred when I realised that Tom Pendry had been overlooked – he had been such a stalwart and successful shadow minister who had earned much respect in the sporting world for his unflashy behaviour and general competence'. Richard Tobias, of the British Incoming Tour Operators' Association, told No. 10: 'Tom Pendry MP was widely expected by the industry to assume [the] role in the new government, having made such an important and significant impact while shadowing the previous office-holders.' There was even a letter from Florida. Warren E. McLaughlin of the Palm Beach County Convention and Visitors' Bureau wrote: 'We do feel a touch of sadness that Tom Pendry, who has been such a good friend to us and shown such an interest in our affairs, is not to be a member of the government. He will be a tough act to follow with the tourism brief.' Most such letters expressed hope that they could work well with Tony Banks.

I certainly did not begrudge Tony Banks's appointment, although I must confess that I did believe, and as it turned out, that the job was not his cup of tea. However, he deserved his crack at the whip as he was a fanatical football supporter, although not necessarily knowing much about the politics of football, or indeed of sports in general. However, Terry Venables, the former England manager and a good friend of mine, did say to me that 'Tony Banks did know his football' – I think he was inferring, and rightly so, that he knew more than I did in that specific area. Tony Banks was a very good and witty companion and he was pleased that I was one of the first to ring him and wish him well when he was offered the job. His period in office was a short one, as indeed was his life. He tragically died while on holiday in Florida in 2006 at far too young an age.

The sense of disbelief at my rejection was shared across the sporting world for many years. On 4 December 2013, during an All-Party Parliamentary Group on Sport special dinner in my honour, many of my colleagues on both sides of the House were still lamenting that I had missed out on the job. Lord Moynihan, as chairman of the British Olympic Association and also a former Tory Minister for Sport who I shadowed for some time, said:

> He was the best Sports Minister we never had! He certainly should have held that office and had he done so it would have been with distinction. A man of conviction, [he has] consistent support for the athletes, a passion for sport and a dedication to improve recreational facilities across the country.

And Peter Lee, chief executive of the Football Trust, said: 'Like many in the world of sport I was so disappointed that Tom was not appointed Minister for Sport. His passion, experience and ideas would have combined to make him an excellent minister.'

Peter Lee's views held considerable clout – and for good reason. He spent twenty-five years in the civil service, including many years working for successive Sports Ministers, and was a key government official at a time when football hooliganism dominated the sports agenda. He chaired the Council of Europe's standing committee on hooliganism, for example. He spent ten years as chief executive of the Football Trust where, in the wake of the Hillsborough tragedy, he was central to bringing about the transformation in safety and comfort of all our professional football grounds. In other words, he was the archetypal unsung hero; a crucial player in the football scene over several decades. For him to express such disappointment over the fact that I was robbed of the Sports Ministership speaks volumes.

Others at that special dinner were former Minister for Sport Gerry Sutcliffe MP; Dame Tanni Grey-Thompson, the most decorated Olympian of all time; Andy Reed of the Sport and Recreation Alliance; shadow Minister for Sport Clive Efford; and others, including three of my former parliamentary researchers – Paul Williamson, Tim Payton and Philip French – all well established in the sporting world and without whose valiant efforts over the years I would never have achieved the sporting recognition that I have to date.

CHAPTER 11

CARERS ACT

A ny disappointment I had experienced in the political world was eventually balanced out by something I remain particularly proud of in terms of lasting achievement. I was lucky enough to win a place in the Private Members' Ballot in 1999 and quickly realised that I had hundreds of friends that I didn't know existed. I received pleas from all sorts of individuals and organisations requesting that I adopt a measure that would advance their favourite charity or cause. I had previously piloted Bills through the House as a whip and a minister, but this was the first time I had the opportunity to introduce a Bill of my own. More importantly, I had to weigh up from a welter of suggestions coming my way and consider if a cause (a) was to my personal liking or (b) whether it would be likely to go through all stages in both Houses and become the law of the land.

Requests came from the very worthy to the sublime, including very laudable entries from Greenpeace and other environmental bodies. Ironically, the amount of paper I received from those organisations would have amounted to a great chunk of rainforests themselves. However, I received a telephone call at my home from John Hutton MP, the Minister of State for the Department of Health, and he convinced me of the importance of having a new Act for carers. The only other one in existence was that of my colleague, Malcolm Wicks, the Member for Croydon North-West, who successfully brought in the Carers (Recognition and Services) Act 1995, seen as a major step forward for carers, giving them important new rights and a firm legal status. In particular, people providing a regular and substantial amount of care could ask for an assessment of their ability to care when the person they are looking after is being assessed for community care services. Malcolm, who sadly died on 29 September 2012, was greatly admired by parliamentary colleagues on all sides of the House.

The importance of carers has always been close to my heart. Within my own constituency, Tameside Council had a particularly good department for carers and I had a great number of dealings with them over the years. In view of those experiences, and John Hutton's overtures, I decided to introduce a Bill based on carers and disabled children. According to my research, 76 per cent of carers had stated that their health has suffered since becoming a carer. It was also estimated that carers saved the state a staggering £57 billion a year. At the time, there was an estimated 5.7 million carers in the UK, which is the equivalent of one in six people. Moreover, 1.7 million devoted at least twenty hours a week to caring. With that knowledge in mind, my decision to plough on and get the Commons and Lords on my side was reinforced.

And so, on the morning of Friday 4 February 2000, after canvassing support from all sides, I launched my Bill in the Commons, stressing: 'This is truly an all-party measure and if, as I hope, it gets onto the statute book, it will reflect a great deal of credit on the House.'

From the start it was clear that I had cross-party support. Particularly helpful was Philip Hammond, the Conservative MP for Runnymede, who went on to become Foreign Secretary. During the committee stages he, a political opponent, made the point that I had won many cross-party friends through the introduction of my Bill. He said:

> We as a society have not only a moral obligation to support carers in what they do, but an economic imperative. The care that is provided informally in our society underwrites our national health service and underpins our social care system. The great silent army delivers care that would simply be unaffordable if it had to be provided through the formal system. There has been a lack of recognition of family and informal care from the inception of the modern welfare state, in marked contrast with other European countries where the obligations of family care are enshrined in law … It is common sense that we should be able to address the needs of carers directly where that represents the least costly and most effective way of meeting the objective of ensuring the proper continuation of informal care for a person who needs it. The dual objectives of the Bill and the strategy are to support carers in carrying out their caring more efficiently and effectively and to maintain their health and well-being to ensure that they do not, in turn, need care. Overall, we feel that the Bill is an important contribution in terms of taking the agenda of carers and their needs forward.

I was particularly delighted that the government had urged total support for the Bill and was reasonably confident that we might be able to celebrate a stunning victory for carers. Not only would it be a victory for them, I thought, but for parliamentary democracy, as the Bill was about freedom, choice and flexibility. The overall aim was to give carers the help and support that they need to enable them to continue caring.

I told the House: 'I chose the Carers and Disabled Children Bill because I, like most Members, have recognised over the years that the carers in our society should be given more choice and flexibility to allow them to carry out their caring role.'

I gave due credit to Malcolm Wicks and his 1995 Act but said that I felt my Bill went somewhat further insofar as it would help all kinds of informal carers – husbands and wives caring for their spouses, parents caring for their ill or disabled children and adults caring for elderly patients, to name just a few. I concluded: 'It would do that by allowing local authority social services departments to assess their need for support and help them in their caring role by giving them what they needed in the form of services.'

In a nutshell, it gives carers enhanced rights to assessment of their own needs; it gives local authorities powers to provide services to carers in their own right; it builds on the freedom and the choice that direct payments give people by allowing carers direct payments for their services, and it ensures that parents, too, can receive direct payments for services to their disabled children.

Many of us, at some time in our life, will care for someone else. We give care willingly to our nearest and dearest because we love them. For some, this caring role will become a larger part of their life, taking up more of their time, because someone close has become ill or disabled. The care provided by carers is not provided on a formal basis by organised, paid professionals. Informal care delivered by family and close friends is provided on an unpaid basis. It is care that draws on feelings of love and duty. Caring is often very hard work, and can be emotionally draining. It takes many forms within a range of relationships. Although the circumstances that lead people to become carers may be different, many of the difficulties faced by carers are common. The impact on their lives of caring can be similar: distress at seeing a loved one in pain; emotional loss as the nature of the relationship changes; effects on other relationships; a sense of isolation and loneliness; and feelings of stress and depression.

In recent years, there has been a growing recognition of the importance of informal care and its effects on carers. I have known many carers over the years. In Stalybridge and Hyde alone, there are perhaps just under 9,000 carers – roughly one in eight of my constituents. I have been amazed by the amount of support that they have given to elderly, sick or disabled relatives. I have been struck by the fact that, even though they are providing substantial amounts of care, relatively small changes can improve the quality of their lives. I hope that my Bill will go some way towards doing that.

I do not believe that we can afford to ignore the needs of carers. There is a strong social and moral argument for supporting them, but there is a clear economic imperative as well. There are an estimated 5.7 million carers in the United Kingdom. The support that they provide for their elderly, sick and disabled relatives is estimated to be worth £34 billion a year. If we ensure that carers are able to care and are given the means to care in ways that preserve their health and well-being, we shall avoid the enormous costs that would be associated with any breakdown of caring.

My Bill was concerned with carers at the 'heavy end', those who provide regular and substantial care. I referred to one case in particular, that of a lady called Sheila, who had cared for her daughter for thirty-seven years. That job had proved enormously stressful, and she spoke at the public launch of the Bill about the many times when she had been desperate for support after nights of broken sleep, worry and constant care. Sheila's daughter had epilepsy and mental health problems and over the years she had developed a deep mistrust of professionals. 'I want people such as Sheila to have their needs met in ways that give them more choice and flexibility,' I said.

At times like these, a passage of a Bill of this kind finds politicians across the party divide being seen at their best. Sterling support was given by such fellow Labour MPs as Tom Clarke and Llin Golding, Conservatives Virginia Bottomley, Caroline Spelman and Philip Hammond, as well as Liberal Democrat Paul Burston. I received a first-class response to the Bill both at the Committee Stage and in the Chambers of both Houses.

In the Upper Chamber, Baroness Pitkeathley introduced my Bill, saying:

> Carers' needs are diverse. As individuals they have particular needs, relationships and support to enable them to continue with their chosen role – I emphasise that most people care willingly and lovingly and want to continue to do so – while maintaining their own health and well-being, which is also important. The Bill offers local councils the opportunity to be innovative in the ways that they support carers, thereby helping them to maintain that caring role.

And Lord Rix, who as Brian Rix was famous for his Whitehall farces but who was ennobled for his campaigning on behalf of the disabled, contributed, saying:

I am delighted that, over the years, there has been a growth of awareness of the issues facing carers, and greater attempts to recognise and support their worthwhile practical and emotional commitment to others. We have in place a National Carers Strategy, which has injected some resources into help for carers, but there is still a long way to go. We cannot be complacent when hundreds of thousands of 'unsung heroes' – to quote the Prime Minister – are not receiving any support to minimise their social exclusion. Giving carers the right to an assessment for themselves is an important step, but it is only part of the solution to a much bigger problem. Without an expansion of provision, assessed need will rapidly become unmet need, which is unsatisfactory, to say the least, for all involved.

Former Minister for Disabled People Lord Morris said:

I am convinced that this Bill will help carers and parent carers of disabled children to achieve a better quality of life. For the first time, carers will have their own needs met. Moreover, the support carers receive will be delivered in ways sensitive to the needs of cared for people, recognising that carers often care in difficult circumstances and need support that is tailored to their individual needs. Of course, there will remain much more to do when this Bill becomes law; but it is undeniably an important step forward for carers.

To reinforce that point, a survey carried out by the Carers National

Association entitled *Caring on the Breadline* found that 33 per cent of carers who responded were in receipt of income support but still had to contribute towards charges for services. The other problem highlighted was the tremendous lack of consistency and varied interpretation of charging policies, with poorly written and, in places, contradictory guidance.

As a result, my Bill received Royal Assent on 20 July 2000 and became the Carers and Disabled Children Act 2000. It was gratifying to recall what Alf Morris said during its Lords stages:

> I congratulate my honourable friend Tom Pendry, both on his good fortune in the ballot for Private Members' Bills in another place and on the humanity of his choice of Bill. 'Tom Pendry's Bill' – as this measure will inevitably be called – offers significant new benefits to carers and parent carers of disabled children; and I feel sure that your Lordships' House will want to facilitate its early enactment. My noble friends Lady Pitkeathley and the minister know why Tom Pendry has kept in close rapport with me on his Bill. He said, in commending the Bill to another place, that our friendship 'goes back a long way' and that he was sustained in the work of promoting his Bill by my encouragement. We have been friends for fifty years and very few of his friendships or mine can go back much longer than that. We first met when Tom was fifteen, when I called him to speak at a meeting that he was too young to attend. I am delighted now to support him again and that he asked me to advise him on his Bill's progress.

He was of course referring to the episode related in an earlier chapter, when he allowed me to speak on a motion to reduce the age limit for joining the Labour Party from sixteen to fifteen when I was fif-teen years of age, when he was the National Chairman of the Labour League of Youth.

Alf went on:

New freedoms are conferred by this Bill for the local authority to deliver the services best suited to the needs of carers and most likely to help them to maintain their caring role; but they are limited to protect the independence of disabled, learning disabled and frail elderly people. Thus, help for carers that takes the form of a service delivered to the person cared for may not, except in prescribed cir-cumstances, include anything of an intimate nature. Carers and those they care for alike will want to know how 'prescribed circumstances' will be defined. I have been given by Tom Pendry the example of a non-intimate sitting service being delivered to the person cared for. If the carer's return to the house is delayed, the person cared for may need to be lifted and helped with toileting, and clearly it would be illogical if a paid sitter could not give that help in an emergency. A second limitation on the new freedoms for the local authority to provide services to carers is that, while the Bill gives carers the right to services, even when the person they care for has refused an assessment or the delivery of services following assessment, services will not be provided to cared-for people against their wishes. Where a person being cared for has refused services, she or he might, of course, be happy to have a person they already know well come and sit with them while their normal carer takes a short break. In such circumstances this non-intimate sitting service could be delivered as a carers' service. I am very glad that in this way the Bill addresses the important issue of the balance to be struck between the needs of carers and the important principle of defending the independence of disabled people; and indeed that it does so in such a thoughtful way.

We know what carers want. They want good quality services for the person they care for so that she or he will have the best quality of life possible. Carers and parent carers want recognition of their caring role and practical help to maintain that role without detriment to their own health and well-being. They want to be supported so that they may still have a life of their own outside of their caring responsibilities without being made to feel guilty for wanting to stay in work or for needing a break from time to time. I am convinced that this Bill will help carers and parent carers of disabled children to achieve a better quality of life. For the first time, carers will have their own needs met. Moreover, the support carers receive will be delivered in ways sensitive to the needs of cared for people, recognising that carers often care in difficult circumstances and need support that is tailored to their individual needs.

The Act was warmly welcomed across the land from social service departments and, most importantly, from the National Care Association. A special mention should be given to Emily Holzhausen of that association for her tremendous help throughout all stages of the procedures.

My Carers Act made four principal changes in the law enabling local authorities to have the power to offer new support to carers. First, the Act enabled 'a local authority to carry out an assessment in circumstances where a person cared for has refused an assessment for, or provision of, community care services'. Second, the Act 'empowers local authorities to make direct payments to carers (including sixteen- and seventeen-year-old carers) for the services that meet their own assessed needs'. Third, the Act 'provides for local authority social services departments to run short term break voucher schemes', allowing for flexibility. Very often, carers were not able to choose when to have a break or given a choice in how services would be delivered to the person cared for when they did go on break. Finally, the Act 'gives local authorities a power to charge carers for the services they receive'. This Bill, being so well received by carers, makes me feel that I, and those parliamentary colleagues who supported the Bill, were able to make a real difference to the carers and those they cared for.

I was pleased that Malcolm's and my Acts were followed up by another Labour MP, Hywel Francis, who had similar success in his Private Member's Bill, which eventually became the Carers (Equal Opportunity) Act 2004.

Hywel, with his background, was able to sum up his Act by telling of the fears and frustrations that he had experienced over the years. Hywel and his wife Mair had been carers for sixteen years of their son Sam, who had Down's Syndrome, and who had died in 1997. He said later:

We knew something of the problems faced by carers, but since becoming an MP I learnt more of the tremendous work of carers and their organisations, local authorities and the campaigning work of Carers UK and Carers Wales. I also learnt of the parliamentary advances made in the last decade which have improved the quality of life of carers. The Carers (Recognition and Services) Act 1995, sponsored by Malcolm Wicks MP, established rights of carers to an assessment of their needs and the Carers and Disabled Children Act

2000, sponsored by Tom Pendry MP (now Lord Pendry) extended carers rights, including allowing local authorities to give carers direct payments.

The Carers Trust reported that, between them, the three acts:

> Give all carers the right to have their needs assessed. Carers over sixteen, including parent carers of disabled children, are entitled to an assessment in their own right; Place a duty on authorities to ensure that all carers know they are entitled to an assessment of their needs; State that carers assessments should always consider a carer's outside interests (work, study or leisure) when carrying out an assessment.

Not wishing to make a party-political point, but, although in all of our deliberations during the passage of these Acts we had received true all-party support to bring them into being, it has to be said that it still took three Labour MPs, through the Private Members' Ballot procedure, to bring them about.

CHAPTER 12

STEPPING DOWN FROM
THE FRONT BENCH

Immediately after being denied the Sports Minister's job, I was at something of a loss as to how best I could occupy my time. I thought I was still capable of doing an effective job as an MP, so I carried on with my former shadow responsibilities after the election in my two areas of interest: sport and tourism. After an initial period, I was invited by the football world, which included the FA, the Premier League, the PFA, Sport England and, importantly, of course, the government itself, to became the chairman of the Football Foundation, the UK's largest sports charity, investing £60 million into improving the country's grassroots sports infrastructure each year with money provided by its funding partners – the Premier League, the FA and the government (via Sport England). Its chief executive was my old friend Peter Lee, who had been central in developing and implementing its policies of social inclusion, supporting anti-crime and anti-drug crackdowns, health, community and education work. It awards grants to applicants that go towards building new local sports facilities, such as changing rooms, grass or all-weather football pitches or multi-use games areas for schools, local authority facilities or sports clubs. Before accepting the post, however, I had to see whether this new job would allow me to carry on as the Member for my constituency in the way I had done so for some thirty years. I had to make a decision about the road that lay ahead for me – staying in the House of Commons, or branching out into the politics of sport.

JAMES PURNELL

While pondering this question, I received a phone call from an old Ramsgate friend, the actress Cheryl Hall who starred in the TV series *Citizen Smith*. She played the girlfriend of Robert Lindsay and later became his wife in real life. In her new capacity as Parliamentary Labour candidate for Canterbury, she was to attend a conference on Europe in Manchester. She asked in a telephone call to my secretary if I would show her around the city, as she was not too familiar with it, and also asked if we could meet up at a Neil Kinnock meeting at the Midland Hotel.

Come the evening in question, I had booked a table at what was considered the very best restaurant in Manchester, in the Midland Hotel itself. When I arrived at the Kinnock meeting, however, there was no sign of Cheryl. After the meeting concluded, I went down to the restaurant floor below hoping that she had made her own way there. As I waited, I observed James Purnell, who I had met very briefly at Wembley Stadium when he was with Alastair Campbell. At the time, James was an adviser to the Prime Minister on sporting issues. I witnessed him walking around in a circular fashion. Eventually, I approached him with the words: 'Why are you walking around like a spare part?' He replied: 'I think I have been stood up.' I responded: 'Join the club – I think I am in the same boat. If your host hasn't turned up in ten minutes and my guest hasn't turned up either then

I've booked a table here, so be my guest.' As it turned out, neither of our dinner companions arrived, so that's what we did. I knew little about James but I found out over dinner that he had been educated mainly in France before going to Balliol College, Oxford, to study philosophy, politics and economics.

During our meal, I said: 'James, I hear you're looking for a seat in the south. Readjust your sights and look to Labour's heartland here in the north.' I told him of Bob Sheldon MP's decision to retire at the next election. As Bob's constituency was next to mine I invited him to come up to Tameside, where I would introduce him to a number of Bob's party members whom I knew well. I further made the point that, since my appointment as chairman of the Football Foundation, I had to judge whether I could carry on as I had over the years as the MP for Stalybridge and Hyde.

On learning that I would be expected to attend football functions at weekends, meaning that I would miss my surgeries, something I valued as an essential part of my job, I decided after much soul search-ing to stand down at the following election – but only after discussing the issue with my constituency party. They reluctantly agreed, as they knew how much being overlooked as Sports Minister had been a bitter blow personally. No one in my constituency party had ever expressed to me an ambition to succeed me, even after I had informed them that I felt I should give way to a younger person and that I would feel relatively happy to focus my work in the field of sport.

With that in mind, I then informed James Purnell of my deci-sion and invited him to go not to Bob Sheldon's patch, but to meet my contacts instead, notably the leader of the council and my best friend Cllr Roy Oldham and his wife Margaret. After some initial hesitation, especially from Margaret, who didn't want 'a Blairite here', they eventually warmed to James and, indeed, he lodged with them for some time during his many visits to the constituency. I was determined that, if James wanted the seat, he would have to work for it. I did not wish my successor to be parachuted in, as had happened to others in the past.

So, a proper selection process proceeded. Most people who thought that I shouldn't go nevertheless decided that they would support the candidate of my choice. I have always been involved in sport politics so thought it would be good to throw my support behind James Purnell, a keen sportsman who played soccer for the parliamentary team. I might have had second thoughts after he confessed to being an Arsenal supporter, but it was too late to change my mind, especially as it seemed at the time that there was no other local candidate willing to step into my place. After I committed myself to supporting James Purnell, three more locals decided after all to enter the race: Kate Cruickshank, a sales consultant with B&Q and a mother of two who was a Tameside councillor; Jim Fitzpatrick, a long-serving Tameside councillor from Hyde; and Jane Milton from Stalybridge, a project director with the company working on the east Manchester regeneration scheme. I proceeded to introduce James to my party workers and they were pleasantly surprised with the way in which he was adapting himself to the area. When the selection conference took place some nine months after I announced my retirement, he won overwhelmingly over the other candidates.

It later became apparent that one of my biggest mistakes was ensuring that Purnell secured the Labour candidature of my seat in Stalybridge and Hyde. Some, including members of my constituency party, believed that I supported Purnell at the behest of Tony Blair – I can absolutely refute that charge and I'm sure that James will concur. In fact, Tony did not know of James's ambition until a conversation I had with him about some sporting issue he was facing. He said: 'I understand James Purnell is seeking to be the candidate in your constituency. What chance has he got?' I replied: 'He has every chance because I am backing him.'

Later, when I arrived with my wife at my first visit back to the constituency party AGM, I received an ovation. At the end, the chairman came to thank me for attending and I asked him why he hadn't welcomed me himself from the chair. He replied: 'James told me not to.' I could not for the life of me understand why at that stage in our relationship.

James was elected at the subsequent general election of 2001, but with a reduced majority from the one that I left behind – of 14,800 to 8,859 in that election. James duly made his maiden speech, and in a letter dated 18 July of that year, Tony Blair wrote to him:

> Well done on your maiden speech. I hope you will enjoy the transition from Downing Street to the House. I know that Tom Pendry made his Lords Maiden Speech on the same day as you, which must surely be unique, and your tribute to him and his sporting prowess was a highlight. I am sure that you have a great future in the House.

Tony added a hand-written note: 'I was so proud of you. It was a superb speech. Very good section on Europe. Keep it up!'

James progressed rapidly through the Parliamentary Labour Party ranks to the point where he became a junior Work and Pensions

Minister and was eventually given a Cabinet post as Secretary of State for Culture, Media and Sport. On his very first day at his ministerial office desk he wrote to me stating that this was the first letter that he had written from his Secretary of State desk; as he would never have got there without my endorsement. I had many other nice letters from him during his brief parliamentary career, but the friendship between us diminished more and more as time went by as I felt he was not as active a constituency member as he should and promised to be. Certainly, some of his constituents felt that way right from the beginning. Tony Booth wrote in his book of having an al fresco cigarette during the 2001 election when a car squealed to a stop beside him:

> Out climbed James Purnell. This was the first time I had seen him during the election campaign, and lost no time in pointing this out … he immediately began to claim he had of course tried to visit us, but we were always out when he called. Tom Pendry made a point of visiting me at least a couple of times during an election campaign and it was effort like this throughout the constituency that ensured him a large personal vote.

Booth also wrote: 'Tom and I have not always seen eye to eye over the years, but despite our occasional differences he has helped me with more than one difficult decision. He was always a hard-working and committed constituency MP.'

Purnell abruptly resigned from his Cabinet position in June 2009 – by then he was Work and Pensions Secretary of State – giving the news to the press in the morning, embargoed until the polls had closed at the European elections. He didn't even share his decision with his

Prime Minister, Gordon Brown, before telling the press that morning or, as I understand it, the officers of his constituency party. His resignation came only days after that of Home Secretary Jacqui Smith and Communities Secretary Hazel Blears, who had both been caught up in the expenses controversy. And Labour did badly in the European elections. It was a low point, compounded when Purnell, in a resignation letter distributed widely to the newspapers, called on Gordon Brown to resign as well!

James Purnell without doubt is a very intelligent and bright individual, but I've always held that in politics there is no substitute for common sense and an ability to relate to the everyday problems of people. I felt I was partially responsible for my lack of judgement in introducing James to a constituency full of people who expected their representative to relate to them and their needs.

I must plead *mea culpa* and *maxima culpa* for my part in bringing James Purnell to Stalybridge and Hyde. However, I do wish him well in his very lucrative current position within the BBC, which he rejoined as its Director of Strategy, and from which he probably should never have left all those years ago after leaving Oxford.

JONATHAN REYNOLDS

Following Purnell's shock decision to resign from the Cabinet, which went down badly with many in his constituency party, he further announced weeks before the 2010 general election that he was to stand down as their MP. He left his local party with the difficult task of finding another candidate and with no time for a normal selection procedure to take place. The General Secretary of the Labour Party informed the members of the Stalybridge and Hyde party, of which

I was of course a part, that a normal selection process could not take place – something that James almost certainly had planned on. The National Executive of the party convened a panel consisting of Tom Watson MP, Keith Vaz MP and a trade unionist member of the National Executive Committee to interview would-be candidates. The local party were informed that their panel's decision on a shortlist of candidates was sacrosanct and appeals were not allowed.

The panel duly came forward with a shortlist that did not include James Purnell's office manager, Johnny Reynolds – his favoured candidate. Not to be thwarted, Purnell, together with some assistance from Peter Mandelson MP, went over the head of the interviewing panel. It was revealed in *The Times Guide to the General Election of 2005* that Mandelson then pressurised the National Executive to include Johnny Reynolds on the shortlist, which they dutifully did.

As Johnny Reynolds had managed Purnell's office, he had a great advantage over the other candidates regarding access to the names and addresses of local party members, which greatly helped with canvassing and postal votes. Johnny became the candidate, and subsequently MP. I was asked three times to go on BBC's *World at One* with Mandelson to discuss whether there was any malpractice, but I refused as it could have harmed Johnny's chances had I done so. Peter did go on and, as I understand, he said he didn't intervene in the selection process – if that is what he said then that would be a blatant distortion of the truth, as pointed out in *The Times Guide* that stated that Jonathan Reynolds was 'selected amid a huge row with Peter Mandelson's involvement after failing to make the initial shortlist'. Having said all that, I think Johnny has demonstrated since his election that he is a first-class constituency MP – something that James never was! He will continue to receive my full support; after all, he could not be blamed for the actions of both James Purnell and Peter Mandelson and also General Secretary Roy (now Lord) Collins for allowing this malpractice to take place. In all probability, Johnny would have been selected had Purnell done the decent thing as I did when I announced my retirement – I was determined not to have someone shoehorned in but wanted to ensure that whoever was to be selected would have to prove themselves over a period of time beforehand. In my case, it was some nine months. Johnny would have been allowed to prove that himself, but his employer Purnell used his muscle to ensure selection for him.

Johnny went on with my support, but his majority unfortunately slumped lower than the lowest majority I ever had in 1970 of 2,849. Johnny won the 2010 general election with a majority of a mere 2,744. I reiterate that those who may have broken the rules set by the National Executive were Purnell and Mandelson, not Johnny Reynolds, who will, God-willing, go on in the next Labour government to be an effective minister. Reynolds is doing the opposite of James and getting down to representing the good people of Stalybridge and Hyde. He also did a commendable job as shadow Minister for Energy and Climate Change. Unfortunately, my hopes for Johnny becoming a minister were thwarted by Labour's May 2015 general election defeat, although happily his majority jumped from 2,744 to 6,686 thanks to the hard work he put in during his five-year tenure of his seat.

I was proud of my record in building up the Labour vote during my time as MP. In 1969, Philip Noel Baker predicted at a meeting in Hattersely, Hyde that I would eventually enjoy a 15,000 majority. The prophecy came true as I won a majority of 14,806 at the 1997 general election.

For my part, after the 1997 election, I never left Tameside. Three years after I stood down I told *Cheshire Life*: 'I'm part of the fabric here and I love this place. There is a warmth and an empathy here you just don't get in a city, not even just a few miles down the road in Manchester.' I still love it and regard my best achievement as hopefully being a good constituency MP over the thirty-one years I served there.

I seemed to have done a fair job in the eyes of the constituents, too. I was made Freeman of the Borough of Tameside and the football ground at Stalybridge Celtic has the 'Tom Pendry' stand. Okay, I didn't achieve my dream of becoming Minister for Sport, but I don't think my teenage dream simply to become an MP was wasted.

CHAPTER 13

HONOURS

PRIVY COUNCILLOR

On 20 November 2000, I received a special letter from Prime Minister Tony Blair:

Dear Tom, I am writing to let you know that I propose to recommend to the Queen that she may be graciously pleased to approve that you be sworn of Her Majesty's most honourable Privy Council. It would be helpful to know as soon as possible if this proposal would be agreeable to you. If you are content and the Queen approves this recommendation, an announcement will be made on Monday 27 November. Yours ever, Tony.

This was of course not only very agreeable, as being a Privy Councillor is the greatest honour any politician can ever receive. When a Privy Councillor is notified that he or she has received the word of approval from Her Majesty, the duties and responsibilities are then conveyed. A Privy Councillor is part of the Queen's own council – her inner circle of trusted formal advisers advising on matters of state. It dates back to some of the earliest days of the monarchy but has adapted to reflect the constitutional monarchy that exists today. The Privy Council is involved with the affairs of Chartered Bodies, charities and companies incorporated by Royal Charter, and also plays a part in some UK statutory regulatory bodies across a number of professions. The Queen also uses the Privy Council to approve Proclamations and a number of orders put forth by its members. The judicial arm of the Privy Council also acts as a Court of Appeal for crown dependencies, UK overseas territories, and Commonwealth countries that have still retained that form of appeal process. It is an honour bestowed on a politician for life, whereas you can live out your glory days as a minister for only a short period of time.

The swearing-in ceremony took place on Valentine's Day, 14 February 2000. It was a very short ceremony and involved me taking the Oath of Allegiance before the Queen, and the president of the Privy Council, Margaret Beckett MP. It also entailed at one point kissing the Queen's hand. At the end she bestowed upon those of us present the privy councillorship. It was certainly a memorable occasion.

The next day in the Commons, I was with a group of colleagues and thought that I would play some tomfoolery with them. I said: 'What did you do on Valentine's Day?' They all looked a bit puzzled and one said: 'I rang the wife and we planned going out for dinner on the weekend.' Another said: 'I sent my wife flowers by Interflora, and we will also meet up on the weekend.' All the others said something to the same effect, adding: 'It's not like you, Pendry – why are you asking this of us?' I said: 'I'm sorry, boys, but I just upstaged all of you. I kissed the Queen on Valentine's Day at Buckingham Palace.' Only then did it dawn on them what a saucy question I had asked them – and it certainly did help to lighten the day for me, if not for them.

LORD MOTTRAM IN LONGDENDALE

To receive the Freedom of the Borough of Tameside was very much an honour, but it has changed considerably since the sixteenth and seventeenth centuries. Being a 'freeman' meant that one was free from having to pay taxes, tolls and could stand for election. Of course, with the passing of the honorary Freedom of Boroughs Act in 1885, all the material rights and privileges associated with freemanship vanished and the title became purely an honorary one. I was then recognised by my constituency for my years in office with the title of Lord Mottram in Longdendale, a title that had been bought by Tameside Council on 14 September 1987 from the Rt Hon. Timothy John Edward. A special ceremony was held for me on 21 July 1995 to mark this honour and I remember the leader of the council at one point told everyone to move out into the square outside the Civic Hall for an unusual event. The leader of the council then held up a signpost that read 'Tom Pendry Square' – and it's been called 'Lord Pendry Square' since my elevation to the House of Lords. Even though having the square named after me was such a treasured and memorable occasion for me on its own, I soon learnt that was only the very first of many surprises. During the ceremony, the Mayor presented me with a framed illuminated scroll and a commemorative gift before we attended a special dinner in Civic Hall in my honour.

The title of Lord Mottram in Longdendale goes back many centuries – to the Black Prince and beyond. The date of the lordship was probably established in the late Anglo-Saxon period but by 1086 had in as its landowner, William the Conqueror. The title passed through many Lords from the Black Prince in 1357, one of which was Thomas Bremlan whose enormous wealth and power eventually led to his downfall and execution for being a supporter of Anne Boleyn's court faction. (Along with others he was accused of adultery with the Queen and was beheaded on Tower Hill in London on 17 May 1536). In fact, the title was given back to the Crown five times in 1322, 1374, 1488, 1495 and 1536 with three of those accounts over acts of treason. Robert Holland, Robert Holland II, Francis Viscount Lovell, Sir William Stanley and William Brereton were all individuals who held the title of Lord Mottram of Longdendale before it was forfeited back to the Crown.

In those days there were certain rights that a Lordship carried like hunting rights, fishing rights and a right that I am very happy that doesn't exist today, which is the right to sleep with the bride on the first night of any marriage that took place within the manor. Now I do not mean to be disparaging of the brides in my manorship, but I think it would be best for them to sleep the first night with their husbands! But I seriously owe this historical title to a Labour council led by my dear friend the late Cllr Roy Oldham, and of course the title will return to Tameside Borough Council when I pass on.

At the civic ceremony, Cllr Oldham praised my commitment to the local people, saying: 'Your dedication to those you represent is legendary and you have excelled in your duty for twenty-five years.' His comments were echoed by the deputy leader of the Conservatives, Cllr Margaret Eddowes, who said: 'I give my congratulations from this side of the House, as a resident I remember Mr Pendry being elected and have seen over the years his commitment to the electorate – although not born a northerner, he has become one.'

Although one can be accused of some vanity – what politician is not guilty of that from time to time? – the way that a council can give someone such an award with remarks from political friend and foe makes being a representative in public life so worthwhile.

ELEVATION TO THE HOUSE OF LORDS

After deciding not to seek another term in the Commons, I admit I would have been disappointed not to have been elevated to the Lords, but when a letter arrived from Prime Minister Blair informing me of my good fortune, I was naturally delighted and my earlier doubts evaporated.

I was never one to knock the Lords as an institution, but I was highly critical of the heritage principle. I have never believed that a peerage should be bestowed on those simply because they had a great- or great-great-grandfather who was a peer and who was no doubt well deserving of the honour at that time.

I also believed that the second chamber had a great value. From time to time, I had given my blessing to it when I spoke from the Despatch Box as either a minister or as an opposition spokesman if I believed that the Bill in question could be improved. The reduction now to only ninety-two hereditary peers is a step in the right direction, but I still refuse to accept the principle. Having said that, I think, with a better appointment system, some of those ninety-two peers who really do participate in the workings of the House could be offered life peerages because of the wisdom and expertise many can bring to its debates. This would ensure that the second chamber still had a real value without the hereditary principle being sustained.

Although I have the title of Lord Pendry of Stalybridge, and I am of course honoured to have that name attached to mine, I had hoped to have the title Lord Pendry of Stalybridge and Hyde – bearing in mind that I had been their Member of Parliament for some thirty-one years. However, I wasn't allowed under the rules because someone who was already a Member of the House had the Hyde title and in fact was sitting on the Tory front bench – Baron Ashton of Hyde. He is an old Etonian, city underwriter and a member of Lloyd's – all the things I am not! Because of the rivalry between the two major towns in my then constituency, albeit a friendly one, I had hoped that Hyde would not take umbrage at the fact that they weren't in my title. I've tried to explain it to many, but whether it's been accepted by all I am not so sure.

However, in order to emphasise my impartiality over the years, whenever Stalybridge Celtic played Hyde United at football, I was very mindful of that rivalry, so much so that I stayed neutral when those games took place. Hyde itself had a very chequered sporting history, from its moments of glory winning the Cheshire Senior Cup, the Cheshire League Cup and later the League Challenge Shield, to a very unfortunate game on 15 October 1887 in Deepdale, Preston. During an FA Cup first round game, a match probably best forgotten by Hyde townsfolk, Hyde United created an all-time record when they were defeated by the 'Proud' Preston North End 26–0; a record that stands to this day, 128 years on. In that game, twelve goals were scored in the first half, with the remaining fourteen in the second. The incredible assessment of the game was that the player voted Man of the Match was none other than the Hyde goalkeeper, Charlie Bunyan, who saved seventy-six shots and was winded three times. The *Preston Guardian* reported:

It would be folly to enter into a comparison of the play of the two teams, but it is only fair to the Hyde custodian to say that had he been a less able man there is no telling what the score might have

been! Times innumerable he stopped shots which brought forth
cries of 'bravo' and was repeatedly cheered quite lustily.

A hundred years later, I organised a return match at the Ewen Fields
Ground in Hyde to commemorate the game of 1887. The score was
a much more modest one on that occasion. Following the centenary
match between the teams at Hyde, Preston organised some time later
a return game that the great Tom Finney, the legendary Preston and
England winger, kicked off – again Preston won, despite the fact there
were some eminent parliamentarians playing on the Hyde side, notably Andy Burnham MP and James Purnell MP. Despite that one
unfortunate football game, Hyde United did reach the FA Cup first
round in 1954, only to lose 5–1 away to Workington, who were at that
time managed by the great Bill Shankly. Hyde were founder-members
of the Northern Premier League in 1968 but could not afford the cost
of travel to places like Ashington and Scarborough and re-joined
the Cheshire League in 1970, where they remained for twelve years.
They reached the first round of the FA Cup in 1983 and played against
Burnley, opting to play away on Burnley grounds in order to have a
more prestigious ground to play on – Hyde lost 2–0, which was a very
commendable performance on their part.

Other sports have also played a major part in the history of the
town. The Hyde Seals water polo team was from 1904 to 1914 regarded
as the finest in the world, winning the world championship in 1904,
1905 and 1906. World champion boxer Ricky Hatton was brought up
on the Hattersley Estate and now lives in Gee Cross, Hyde. His association with the town led to the creation of a boxing gym and health
club in Hyde.

Other people of whom the town are proud include artists Harry Rutherford and Trevor Grimshaw, *Shameless* screen writer Danny Brocklehurst, and footballers Warren Bradley, Lee Martin and Alan West.

Like Stalybridge the population of Hyde also increased rapidly during the industrial revolution. At one stage there were forty working mills decreasing to twenty-seven by 1872 – only one remains to this day. Cotton had brought tremendous changes in a relatively short space of time but with it great increases in the population. The working conditions for the workers in the mills were appalling and brought into being some of the earliest attempts to form trade unionism. In 1824, the spinners union formed into local union organisations, after the repeal of the Combination Laws, and a series of strikes took place in Hyde with the involvement of the famous John Doherty, who arrived from Ireland and was described by Sidney and Beatrice Webb as a great activist thinker and one of the staunchest leaders among the workers of his time. Doherty was involved in the Hyde spinners' strike of 1829 and others in Stalybridge in 1830 and 1831.

To commemorate Hyde's working-class heritage and the growth of organised labour, I was fortunate enough, together with Cllr Roy Oldham, to unveil a statue commemorating the birth of the Chartist Movement, which was started in the town. The artwork we unveiled was called 'Pulling the Plug', and it depicted the Chartists' protests during the General Strike of 1842, when the mill workers stopped the boilers from working. Over the years, other notable individuals added to Hyde's rich history. Cllr Thomas Middleton, who was the most notable historian of Hyde at that time as chairman of Hyde's Parks Committee, brought in playing fields and recreational facilities that were relatively unique in that part of the north-west during that time.

Another famous inhabitant, although not born in Hyde, was one of the town's most famous socialists – Barbara Castle, who was a reporter on the *North Cheshire Herald* and was selected and elected to represent Blackburn in the 1945 general election after working for her local Labour Party in Hyde. Hyde also boasted the first socialist church and had one of the first trade's council.

Hyde has, over the years, a great history related to the advancement of organised labour, but it only had its first Labour MP in 1929. The second Labour MP was elected in 1945, with continuous representation since then.

When the day came for me to be introduced into the Lords, I had two peers to introduce me to take the Oath of Allegiance to the Crown. In my case I chose Lord Roy Mason, whom I had served under as his Undersecretary when he was Secretary of State for Northern Ireland, and, indeed, alongside him I had another Yorkshireman, Lord Ken Woolmer, who had been a colleague of mine in the Commons some years before, when he was a Member of Parliament for Batley and Morley. We had always been very good friends ever since.

With that over I had to undertake the next hurdle – to make my maiden speech. By this time, of course, after thirty-one years in the Commons, I was quite accustomed to delivering speeches. It certainly was not the same stressful occasion as it had been back in 1970.

I made my maiden speech in the House of Lords on the evening of 17 July 2001, during a debate on tourism. Moments before I rose, Lord Harrison said: 'I conclude not only by anticipating the maiden speech of the noble Lord, Lord Pendry, a noble warrior in the cause of all things touristic, but also in making a prediction: tourism is an industry whose time has come.'

My first speech in the Upper Chamber was not in any way as good as my Commons maiden speech had been all those decades before, but I hope it was a worthy contribution to the debate. As I said, it was

an opportunity to place on record my affinity with those who work in this important industry, an interest I have had ever since I was given front-bench responsibility for tourism by the late John Smith in another place back in 1992. It was given to me in conjunction with the sports portfolio. I think it is fair to say that, for an industry that employs some 2 million people, tourism has had far too low a profile over the years. In my view, the industry itself should have presented a more powerful and unified voice, demanding an insider status with government as other industries have done. Governments of all complexions, until possibly now, have been too slow to recognise tourism's potential to be one of the real economic and employment driving forces within our country. I can say that governments are at last beginning to recognise tourism's importance because many more parliamentarians and policymakers are taking a real interest in it. I say that also because for the past four years I have been privileged to have been chairman of the All-Party Tourism Group. In that group we have many active and spirited participants.

I concluded by stating that my greatest wish was for tourism and sport and leisure to become a Department of State in its own right. Sport and tourism to my mind are natural bedfellows. Both are vibrant and growing sectors of the leisure economy, and Britain's sporting infrastructure offers huge tourism potential.

By an uncanny coincidence, it turned out that I made my maiden speech on the very same day as my successor James Purnell made his in the Commons. This prompted Prime Minister Tony Blair to write to James, but strangely enough not to the both of us, congratulating him on his speech. Blair wrote:

> Well done on your maiden speech, I hope you will enjoy the transition from Downing Street to the House. I know that Tom Pendry made his Lords Maiden Speech on the same day as you, which must surely be unique, and your tribute to him and his sporting prowess was a highlight.

For that, of course, I thanked him.

I didn't feel moving from the green to the red carpet was as much of a wrench as I thought it might be. I continued to chair both the Sports and Tourism Backbench Groups and therefore was able to participate, and in many cases initiate and lead, in debates on those subjects as clearly I felt I had considerable knowledge in both those areas. I felt very much at home from the first day I entered the Lords.

CHAPTER 14

MANDELA AND ANTI-APARTHEID

During the 1960s, I became an active member of the anti-apartheid campaign to boycott South African goods until the apartheid system was eradicated. Although the boycott was partly successful, because the UK was around this time South Africa's largest foreign investor, the full effect of the boycott was not realised fully until the Sharpeville Massacre on 21 March 1960, where sixty-nine unarmed protestors were shot dead by the South African police. After that, there emerged a more concentrated effort to boycott trade to South Africa. The sight of so many human beings gunned down from armoured cars showed the true, evil face of apartheid, a system under which the opportunities for you and your family were governed by the colour of your skin.

As a consequence of this, the trade boycott became rather more broadly based, with the birth of the Anti-Apartheid movement (AAM), focused on the total isolation of South Africa and its apartheid policies, including notably sporting events.

So much was the campaigning success of the AAM that it secured a major victory when South Africa was forced to leave the Commonwealth in 1961 and, in 1962, when the United Nations passed a resolution calling on all member states to impose economic sanctions against South Africa.

I formed a branch of the AAM in Derby where I was living and working as a trade union officer for the National Union of Public Employees in the early months of 1962. However it was in June 1965 when I received a phone call from Ethel de Keyser, the executive secretary of the Anti-Apartheid Movement in Britain based in London. As a leading member of Anti-Apartheid in the East Midlands, Ethel asked if I would lead a boycott against the impending visit of the all-white South African Cricket sides tour to England, which was to take place at Chesterfield, near Derby. Ethel said it was important that the message got through loud and clear how morally wrong it was that South Africa was discriminating on the grounds of colour when selecting their all-white cricket team. I readily accepted the challenge and my first point of call was to meet the Executive Committee of the Derbyshire branch of the National Union of Mineworkers (NUM), the largest workforce in that area at that time. The leader of the local NUM was a wily communist called Bert Wynn, who immediately invited me to address his Executive Committee. Notable among them was a very bright and future MP Dennis Skinner. The committee accepted the importance of this kind of non-industrial action.

The picket line was assembled outside the grounds of Queen's Park in Chesterfield on the morning of 28 June 1965. The line not only had miners, with Dennis Skinner at the fore, but other workers in the area, as well as Anti-Apartheid supporters from Derbyshire and Yorkshire. A well-known actor, Stacy Davies, who was appearing as Billy in *Billy Liar* at the Nottingham Playhouse at the time, also joined the picket line. Stacy's presence did bring a smile to our faces when, in the evening on *Radio Newsreel*, Stuart Hall, who covered the picket line protest for the BBC and was not too happy at being forced to turn his back on the cricket, mentioned that Stacy had to leave at lunchtime as he had received a telephone message from his wife that their Manx cat had given birth to five kittens. That distraction aside, the demonstration was a great success.

That evening, and after hearing the BBC's account of the success of the boycott, I received a telephone call from Ethel congratulating my team and me. She then invited me to speak the following day at Trafalgar Square in another anti-apartheid rally. Not yet an MP, or, indeed, even a parliamentary candidate, I was thrilled and honoured to be asked to say a few words about our mission at Chesterfield. My train journey down to London was also a highlight as I shared a compartment with Philip Noel Baker, who was also to speak at the rally. When at the square, I found that, in addition to Philip, there were also a number of luminaries in attendance, including the Bishop of Johannesburg; David Ennals MP; Patrick Wymark, a famous actor who appeared in the popular TV series *The Power Game*; Jeremy Thorpe, the then leader of the Liberal Party; and Ruth First, a South African anti-apartheid activist who was later killed by a letter bomb in August 1982. In the square, Ruth spoke with eloquence and passion, saying that South Africa was isolating itself from the world. 'Her recovery lies with associating with the world, joining the community of nations and following their practices,' she said, adding that it would be a long and painful struggle, but one that could be shortened by pressure from the British government. 'You must pass from verbal condemnation to practical action,' she urged.

The people of Britain must see that their government stops dragging its feet at the United Nations whenever the question of South Africa comes up. The guilty men of apartheid are not only those who make the laws in South Africa, they are among us here in Britain – those who draw profits from apartheid.

Patrick Wymark spoke of his recent tour of South Africa, where his eyes were opened by what he saw – so much so that he and many of his actors refused to play in South African theatres where apartheid barriers existed.

Both Jeremy Thorpe MP and Philip Noel-Baker MP spoke of the bestiality of South African racial policies. In fact, Noel-Baker stressed the need for an oil sanction against South Africa, which could avert a holocaust and bring apartheid to an end.

My part in the rally was small but well received, as it demonstrated that sport-loving people were prepared to forego their natural desire to attend a favoured sport in the interest of a greater ideal – namely, the conquering of racism in sport, and we would do so whenever racism reared its ugly head.

By now, sport was a hugely important aspect in the struggle against apartheid. Abdul Minty, who became the AAM's honorary secretary in 1962 and was also a representative of the South African Sports Association, a non-racial body set up in South Africa by Dennis Brutus, presented a letter to the International Meeting in Baden-Baden, Germany. The letter, outlining the racism engulfing South African sport, led to a ruling by the IOC to suspend South Africa from the Tokyo Olympics in 1964, and ultimately its total expulsion from the Olympics in 1970.

At the Trafalgar Square rally, beneath a banner hung from Nelson's column proclaiming 'Freedom from Apartheid', Mr Minty condemned apartheid in cricket. The Trafalgar Square demonstration hit TV screens around the world and was credited as a key part of the long battle to dismantle the apartheid regime.

Following Chesterfield and Trafalgar Square, there were many other demonstrations that had an impact on President F. W. de Klerk's eventual and long-overdue decision to abandon apartheid in his country. The reasons for such actions were often attributed to the decision by the South African Cricket Board not to allow Basil D'Oliveira, who was of Indian Portuguese heritage, to tour with the MCC to South Africa in 1968/69. After a hesitant start, the MCC refused to yield and the tour was cancelled. D'Oliveira, as a 'coloured' South African, was refused permission to play for the South African team by the government and instead opted to play for England. If chosen, D'Oliveira was one of the more likely players to be selected following his performance against Australia in the previous year's Ashes. We all thought that the MCC's decision was a capitulation to the apartheid regime. Peter Hain – now a Labour MP, then the leader of the Young Liberals – together with other Young Liberals, helped to ensure the cancellation of the 1970 cricket tour by Springboks. The International Cricket Conference (ICC) imposed a moratorium on tours in 1970. There were several private tours in the 1970s and 'rebel' tours in the 1980s. Participants in the latter were banned by their national federations upon returning. World Series Cricket, run outside the auspices of the ICC in 1977–79, included South African players in its 'Rest of the World' team.

And it was not just cricket, but also the Olympics and other sports that saw rising anti-apartheid activism. There were strong demands by African nations to suspend New Zealand from the IOC due to its continued contact with apartheid South Africa. However, this proposal was rejected by the IOC, which led to the African countries themselves withdrawing from the games. All of this contributed to the Gleneagles Agreement being adopted by the Commonwealth in 1977. As a response, the IOC declared the total isolation of apartheid in sport on 21 June 1988.

Other sports followed. For example, the Greek government banned South Africa from competing at the golf World Cup of 1979, which was to be held in Athens. While South Africa did compete in the 1980 edition in Caracas, the prospect of it competing in the 1981 edition in Ireland led to the event being cancelled. South Africa did not appear in golfing events until the post-apartheid era in 1992.

Shamefully, South Africa remained a member of the International Rugby Board (IRB) throughout the apartheid era. Although contacts were restricted after the Gleneagles Agreement in 1977, there were controversial tours in 1980 by the British Lions and by France, in 1981 by Ireland, and in 1984 by England. In 1986, though a Lions tour was cancelled, South Africans played in all-star matches in Cardiff and in London marking the IRB centenary. South Africa was excluded from the first two Rugby World Cups in 1987 and 1991.

In contrast, on the footballing front South Africa was suspended from FIFA in 1963. While attempts were made to renegotiate its reinstatement into FIFA, notably by the then FIFA president Stanley Rous, South Africa's proposals of entering an all-white team in the 1966 World Cup and an all-black team in the 1970 World Cup were rightly rejected by the footballing body.

As far as tennis was concerned, and partly thanks to a campaign by the great black player Arthur Ashe, the South African Davis Cup team were ejected from the 1970 competition. However, it was duly reinstated in 1973 and in 1974 won the competition, albeit only after India refused to travel to South Africa for the final. Subsequently, South Africa was banned from team competition, although South African players continued to compete on the pro tours.

With the end of apartheid, sports organisations rapidly ended their boycotts. During a 1995 visit with a parliamentary rugby team to celebrate South Africa winning the World Rugby Championship, I, together with other colleagues, was invited to the lawns of the presidential palace to meet the newly elected President Nelson Mandela. He walked towards the line of dignitaries and asked: 'Which one of you is Tom Pendry?' With a broad smile, he thanked me for my part in the Trafalgar Square protest. He must have been well briefed. He then gave me his book *Long Walk to Freedom* with an inscription highlighting my work for the Anti-Apartheid Movement. I understand he arranged for all of our delegation to be sent his book, each of which was signed by him personally.

Mandela, of course, needs no introduction here. He was acknowledged as one of the greatest figures of the century. After twenty-seven years' imprisonment by the apartheid regime, he was elected President of South Africa in 1994 and served for five years. During that time he did his utmost to heal the old, deep wounds created by apartheid. He invited other political parties to join the Cabinet, and promulgated a new constitution. He also created the Truth and Reconciliation Commission to investigate past human abuses. His administration also introduced measures to encourage land reform, combat poverty, and expand healthcare services.

At a subsequent meeting, following our meeting with Mandela, we met F. W. de Klerk. Many had poured scorn over the importance of sport demonstrations over the years and its impact on the abolition of apartheid, and de Klerk was very much in that camp, in public at least. But those who believed he genuinely held such views would have been flabbergasted on hearing the words at that meeting by de Klerk in answer to my question: 'What was the most compelling reason for abandoning apartheid?' He replied that the trade boycotts were relatively easy to overcome, but that his country was a sport-loving one. The people yearned for a return to international competitions that they had been denied entry to. He told me: 'What people like you and your colleagues did meant we could compete on the global stage again.'

To confirm that view, a survey in 1977 taken of white South Africans ranked the lack of international sport as one of the three most damaging consequences of apartheid. In June 2008, at Lord's Cricket Ground, Dr Desmond Tutu also spoke of 'the sports boycott playing a crucial part in our liberation'. From the first boycotts in Chesterfield, and all those who took part in demonstrations against the evils of apartheid in sport, we can take great heart from Desmond Tutu's words. I was one of those in Parliament who had been active in supporting Nelson Mandela through his period on Robben Island and since his liberation from that prison.

After that meeting with De Klerk, my colleagues and I went on to Stellenbosch University, where I gave a lecture on the evils of apartheid. The audience there would not have been possible during the days of apartheid, and there were almost certainly former supporters of that regime on the platform, who put on a brave face as I spelt out the evils of apartheid and talked about the instrumental role sport played in its collapse. My talk was warmly received and one of my colleagues in the audience was Charles Kennedy, who afterwards kindly sent me an article he wrote in his local newspaper in Scotland, in which he stated how he was moved on that occasion by my address.

Mandela was a truly inspirational politician, and his book *Long Walk to Freedom* should be seen as a template for any aspiring politician.

He had a Gandhi-type approach, namely, forgiving those who trespassed against his human dignity. Both, on different continents and in different ages, subscribed to a political, economic and religious philosophy and view based, despite the utmost provocation, on an un-dying faith in the goodness of human nature.

Mandela's policy of reconciliation after decades of bloody repression echoed Gandhi's famous quote: 'An eye for an eye will only make the whole world blind.'

On 5 December 1993, Nelson Mandela died at the age of ninety-five in his home in Johannesburg and on 12 December 2013 a commemoration ceremony was held in Westminster Hall, which I attended. Tributes from various parliamentarians were given, including words from David Cameron and Gordon Brown. Cameron said: 'Nelson Mandela was a towering figure in our lifetime, a pivotal figure in the history of South Africa, and the world,' while Gordon Brown stated: 'Nelson Mandela had eloquence, determination, commitment, passion, wit and charm, but it was his courage that brought all those things to life.' Cameron's comment was particularly notable considering the historical relationship between the Tories and Nelson Mandela. One can remember Margaret Thatcher's comment at the Commonwealth summit in Vancouver in 1987, when she famously called the African National Congress 'a typical terrorist organisation' whose leaders were all communists. Some would say that the Tories were two-faced, but one should nevertheless rejoice that 'there will be more joy in heaven over one sinner who repents than over ninety-nine righteous persons who need no repentance'.

Several months later, on 3 March 2014, I was privileged to be invited to a special service to celebrate the life and work of Nelson Mandela at Westminster Abbey. In attendance were various politicians, celebrities and members of the royal family. There were some moving tributes and Desmond Tutu gave the Address. Peter Hain MP, who was often chastised for his opposition to apartheid during the 1960s, spoke very poignantly.

CHAPTER 15

BOXING

BRITISH BOXING BOARD OF CONTROL

I was invited to become a member of the British Boxing Board of Control (BBBoC), the governing body of UK professional boxing that was formed in 1929 from the old National Sporting Club. I went down for the interview with Conservative MP Julian Critchley. The General Secretary, John Morris, said: 'We weren't sure about Critchley, but we are certainly sure about you and your background.' We both became stewards, and Julian was a tower of strength on that body and certainly deserved to be there – he had a great love for boxing.

I then became chairman of a medical sub-committee after the Eubank versus Watson fight in which Michael Watson was very badly injured.

It was well-known in our boxing circles that Watson had started his boxing career as a schoolboy and began his professional boxing career in 1984.

His major boxing success was undoubtedly when he beat the British Middleweight Nigel Benn for the British Commonwealth title. A loss for the World title with Jamaican Mike McCallum followed, before meeting Chris Eubank on 22 June 1991 for another shot at the World title, which he narrowly lost.

The fight then that ended his career came on September 1991 at White Hart Lane in a bid for the vacant WBO super middleweight title and again against Eubank. After causing Eubank considerable injury in the eleventh round and seemingly on his way to a comfortable win, Eubank caught him with an undercut that sent Watson to reel back and hit his head on the ropes. In the following round, referee Roy Francis sensibly stopped the fight and Watson collapsed in the ring.

It emerged that there were no doctors or paramedics at the event, and the doctors that arrived some eight minutes later appeared to have been off duty. During this period, Watson received no oxygen and it was a total of twenty-eight minutes until he received treatment in a hospital neurosurgical unit. Following that tragic event, he spent forty days in a coma before spending over a year in an intensive care unit. It took another six years before he began to slowly regain some move-ment and eventually an ability to speak and write. Eventually, through extraordinary willpower and courage, he was able to walk again.

In response, the BBBoC set up the subcommittee, with me as its chairman along with eminent surgeons and neurologists, and we were able to, as a result of our deliberations, create a much safer situation for boxers, in that all boxers had to have a scan after being knocked down. Funding came in from a number of quarters, but the surprise was that the largest amount came from the boxing promoter Frank Warren. Frank was notorious for not attending meetings when I first sat on the board as the chairman, but, as I said, he became quite an 'angel' with his generous contributions to the medical committee.

At one particular meeting, my niece's husband, Simon Lewis, wit-nessed a disagreement I had with John Morris. I walked out with every intention of resigning from the BBBoC for something John had done or said. When I got back to my office I phoned the then chairman to inform him, but he told me to hold fire and then called John Morris. Simon later told me that when John came back after that phone call he said: 'We've all got to be nice to Tom Pendry.' Just as well, because within a day or two I was appointed the shadow Minister for Sport. John Morris and I have had a very constructive relationship since – so much so that I am his vice-president on the Schools Amateur Boxing Association.

Everything went swimmingly from then on until the BBBoC had to pay Michael Watson by way of damages over the Eubank–Watson fight. Watson sued the BBBoC for negligence and won his case. The High Court ruled that the BBBoC bore responsibility for inadequate medical provision at ringside suitable for dealing immediately with the type of injury (brain haemorrhage) that Watson had sustained during the contest, sufficient to limit the potential for permanent brain damage. It was successfully argued that, had more advanced provision been in place prior to his transfer to hospital via ambulance, there was a likelihood that on 'a balance of probabilities' his eventual post-surgical recovery would have been more sustained. As such, the BBBoC was in breach of its 'duty of care' owed to Mr Watson and was liable for the payment of damages to be claimed by him. The Judge, Mr Justice Kennedy, ruled that his decision was made under existing 'duty of care' laws. The amount of damages to be payable was not determined in this case but was reliably predicted to be in excess of £1 million, an amount the BBBoC would be unlikely to be able to pay. Although leave for an Appeal against this decision was not granted by Mr Justice Kennedy, the Court of Appeal independently agreed to hear an appeal from the BBBoC. Their resultant verdict upheld the decision of Mr Justice

Kennedy but disagreed with his judgement that existing interpretation of law covered this case. Exercising their powers under 'laws of precedence' their interpretation extended the boundaries of 'duty of care' to be applicable to Mr Watson's circumstances. As new law had been made, leave for a further Appeal to the House of Lords was granted by the Appeal Judges. However, with regard to Mr Watson's clear disability and the fact that they had already lost two cases, the Stewards of the BBBoC decided it would not be in the best interests of their own standing in the eyes of the general public, the sport itself or Mr Watson in particular to pursue the case and it remained only for the quantum of damages to be negotiated. The BBBoC was compelled to put itself into administration and eventually after negotiations involving all parties a staged settlement of £400,000 was agreed. As a consequence, the BBBoC was compelled to sell their London headquarters to meet the first stage of that settlement. Unfortunately, the BBBoC then had to move their headquarters to Cardiff and, as I could not afford a whole day away from my parliamentary duties, I had to resign from my position.

I also remember well another boxing character, Frank Maloney, previously best known as the manager of Lennox Lewis, the former heavyweight champion of the world. Frank, as he was then, had boxed as a youth and had taken up training alongside Frank Warren. After parting ways with Warren in the 1980s, Maloney became involved in management and began promoting professional fights, becoming Lewis's manager in 1989, and this relationship lasted until 2001. I met him at the British Boxing Awards function when I was the guest speaker. After my speech, Frank came up to me and told me what a marvellous speech I had just made and that he would like to become a politician and join the Labour Party. I ensured that he became a member of the party in line with his wishes. This was of course during the Blair years, but then I read in his newspaper column in the *Star* soon after that he regularly attacked the Labour government. Frank then went on to contest the London Mayoral elections as a UK Independence Party (UKIP) candidate in 2004, and during the campaign was criticised for claiming there were 'too many gays' in Camden. He finished up by losing the contest but remains an active Ukipper. In August 2014, he announced that he would from then on be known as Kellie and was undergoing gender-reassignment surgery. While at first Lennox Lewis was shocked at the news, he later expressed respect and support for Maloney's decision. The things that happen in the world of boxing!

The danger inherent in boxing was an issue that came up on a regular basis during my time both as shadow Sports Minister and as an active member of the BBBoC spanning this period. Not least in April 1994, following the death of British title contender Bradley Stone. The 23-year-old collapsed hours after being stopped in the tenth round of his fight against Richie Wenton for the new British super-bantamweight title. He had a blood clot removed from his brain, but never came out of a coma.

Despite demands from the British Medical Association for an independent inquiry into boxers' safety, the government ruled out a ban on boxing. I said at the time that such calls for a ban were a 'knee-jerk reaction': 'Where there is room for improvement, there should be improvements. But you cannot wrap up the nation in cotton wool and say you cannot have any contact sports,' I said, defending the board. I went on to describe British boxing as 'the best controlled in the world'.

Minister for Sport Iain Sproat said: 'The government's line is that as long as there are proper medical safeguards anybody is entitled to pursue the sport that they wish. We have done something about it, which is to see that proper medical controls should be in place.'

As the 1990s progressed there were numerous attempts to ban boxing, not least with a 1991 House of Lords Bill, which was, thankfully, unsuccessful, having been defeated by just two votes.

My Labour colleague, the late Sam Galbraith, consultant neurosurgeon and MP for Strathkelvin and Bearsden, called for an urgent programme of research into brain damage caused by professional boxing. 'If we cannot get it banned, the least we are entitled to demand is research which will lead to inescapable conclusions which nobody will be able to hide from,' he said. Though the president of the Professional Boxers' Association and former boxing champion Barry McGuigan said that, statistically speaking, boxing produced fewer serious injuries than other sports. Indeed, according to figures released by the Royal Society for the Prevention of Accidents, three boxers had died in action between 1986 and 1992. In comparison, there were ninety-two deaths from horse riding, ninety-one from motor sports, sixty-nine from air sports, fifty-four from mountaineering, and forty from ball games.

Once again, I joined the fray, saying that if the sport was banned, it would continue underground without controls. Harry Greenway, Tory MP and vice-chairman of the All-Party Parliamentary Friends of Boxing, said it would be wrong to ban the sport in the 'heat of the moment'. Some in the medical arena criticised the BMA's policy, such as Dr Nigel Warburton, a professor of philosophy, who argued in the *Journal of Medical Ethics* that the policy is 'inconsistent, paternalistic, and too weak to justify a change to criminal law'.

My view, then and now, was that boxing is a sport that allows people

from all classes and backgrounds to excel. It is of particular value for
those from deprived backgrounds. Of course, there are risks – there
are other sports with a more serious level of injuries than boxing and
the Sport England list includes skiing, snowboarding, cycling, soccer,
water sports, motor racing and horse riding – but it helps build character and respect for others.

MUHAMMAD ALI

Thanks to my numerous sporting interests and roles, I have been
privileged to meet many of my own sporting heroes. Of course 'The
Greatest' was Muhammad Ali.

In December 1999, the boxing legend was crowned Sports Personality
of the Century at the BBC's final sporting awards ceremony of the millennium. Ali, the three times world heavyweight champion, received
a standing ovation as he collected the trophy at the event in London.
Despite Muhammad's ailment – Parkinson's disease – he overcame his
impediment on the night with charisma and charm and the ceremony
went very well. Ali collected more votes from BBC viewers than the
other contenders – soccer stars George Best and Pelé, cricketer Sir
Donald Bradman, golfer Jack Nicklaus and athlete Jesse Owens – put
together. On receiving the award from former world boxing champion
Evander Holyfield, Ali said: 'I would like to thank the British people
for giving me such a big welcome and all the people concerned with the
award,' before jokingly adding: 'I had a good time boxing. I enjoyed it –
and I may come back.' In a statement following the ceremony, he said:

Ever since I first came here in 1963 to fight Henry Cooper, I have
loved the people of England. They have always been extremely warm

and welcoming to me, which is why I am especially honoured to accept the BBC's Sports Personality of the Century. I give thanks to God and to all the people in the UK who have supported me over the years.

After the ceremony, Jarvis Astaire, a former boxing promoter and a very good friend of mine and of Muhammad's, came to me and said: 'Tom, I'm taking Muhammad, his wife and a friend of theirs to the Savoy for supper – would you like to join us?' Would I like to join them? Gosh! 'Of course I would!' I said. What an honour.

So, there I was at the Savoy, sitting at a table of five enjoying the conversation when it was interrupted by Jarvis who said to Muhammad: 'Did you know that Tom was a boxer?' God, I could have killed him – not only was I sitting at this table with the best boxer of the millennium, but he was also the best sportsperson of the millennium. In his stuttering voice, Muhammad turned to me and said: 'Show me your left hand.' I thought, my God, my last fight was for Oxford University about forty years earlier and here I am, expected to show how good my left hand was – although to be fair, it was always my best hand and I won most of my fights because of it. When I showcased what I thought was a very good jab with my left hand, Muhammad's wife, Yolanda Williams, who was sitting to the left of me, exclaimed: 'You nearly knocked me out then!' I then turned to Muhammad to find him nodding in approval, muttering something about Henry Cooper. We all remember Henry Cooper nearly beating Muhammad Ali in a fight in London before Muhammad's gloves were split by his trainer Angelo Dundee, allowing him to recover in time to go back for the next round and eventually win.

It was a praiseworthy comment indeed, but what I could not tell

Jarvis's guests at the time was that I had actually dislocated my shoulder as a result of that demonstration of my left jab. I refused to let on, so I finished my meal with a pretty brave face, eating with the fork in my right hand. The next morning, I ended up having my shoulder sorted out at Westminster hospital before I went on to meet Muhammad's wife and her friend to show them around Parliament. Unfortunately, Muhammad was doing something else at the time and could not join us. I remember saying to his wife: 'You know your friend around the table last night had a camera and I was stupid in not asking if he would take a photograph of me and Muhammad.' She replied: 'Don't worry, when he comes back to London next I'll make sure a photograph will be taken of you both.'

A few months later I received a phone call from someone in my constituency asking my whereabouts – I was busy interviewing secretaries at the time in London. This person then said: 'Muhammad Ali is here in your constituency and he has been told to look out for you to be photographed as his wife so instructed.' Muhammad was there in my town seeing one of my constituents, the famous local boxer Ricky Hatton who was at that time a world champion himself. Unable to get away from London, I missed out on the opportunity to have that picture of Ali that his wife promised me at that earlier encounter in London at the Savoy Hotel and I doubt there ever will be another chance since, at the time of writing, he is not well enough to travel. I am still hopeful, though, that a photograph can be found of that precious evening at the Savoy.

CHAPTER 16

FOOTBALL

ALL-PARTY FOOTBALL GROUP

When I arrived at the House of Commons in 1970,there was already an All-Party Sports Group based on sports that related to those of the Sports Council, as it then was called. The sports that were recognised by that body seemed to be the only sports that group could discuss. In 1973, I raised a problem in the world of association football concerning West Midlands football clubs. The chairman, Hector Munro MP, later knighted and Minister for Sport from 1979 to 1981 ruled me out of order on the basis that it was outside the Group's remit. Regarding this as ridiculous, I approached the Tory MP Jim Lester, a fervent Nottingham Forest supporter and a Nottingham MP, and invited him to join me in forming an All-Party Football Group to discuss problems relating to our national game. As a result, the group was formed and I became its first chairman, with Jim Lester its first secretary.

In England, the world of football's reaction, notably from the Football Association and the Football League, was wariness. They believed that there should be no room for parliamentarians to interfere in the running of the national game, as they put it, or a way for politicians to poke their noses into football affairs generally. Regardless, the All-Party Football Group continued to grow apace to the point where the numbers became so large that it soon became the largest back-bench group in the Houses of Parliament – and probably still is to this day!

We attracted a lot of attention in the football world and the guest speakers at our meetings were in many cases prominent household names, in particular Gary Lineker and the infamous Robert Maxwell, who was then the chairman of Derby County FC. Both these speakers, and others, attracted large numbers of attendees and we had around fifty to seventy members at the meetings in those days. Others, like Colin Moynihan, the famous manager of Derby County Brian Clough, gold medallist Olympic swimmer Duncan Goodhew, Tom Daley and Karren Brady, were also star performers. When Gary Lineker, then the captain of the England squad, was guest speaker on 20 November 1990, there was a real clash of interests as this was also the day of the first ballot in the leadership contest between Michael Heseltine and Margaret Thatcher.

I dispatched my researcher Joe McCrea to the committee room corridor to obtain the result. When Joe returned he handed me the envelope, but I decided to keep quiet myself. I thought it would be something that Gary would like to do, so I handed it over. He said: 'It's nice to be here on the night of the biggest mid-week match since we played West Germany.' Then, with a devilish grin, he announced the result. The cross-party group of around twenty-five MPs present murmured their appreciation. Later, Gary remarked: 'It was easier than reading the football results on a Saturday night. After all, there was only one game, wasn't there? That seems to have gone into extra time. If it gets to penalties, I hope they don't ask me to take any.'

Neither Heseltine nor Thatcher got the votes needed for outright victory in the first ballot. Heseltine polled 152 (40 per cent) and Thatcher polled 204 (55 per cent). The pundits thought Heseltine was on course to beat her in the second ballot as it was thought that many Tory MPs were ready to switch. Thatcher clearly saw the warning signs and threw in the towel, thus ending her eleven years as Prime Minister and fifteen years as Conservative leader. This allowed John Major, who was at home in Huntingdon recovering from a minor operation and as a consequence held back, to sign both Thatcher's papers and a set of papers for his own candidacy in case she withdrew. Unlike in the first ballot, a candidate only needed a majority of Conservative MPs to win, in this case 187 of the 375 MPs.

So that ended a momentous All-Party Football Group meeting, which I am sure will be remembered by all those present, Lineker beating both Heseltine and Thatcher and being the real star that night. He spoke eloquently of the need for the government to improve sports facilities, and delivered a clear summary of the struggle against hooliganism.

The sports reporter Michael Calvin, who had covered the event, drew comparisons between Gary and politicians:

The Tottenham striker is in the mould of Sebastian Coe, whose athletic activity has been sacrificed to the demands of defending a 5,039 Conservative majority at Falmouth and Camborne. Sufficiently clean-cut to appeal to any constituency selection committee, Lineker is articulate, diplomatic and, through his spell in the Spanish League, a proven Europhile. On the pitch he evades tackles with the dexterity of a potential Prime Minister avoiding awkward questions; off it, he does his best to answer the accusations that footballers have their brains in their kid leather boots.

Gary himself said: 'There are some similarities between professional sport and politics, I suppose. There's a lot of ambition in both. I knew a few players who talk a good game; they'd do quite well here in Westminster.'

I had admired Gary as a dashing goal-scoring centre forward and he was equally a likeable young man, but I could not compete with the feelings held by my fourteen-year-old daughter Fiona – he was her pin-up crush. When I told Gary how much of a fan she was, and how she had put up photos of him on her bedroom wall, he said: 'Give me her telephone number.' He then went to the nearest phone booth and, when she answered and asked who it was, he said: 'It's Gary,' looking and sounding a bit put out with her response. She told me afterwards that at first she thought it was a Gary in her school that she couldn't stand. I knew that this besotted young girl couldn't wait to get to school to tell her school friends of her 'new boyfriend'. In fact, a few weeks later, I took her to a function where Gary was in attendance and he met Fiona, gave her a little peck on the cheek and took her for a spin on the dancefloor. She, again, couldn't wait, I'm sure, to tell her story when she returned to meet her friends. Surely a man of the people is Gary!

That kind of informality aside, we as a Group were determined to make an impact and it soon became obvious, even to the Football Association and, in particular, to its chief executive Graham Kelly and its chairman Bert Millichip, that, far from being an obstructive nuisance, we knew about the world of football and wanted to help rather than hinder the FA and the Football League. This became very apparent during the Thatcher years with her lack of feeling for football and her introduction of harmful measures like membership cards to gain entry; the prohibition of alcohol in executive boxes; and the imposition of all-seated stadiums for the smaller clubs. However, we were successful in stopping the latter, thanks in part to the efforts of David Mellor as Secretary of State, leaving only the top two divisions to comply with that particular edict from government – clearly the smaller clubs were not in the position of the larger clubs to go down that road. In the face of the Group's constructive approach to football issues that stemmed from the united voices of soccer-loving parliamentarians, the FA did a complete volte-face, moving from a feeling of hostility to the point where they actually began sponsoring the annual dinner of the group. They do this together with the BBC to this day.

So popular was the group becoming within Parliament that it became inevitable that my chairmanship would be challenged, and indeed it was by Joe Ashton, the Member of Parliament for Bassetlaw and a Sheffield Wednesday supporter. He was ably assisted by Alan Meale, now Sir Alan Meale, the MP for Mansfield, as his campaign manager. So highly valued was the prize of chairing the group that it soon became the talking point around the corridors of power.

One surprising event that I have never been able to come to terms with was when, a few days before the crucial chairmanship vote at the group's AGM, I received a phone call from a very eminent MP from another party. Before making his point, he said: 'I will deny this conversation ever took place if it is ever raised by you.' He informed me that there was a very active campaign to oust me. 'Thank you for telling me,' I said, 'but hopefully I will overcome the challenge.' When the

AGM took place in a crowded room, to my surprise the very Member who had warned me of the attempt to 'defrock' me was standing at the back of the room, and – hoping, I suppose, that I wouldn't see him – when the vote occurred, raised his hand in support of Joe. Eventually, because the numbers in the room were so large, it was decided that we would have a balloted vote, rather than a show of hands. When the results came through, I was declared the winner and I'm certain that those who opposed me did not reckon on the number of my support-ers, who had turned up to block their manoeuvres.

I never held any animosity to those colleagues and I know that they had a real genuine love of the game, although they clearly had different views from mine on how to go forward with the group. In fact, Alan Meale made a statement to the *Mail on Sunday* in which he explained why they had wanted Joe Ashton over me. It seemed in their eyes that Joe would give the group more 'flair'. If by that they meant that the group would have the kind of flair that Joe wrote about in his column in the *Daily Star* then, yes, it would have been be a different kind of chairmanship to mine, flair or no flair.

My chairmanship eventually did come to an end when I was made the shadow Minister of Sport in 1992. Before standing down, however, I took a chairman's prerogative and proposed Joe Ashton to take my place in view of his longstanding membership of the committee. The recommendation was duly agreed 'nem. con.'.

What hurt me somewhat was that, despite what I thought was a magnanimous gesture, I did not get a thank-you from Joe. Instead of saying something positive about the fact that I had formed the group and had done a good deal of work, he merely said: 'Next item on the agenda is...' He was about to proceed until one of the vice-chairmen,

Conservative MP John Greenway, said that we couldn't proceed without recognising the founder of the group's work and went on to list some of its achievements. I hope Joe was suitably shamed by that.

HENRY KISSINGER

In 1986, I attended the FIFA World Cup tournament in Mexico and had the good fortune to sit in the VIP box watching England play with none other than Henry Kissinger, the presidential fixer, diplomat and negotiator on major international issues. The referee made an offside call that Kissinger queried, firmly shouting: 'That was not offside!' I turned to the great man, and, using salt and pepper condiments to demonstrate, I explained the offside rules to him. Kissinger himself was an ardent soccer fan and I thought not new to the rules of the game, although many years later my own personal assistant, Gee, who had played women's soccer in Canada under the NASL rules, informed me that they had different rules for offside and, no doubt, those were in Kissinger's mind when he made his outburst. Prior to the 1986 World Cup, the North American Soccer League (NASL) adopted new rules that were contrary to FIFA's and so became a source of contention between the two organisations. The NASL moved the offside line from the halfway line to the 35-yard line, allowed for three substitutions instead of two, created an elaborate point-scoring system and allowed shootouts to decide tied games. When Colombia was stripped of its rights to host the 1986 World Cup, Mexico, Canada and the United States were in the running to take up the spot. Kissinger was at the helm of the US bid, but with the animosity between the NASL and FIFA, it was unlikely that the US was going to win the bid.

In the end, Mexico played host to the World Cup once again, having previously hosted not long before in 1970. I was fortunate to have been able to travel to the Mexico Games as a guest of the FA's secretary, Ted Croker, and I thought the whole scenario was incredible: there's Kissinger, a big star solving all kinds of international crises, and me, a humble Pendry, having to teach the offside rules to him. Life certainly has its curious twists and turns.

THE BRADFORD, HEYSEL AND
HILLSBOROUGH DISASTERS

It was at Bradford City that the worst football fire disaster in the UK took place on 11 May 1985, killing fifty-six people and injuring at least 265. The Valley Parade stand had been officially condemned and was due for demolition. The match against Lincoln City had started in an atmosphere of celebration and good cheer all round, with the home team receiving the Football League Third division trophy. A small fire was reported by TV commentator John Helm and at first no-one took much notice, but in fewer than four minutes winds had whipped it into an inferno. In the panic, fleeing spectators had to break down locked exits to escape. There were many cases of heroism, with more than fifty people receiving police awards or commendations. Less than two weeks later, the Heysel Stadium disaster took place in Belgium on 29 May 1985; thirty-nine people died and 600 were injured when they were crushed into the walls at the Euro Cup Final between Juventus and Liverpool. The disaster happened before the match started when a large group of Liverpool fans breached a fence separating them from a 'neutral area', which contained mostly Juventus fans. Despite the trouble that was taking place, the game proceeded. The decision controversially was to prevent further tragedies taking place. I later described the disaster as the 'the darkest hour in the history of the UEFA competitions'.

However, the result for English football was devastating. UEFA banned all English clubs from taking part in all European competitions indefinitely. Thankfully, it was lifted in 1990–91, but with Liverpool excluded for three years, which was later reduced to one on appeal.

But there were more horrors to come.

That proved to be the biggest disaster of all – at Hillsborough in Sheffield, where ninety-six people died and over 700 fans were injured. It happened on 15 April 1989 during the FA Cup semi-final match between Liverpool and Nottingham Forest and I remember that day quite vividly. I was travelling with one of my local football clubs, Hyde United, en route to Telford United in Cheshire for a cup game.

It later emerged that the Liverpool fans had been allocated the Lepping's Lanes stand, but entry into it was made more difficult as the turnstiles were antiquated, which, as it emerged, resulted in the overcrowding.

The senior police officer in charge, Superintendent David Duckenfield, who was to bear the brunt of the criticism that ensued after the tragic events had unfolded, had ordered a tunnel to be the exit route to relieve the overcrowding. Unfortunately, that tunnel was unmanned and the pressure was such that when a crash barrier collapsed, fans were crushed, some fatally and the game was stopped after six minutes in order for the injured and the dying to be administered to.

It was only at half time at the game at Telford did I observe in their Directors' Room the disaster unfolding on television.

It transpired that of the ninety-six who died, only fourteen had been admitted to hospital. Duckenfield falsely claimed that the supporters had 'rushed' the gate, however in the Lord Justice Taylor report into the Hillsborough disaster, it was concluded that the main reason for the disaster was failure of the police control.

ALL-SEATED STADIA AND THE TAYLOR REPORT

Following the terrible tragedies at Bradford, Heysel and Hillsborough, there was a great deal of talk about all-seated stadia, and Lord Justice Taylor's report did recommend them. At that stage the recommendation included smaller grounds across all divisions, from the Premier Championship league down. It was a very contentious issue and in my capacity as chairman of the All-Party Football Group I went to Risely, near Warrington, Lancashire, at the invitation of the nuclear industry. They had asked me to see safe standing areas that they had developed and I went to take a look because, after all, the nuclear industry of all industries was very safety conscious. There I saw their designs which, if adopted, meant that when the pressure built up, the gates would close and there would be no problem of crushing of the kind that had caused the problems at Hillsborough. I was so convinced that this design was part of the answer to the problems that had been witnessed at Hillsborough – even if it was just a section of the ground that could be designed as a safe standing area. I recognised that there would always be risk on the odd occasion, in particular during a Christmas and holiday period when people would come from all over the country to be with their families to see a football match together – something that would have been impossible if separated by a membership card system. In more cases than not, they wouldn't be able to do that if it was just all-seated stadiums. By definition, they would not be able to go on a casual basis to be with their friends and family, especially during holiday periods.

I engaged the support of the Minister for Sport, Iain Sproat MP, and asked if he would come up and see the proposed safe standing system I had witnessed in Risley. To his credit, he agreed, and we both went up together. He was also convinced that the design was a worthwhile development. Unfortunately, we both had to concede the point when we went back to Parliament and found out that Arsenal and other football clubs had already gone down the route of ploughing up their terraces and pulling down cables to make way for all-seated stadia.

I do blame to some extent those brilliant nuclear engineering experts for not recognising the importance of promoting their product of safe standing areas before, or during, the Taylor Inquiry and marketing their own scheme. Even Lord Justice Taylor, who took me to the Garrick Club for lunch one afternoon, said: 'That could well have made a big difference to my report.' We lost the battle there and the unfortunate thing was that it has not stopped people from standing. Now, whenever anything happens down in one corner of the pitch, everybody still stands up. It is an issue that is now being discussed and I suppose eventually they may well see the benefit of having a part of the ground as a safe standing area.

On the twentieth anniversary of the Hillsborough disaster, my colleague Andy Burnham MP requested that documents previously not available for the Lord Justice Taylor's inquiry in 1989 be released to the public through various agencies, including the police. As a consequence, the Hillsborough Independent Panel was set up that, on September 2012, concluded that no Liverpool fans were responsible for the deaths. The independent panel also made stunning revelations about attempts at a cover-up by authorities, including the alteration by police of 116 statements relating to the disaster. It further concluded that up to forty-one of the ninety-six fatalities might have been avoided had they received prompt medical treatment and that 'multiple failures' by other emergency services and public bodies contributed to the death toll. A truly shocking verdict.

Following the findings laid out in the Hillsborough Panel report, on 19 December 2012, the Attorney-General Dominic Grieve made an application to the high court. The decision set out by the Lord Chief Justice quashed the original inquest verdicts. In the wake of the decision, Home Secretary Theresa May announced that a new police inquiry, headed by Former Durham Chief Constable Jon Stoddart, would be initiated to examine whether it is possible to charge agencies other than the police over the deaths of the ninety-six Liverpool fans who lost their lives at Hillsborough. At the time of writing, that inquiry, and the new inquests, are still ongoing. Again, it is truly shocking that the families and friends of the victims have had to wait so long for justice.

ALCOHOL AT SPORTING EVENTS

The issue of alcohol at sporting events was another controversial issue. In an attempt to combat the problems of hooliganism within football, the Tory government banned drinking alcohol in areas overlooking football pitches. This was an ill-thought-out response as the ban included executive boxes full of the very people who were pumping a great deal of money into clubs. The stupidity of it all was that potential hooligans were still allowed to drink alcohol in bars *not* overlooking the pitch. So the areas where there was not one hooligan in sight and were previously contributing a lot of money into the game for the many requirements made of them from government itself were now

being penalised. In response, I led a delegation to the appropriate minister at the time, Leon Brittan MP, and eventually we managed to get a
compromise that those in the executive boxes could drink up to fifteen
minutes before kick-off, and then after the game. All alcoholic beverages had to (and still have to) be served in accordance with licencing
laws and consumed within the executive boxes. FA regulations state
that no alcoholic beverages can be consumed within view of the pitch
and so, fifteen minutes prior to kick-off, the blind is lowered until
the players have left the field at full-time. In truth the legislation was
largely ignored because the police who were supposed to monitor the
workings of the Act knew it was nonsense.

GALATASARAY AND MANCHESTER UNITED (1993)

One of the biggest hooligan issues that I, together with others within the
All-Party Football Group, engaged in was to help solve a problem faced
by many Manchester United fans that took place in Turkey at the football grounds of Galatasaray on 3 November 1993. There was tremendous
violence during and after that game, largely brought about by the Turkish
supporters and the Turkish police. It was clear that some United fans also
took part in some violent acts but it quickly became apparent that the
main culprits were the Turks. The spectacle that unfolded caused a good
deal of resentment back home in Manchester. So many of their fans were
victims of violence and were injured in many of the clashes, and some of
them even had their passports taken away by the Turkish authorities. Six
fans were jailed for twenty-eight days and then released without charge.

While I will always condemn violence and hooliganism on and off
the pitch, I was left in no doubt that most of the fans were the victims
of heavy-handed and unjustified treatment. The testimony I received

was compelling. Two Stoke doctors, husband and wife Stephen and Barbara King, were returning from sightseeing when they were bundled into a police van in Istanbul. They were 'taunted and jeered at' by police holding them when the match result was broadcast. Lecturer Adam Brown of Manchester Metropolitan University reported that missiles and abuse were thrown at British fans, money and possessions stolen from them, and their coach attacked with bricks and bottles. Pensioner Joe Metcalf, aged seventy-one and a Man United fan for thirty years, was roused by police from his hotel bed at 5.15 a.m. and detained without water or food for ten hours. A deaf woman was also awoken by police in the early hours and thrown into a cell with six men. There were many such disgraceful stories.

As a result, I attended a meeting at Lancashire Cricket Ground, Old Trafford on 4 December 1993. My son was in the audience, together with a lot of quite angry supporters of United who were tilting their lances in the direction of the club's directors. I was sitting alongside those directors and I rose and told the fans that they were misdirecting their anger. The directors had worked very closely with me and my colleagues on this issue and had been very supportive of their fans throughout. This prompted Paddy Crerand, the great former United player, to get up and say: 'Now we know why Tom Pendry is such a good MP.' He should also have added my parliamentary colleagues, David Mellor and Tony Lloyd, who, although not present, were very supportive. What Paddy said, however, took the heat completely off the Manchester United directors, which they greatly appreciated.

Following that meeting, and prompted by calls from both Manchester United FC and their supporters, I led a delegation to the Turkish embassy alongside two Manchester United supporters and MPs from the city, Stan Orme and Tony Lloyd – the Member in whose constituency Manchester United's ground is situated. As a result of our representations, we managed to get all the fans that had been badly treated free holidays to Turkey, as well as the return of confiscated passports. But that was only after a long correspondence involving the Foreign Office and the Home Office, not forgetting a furious clash with the Prime Minister at the time, John Major.

On 5 November 1993, I wrote to remind him of how he had swiftly telephoned the Dutch Prime Minister to apologise for the conduct of British hooligans at a Holland–England match in Rotterdam when over 1,000 English 'fans' were arrested. He had been right to do so, as I had myself been an eye-witness to those disgraceful events. But now I asked him to be even-handed and call the Turkish Prime Minister to complain about the treatment of English fans on this occasion. I wrote:

> As you will know, a large number of fans were arrested for their supposed involvement in an incident at their own hotel. The vast majority of these fans were then deported without watching the match. Eye-witness accounts indicate that many of those arrested had little part in any criminal behaviour and even the chief liaison officer present said they had been found 'guilty by association'. You will no doubt be aware that no Turks were arrested for their part in events leading up to the match. Furthermore, Brian Robson, the Manchester United captain, needed two stitches to his hand after a Turkish policeman struck him with a riot shield...

The response I got back, from Major's private secretary, was not only anodyne, but also seemed to refer only to the earlier Rotterdam match.

I fired back another letter to the PM, saying: 'I cannot express sufficiently my anger and disappointment at your response.'

I continued to press the case for a European-wide agreement on
how to police international football matches to avoid a repetition of
what happened in Turkey.

THE FOOTBALL TRUST AND TASK FORCE

Many people believed that I was previously offered the job of the chairmanship of the Football Trust in October 1997 because Tony Blair felt
shame-faced and guilty about not giving me the Sports ministerial
post. The writer Tom Bower even suggested it was due to the intervention of James Purnell, by then his special adviser – but, as we shall see,
Bower is an unreliable source. My appointment, according to Bower,
stirred up a controversy. The Trust's vice-chairman, Richard Faulkner,
now Lord Faulkner of Worcester, who was then also a lobbyist for
Littlewoods, fumed that it was a political fix. And Tony Banks insisted it was a decision imposed by No. 10. There were more conspiracy
theories as the new Labour government settled in, and much of the
evidence is contradictory. Some of the claims made then and later were
malicious or the result of ignorance. Others were downright untruths.
Could it be, I say in all modesty, that Tony Blair simply thought I was
the best man for the job I wonder?!

Prior to the general election of 1997, I, together with Peter Lee, chief
executive of the Football Trust, attended a football function at Watford
FC, meeting the manager Graham Taylor, the former England manager from 1990 to 1993. We were accompanied by Richard Faulkner
and, in our informal talks, Richard informed us that the current chairman of the Football Trust, Lord Aberdare, was going to step down

after the election and he, Richard, was to become chairman. I expressed my congratulations – after all, I was expecting to be Minister for Sport and I would have been happy to work alongside Richard who had done an immense amount of good work in the interests of football at every level, especially for the football fan. I think my assessment of Richard's abilities was very much in line with Peter Lee's. However, to my amazement, I was asked by the football authorities to take the chairmanship instead, after my disappointment at not getting the Sports job. I accepted, but I did feel for Richard Faulkner, who was no doubt feeling just as bruised as I had been.

Indeed, when Tony Blair called to congratulate me, I referred to Richard, to which Tony said: 'We will find something else for him.' I felt so happy when Richard was made a Peer of the Realm and I made a point of standing outside the Peers Lobby on his way to be introduced in the Chamber. I found that his work in the Lords on many issues, not just sport, has made him a very valuable Member indeed, and we do now often join forces when sporting issues in particular are debated.

In any event, I was very proud to be asked to serve as chairman of the Trust. It was a government-funded body to improve the safety of UK sports stadiums that had been set up by the Labour government in 1975, with the assistance of the pools companies and the Football League. Millions of pounds were poured into grounds, and those who benefited by more than £4 million apiece included my team Derby County, Sheffield Wednesday, Sunderland, West Ham, Chelsea, Middlesborough, and many more.

The Trust was unique, bringing together all of football's major bodies around one table. Annual contributions from the FA, the FA

Premier League, Sport England, the Football League and the PFA, the Scottish FA and the Scottish Sports Council had been added to the Trust's pools income to allow it to grant aid to football at every level. It distributed over £300 million, built new stadiums, built or refurbished over 160 stands, twenty-two stadium control rooms and twenty-six first aid rooms, and funded fifty-five new community and family facilities for people with disabilities. One of its most important measures was the introduction of CCTV surveillance equipment across football to help combat hooliganism. Over £40 million was allocated to non-professional football throughout the game's grassroots, including the Pyramid, and the Highland and Junior Football Leagues. Our grant awards, large or small, played a fundamental part in guaranteeing a future for football. Our aim was to get cash efficiently and effectively to where it mattered most. In one promotion I wrote:

> The Football Trust is one of the great unsung heroes of British football. Thanks to a great deal of hard work and dedication from our clubs the Taylor report has transformed football and I'm proud to say that the trust has played a huge part in that transformation. Thanks to our investment this country can now boast the finest football grounds in the world. With this stadium rebuilding programme nearly complete the trust is now ready to broaden its remit to tackle new investment priorities at the grassroots of the game and help create a long-term partnership and strategy for our national game.

Meanwhile, the Football Task Force, which I pledged would be set up in our Sports Manifesto in 1997, with an aim to recommend measures to help combat racism, improve disabled access, clubs' involvement with their local communities, and encourage more equitable ticket pricing and merchandising, became a reality. Before the election, in part due to charges of corruption levied against the goalkeeper Bruce Grobbelaar, Labour had committed to an independent regulator for football, and the Task Force was the outcome. But there was a dispute over who should chair it. Banks suggested David Mellor, the former Conservative Sports Minister. Again, James Purnell, as I understand, had an influence as the PM's adviser, opining that Mellor was someone some people loved to hate, but was also a populist choice. Mellor was duly appointed and given the impression that he had been proposed by Alastair Campbell, the PM's football-mad communications chief. Mellor, with the whole-hearted support of the new government and the Football Trust, set out to tackle sleaze in football after a series of allegations about match-fixing, bungs and dishonest management. The Task Force looked at bringing in a code of practice, setting out how clubs should treat their supporters, considered ways of forcing clubs to offer cheaper tickets, change their strips less often and consult supporters on any plans to sell substantial quantities of shares. It produced a report on eliminating racism, improving facilities for the disabled, and investing in the community.

Bower, in his book *Broken Dreams*, wrote that I, due to my disappointment at not getting the ministerial job, then set about undermining the Task Force. He wrote: 'Tom Pendry, in retaliation against Banks, whom he despised, and Mellor, whom he loathed, was reconsidering his allegiance to the fans, football's owners and the regulators. From his offices in Westminster and Euston, Pendry began sniping at the Task Force...' That is a downright untruth. I neither despised Banks nor loathed Mellor; both men have different qualities but a shared love of the game. And as for the charge that I sniped against the Task Force, I have a bundle of correspondence that proves just the opposite. Both Mellor and Banks told me later that Bower's remarks were not true. In the case of David, he had on two or more occasions had me as his dinner guest in his house at Tower Bridge, and a very good host he was too. As far as Tony is concerned, I warmly welcomed him in a speech I made in the House of Lords when he arrived there – again, Tom Bower got it wrong. And how could I be accused of undermining the Task Force, a body I had first recommended be set up in my sports manifesto?

On 7 January 1998, Chris Smith, then the Secretary of State for Culture, Media and Sport, wrote to me:

> I was very pleased to receive your message of continuing support for the final stage of the Task Force's work. The commercial report will be a crucial one, following on from the effective contributions the Task Force has made in other areas. Tony [Banks] and I greatly appreciate the trust's help with this. Many thanks – and Happy New Year!

That hardly suggests I had been sniping from the sidelines, does it?

And there was a lot more to come. In a letter dated 23 July 1998 from Chris Smith, thanking me for a meeting I had arranged partly to sort out differences between Mellor and Gordon Taylor of the Professional Footballers Association (PFA), he said: 'I have been very happy with the positive relationship that has existed between the Trust and the Task Force since it started its work, and I believe it is important this continues. The government values the help and support of the Football Trust in taking forward this initiative.'

If anything, the problem was the government's decision to set too early a deadline for the Task Force to complete its business. And its lack of funding, which meant an extra burden on the Football Trust, as it was providing the secretarial assistance for the Task Force. In a letter dated 15 September 1998, I told Chris Smith that a certain disquiet was felt by the Board of the Trust about it providing the secretariat in its latter stages. I wrote:

> I conveyed to the Trust meeting that it was your intention to wind up the Task Force by November or at the latest December, and in view of that I recommended that the Trust should continue in its present role. I am happy to inform you that the meeting accepted my proposition and the Trust will carry on its duties as before on that basis. I might add that the Trustees proposed that either I or Peter Lee, my chief executive, will continue on the Task Force as the Trust's representative. In the interests of continuity I suggest that Peter represents the Trust at future meetings in view of his current involvement with the Task Force.

Chris Smith agreed, and, in a letter dated 28 September, said: 'I am grateful for your help in this matter.' He added, in his usual hand-written notes, 'PS: Many thanks for your help on this.'

On 24 November I received a letter from Tony Banks, the man who, according to Bower, I 'despised'. He referred to the help that I and my team had given to the Task Force's report on improving facilities for disabled facilities. 'Thank you again for all the assistance...' he wrote. 'Access is a key part of this Department's policy, and I fully endorse the recommendations in the Task Force's report. There are a number of recommendations which fall to the Trust to consider...'

Again, this can hardly be construed as 'sniping' from the sidelines. These were difficult times, but the record shows that I was entirely constructive. In the blurb for the paperback version, Bower's book is described as 'meticulously researched'. On the issue in which I played a part, how then did he get it so wrong? Incidentally, I did ring Tom Bower and offered to meet him and show him in confidence the letters from Chris Smith, David Mellor and Tony Banks, but he declined a meeting and suggested that I send the letters to him, which I would not do.

Incidentally, the recommendations that Tony Banks referred to were of real importance. They included specific conditions of grant aid, including wheelchair access in all grounds, a minimum number of spaces for those who are ambulant disabled or visually/hearing impaired, improved lighting for those who are visually impaired, and an awards scheme rewarding clubs judged to have done the most to improve facilities for disabled supporters.

With my full support the work of both the Task Force and the Trust continued, and I took it upon myself to ensure that was the case until the Trust completed its final commercial report up to the end of the following February. I informed both the Department and Tony Banks of that. But then, in January 1999, I had to report to Chris Smith that a 'nasty bombshell' had hit us. Gordon Taylor, the chief executive of the Professional Footballers Association, resigned from the Task Force. He was upset by not having been invited to the launch of a report on community investment, and by David Mellor's overall approach to such investment. He was also reconsidering with his management committee their membership of the Trust, as it was by now providing the secretariat of the Task Force in the form of Andy Burnham, now shadow Home Secretary. In a letter to Chris Smith, dated 11 January 1999, I said:

I am sure that you will understand my overriding concern is to safeguard the membership and the future of the Trust. Given the sensitivities of many Trustees about the Trust's involvement with the Task Force, providing back-up facilities and staff resources has always been a very difficult area. The appointment of a full-time Administrator meant that it was just about possible to maintain a service. However with Gordon Taylor's departure this has been made virtually impossible. I have therefore been left with no choice but to act upon the Trustees' wishes expressed at our September 1998 meeting and to withdraw the Trust's administrative support to the Task Force.

At the bottom I hand-wrote that I had done so 'with a heavy heart!' Tom Bower, of course, wrote that I had 'switched allegiances' – another misconstruing of what actually happened.

As a result of the Trust's decision, Gordon Taylor recommended to his management committee that the PFA maintained its relationship with the Football Trust. Chris Smith said: 'The support the Football Trust has provided the Task Force is greatly appreciated.' The Trust then followed my recommendation that it should maintain its support to enable the Task Force to complete its final report on commercial issues. The Trust also agreed to my suggestion to let the deadline slip. A few days later Chris Smith wrote to me:

I thought I would drop you a note to register my thanks for all the hard work you have done in maintaining the Football Trust's support for the Football Task Force. As you are doubtless aware, I consider the Task Force to be an important part of our work here at DCMS and I am extremely grateful for your help.

I received similar notes from David Mellor and Tony Banks. So much for Tom Bower's outrageous slur.

The Trust continued to finance the Task Force's administrative costs as spring turned into summer and the final report was still not published. On 27 July, I wrote to the Secretary of State saying we would not demand any more deadlines, having persuaded the trustees that we should 'continue to support the Task Force until the business is complete'.

There was still some way to go. The Task Force was split over how to balance the interests of fans and clubs. Supporters' groups had hoped to shift the balance of power back in their favour but had been resisted by the clubs from the Premier and Football Leagues. Despite the disagreements, Ian Todd, the chairman of the National Federation of Supporters' Clubs, said he was hopeful fans would get a better deal in the end. 'The particular problem for supporters at the moment is they feel the game is slowly being taken away from them,' Mr Todd told BBC *Radio 5 Live*.

> There is a mood for change – what we're dealing with now is the extent to which that change will bring about what we are seeking. I've been heartened by the attitude of the football authorities. I think they are quite intent on bringing in some quite significant changes, particularly in club's relationships with supporters. I am convinced there is a will to bring in codes of practice so that clubs which are being run best can pass that information on to clubs being run not quite so efficiently.

James Purnell was hostile to the concept of a regulator, telling Blair that football 'hated outsiders' interfering in its concerns. The issue caused the Task Force to issue two contradictory interim reports. Purnell told Smith and Task Force administrator Andy Burnham, employed by the Trust, that 'it is a delusion that football will ever be regulated by the government or an independent official digging deep'. And then Kate Hoey, who professed to support reform, refused to attend the launch of the reports, castigating Chris Smith, her superior minister, as indecisive. David Mellor said, with a sigh, that it was all a 'sorry state of affairs'.

There was also an unseemly scramble over who should become the proposed regulator, which caused more chaos, more damaging splits and some vicious internal battles that were all too often played out in the media. First Blair appointed Jack Cunningham, the former Cabinet minister, as chairman of the proposed International Football Commission. Cunningham had at first rejected the offer but changed his mind after a telephone call from James Purnell. The appointment was supported by the football establishment but outraged two men who had each expected the job – the former police chief Sir John Smith and the lobbyist Lord Faulkner, supported by Kate Hoey. Faulkner told everyone who would listen that fans had been 'sold out' and orchestrated protests from supporters groups. The backlash infuriated Purnell and Andy Burnham but they were forced to agree that Cunningham had lost the media battle. His appointment was quietly rescinded.

The hunt was then on for a replacement. The renowned broadcaster and journalist Michael Parkinson was suggested but that idea proved a no-goer. Sir John Smith was briefly reconsidered, but that was scuppered by the hostility of Sir Richard Scudamore, the Premier League's chief executive. He warned that the football authorities would abandon the IFC plan if Smith was picked.

As it turned out, the three main governing bodies – the Football Association, the Premier League and the Football League – refused to support an independent football regulator, to be known as 'Offoot' – and also opposed the mandatory introduction of fans' representatives on club boards. They also opposed mandatory restrictions on ticket prices and quotas on subsidised tickets for young, disabled, unemployed and OAP supporters, saying that clubs needed flexibility to allow for circumstances such as promotion, relegation and ground developments. They said that they didn't believe that the overall well-being of the game will be helped by 'new layers of regulation or bureaucracy [i.e., a regulator]', and dismissed fans' calls for representation as 'unacceptable'.

Eventually, the Task Force was stood down. Chris Smith and Kate Hoey would subsequently be sacked as ministers, while Purnell and Andy Burnham were rewarded. The Football Trust was replaced by the Football Foundation. And the run-up to that, dove-tailing with the demise of the Task Force and all hopes of an independent regulator, was to see more controversy.

THE FOOTBALL FOUNDATION

In early 1999, the Premier League agreed to pay a levy on satellite TV income to fund community sports. The money would be administrated by the new Football Foundation, but there was the question of who should chair it. By then I had decided to stand down as an MP, but Tom Bower's suggestion that I orchestrated the ambitions of James Purnell as my successor in Stalybridge and Hyde to curry favour is another outrageous untruth – the actual circumstances are spelt out in another chapter. My experience in sport, and as chairman of the

Football Trust, made me in the eyes of many an obvious candidate, and I was appointed by the representatives of the governing bodies of football. The Foundation was duly launched in July 2000 on the lawns of 10 Downing Street by Tony Blair and myself in the presence of the then England manager Kevin Keegan.

The newly established Football Foundation immediately became the country's largest sports charity, as it remains to this day. With a focus on addressing this country's chronic shortage of grassroots football facilities, the Foundation awards £30 million worth of grants on behalf of its core Funding Partners: the Premier League, The FA and the government (via Sport England). This investment quickly began to translate on the ground in the shape of a whole new generation of changing pavilions, state-of-the-art all-weather playing surfaces and properly draining natural grass pitches being built in towns and cities across the country for people of all ages and abilities to enjoy playing football, and other sports, purely for the love of it.

When Tony Blair launched the Foundation, he undertook to match the Premier League's contribution, and I was engaged in many funding battles. At the end of October 2002, I met Richard Caborn MP, who had taken the Sports Minister's job, to discuss the FA/Premier League's proposal that a £35 million assistance package be made available to the Football League via the Foundation. The idea was that £10 million should be provided immediately and another £10 million in the 2003/04 financial year. Each tranche would be split between the FA and the Premier League, so that none of the government's annual contribution to the Foundation/FSIF would be involved. The FSIF's annual budget would be reduced by £6.25 million and the Foundation's by £3.75 million for a limited period. The shortfall would come from a £15 million loan. In a letter to Caborn I said: 'The plan is that any loan would be secured by the Football League top-slicing payments to clubs under their BSkyB broadcasting and advertising contract.'

In 2003, my three years as chairman of the Football Foundation had lapsed, as is the norm for a government representative on such a body, so the board kindly made me its first president. In his welcoming letter, the chief executive, my old pal Peter Lee, wrote: 'I look forward to my continuing association with El Presidente!'

When Peter stepped down in April 2006, the Foundation's Trustees appointed Paul Thorogood to replace him. Paul had enjoyed a distinguished career in the Royal Air Force, rising to the rank of Group Captain, before deciding on a mid-career change. More crucially, Paul brought a wealth of specialist experience in operational logistics, systems thinking and organisational performance and change management, which he employed extensively to help transform the Foundation from a charity whose good work people supported, to the highly advanced and very-well-respected organisation that it is today. Paul had no sooner got his feet under the desk before implementing a strategic review that penetrated every area of the operation; he transformed it from top to bottom and created a very strong business culture throughout the charity, which was focused on its strategic objectives. In doing so, he introduced sophisticated delivery systems and capability to the Foundation that rival any business, never mind charity. Most importantly though, Paul applied very strong leadership and boundless enthusiasm, which captivated and galvanised the staff.

Since we launched it in 2000, the Foundation has delivered a staggering £1.2 billion worth of grassroots sports projects, developing more than 500 all-weather playing surfaces, 900 changing pavilions and 3,200 properly drained real grass pitches.

So effective is the Foundation as a delivery vehicle that other major organisations have harnessed its expertise, drawing in further investment into community sport we had not even dreamt of when we set it up. These include the multi-award winning £70 Barclays Spaces for Sports programme, which has created 200 new or refurbished community sports sites across the UK. We have also seen the delivery of the Mayor of London Sports Facilities Fund, creating a stunning Olympic legacy for the capital in the shape of over 100 multi-sport sites.

I have had the pleasure of officially opening scores of Foundation sites across the country and it always gives me a real buzz to see the delight on the faces of local people, young and old, when these stunning new facilities open their doors to their local communities. I often remind those lucky young footballers how, in my day, nothing as palatial as changing rooms with showers and toilets or floodlights ever existed. Getting more and more of our youngsters out into the open air pursuing healthy sports can not only be of great benefit to them, but also to the communities that are in receipt of these facilities.

Many of these are in the most deprived areas in the country and in many cases Football Foundation funding is the first investment that they have received for a long time or, in some cases, ever.

CHAPTER 17

RADIO 5

At 9 a.m. on 27 August 1990, a brand new radio station focusing on young people, sport and other issues that the other stations had long neglected was launched. Medium-wave frequencies, previously used to transmit BBC Radio 2 from 23 November 1978 to 26 August 1990, were then largely unused, and the Conservative government wanted, for their own reasons, the BBC to end its long-standing practice of simulcasting its services on both AM and FM frequencies. This offered an opportunity to provide a home for a number of programmes that were previously broadcast as opt-outs on one frequency only. Radio Sport took the lead and radio sports coverage blossomed on the airwaves as never before.

It was effectively the only 'sports network' in the country and its sports coverage was three-times that of the old days of Radio 2. It broadcast over 2,000 hours of commentary, reports, news and interviews each year, and in 1991 covered forty-five different sports. The Wednesday night football programme, presented by Gary Lineker and Trevor Brooking, won the largest audience of any radio station between 7 p.m. and 10 p.m., including Radio 1. It covered five days of football, from Saturday to Wednesday, every week of the season – in total it covered a record 800 matches, plus every single competitive England match. Its Wimbledon fortnight gave listeners 100 hours of continuous commentary. Radio 5 was the only radio or TV station to cover all five classic horse races as well as the Cheltenham and Aintree festivals – none of the classics were available on BBC TV. The Rugby World Cup final attracted a million-strong audience, while thirty hours of uninterrupted commentary were devoted to the Open golf championship and Ryder Cup. Cricket correspondent Jonathan Agnew won sports reporter of the year at the Sony Awards, while the station's Olympic Games coverage was voted best sports outside broadcast by the Sony panel. Its broadcast of the Cricket World Cup won three-times the audience achieved by Sky TV. It was the only national provider of an hourly sports bulletin – twenty a day from 6.30 a.m. Radio 5's presenters and experts in 1992 included such household names as Gary Lineker, George Best, Stirling Moss, Bill Beaumont, Barry McGuigan, Ian Chappell, Fred Perry, Fred Trueman, Henry Cooper, Barry John, Andy Irvine and Anita Lonsborough. In sports terms, it was a stunning success and all those involved were proud to be part of it. Unfortunately, that pride was not shared by top BBC executives.

Many saw the station as something broadcasting programming the other four main BBC stations did not want, reflected in a speech by Jenny Abramsky, News International Visiting Professor of Broadcast Media at Exeter College, Oxford, of whom we shall hear more later. She said of Radio 5:

The sports output from Radio 2 Medium Wave, all the Schools and Continuing Education programmes from Radio 4 FM, the Open

University programmes from Radios 3 and 4 FM and programmes for children and young people from Radio 4 and some World Service output. This was a network with no audience focus, born out of expediency.

The biggest threat, however, came from the BBC's Director-General, John Birt, whose only priority seemed to be rolling news.

In 1991, Operation Desert Storm was launched as the multinational response to the Iraqi invasion of Kuwait. From 16 January, Radio 4's FM frequencies were used to provide an all-news network for the coverage of that first Gulf War. It was dubbed 'Radio 4 News FM', but was known more popularly in the media as 'Scud FM'. Despite protests from Radio 4 listeners, the BBC mainly received praise for the quality of the service and the speed with which it was set up. Following the end of the conflict, Radio 4 resumed its normal schedule but the positive response to 'Scud FM' made the BBC start a review into the possibility of providing a full-time news station, leading to the broadcast of a similar service on long wave during the 1992 UK general election campaign. Due to the resistance to any use of Radio 4 FM or LW frequencies, it was decided that Radio 5, criticised by Birt as 'improvised and disjointed', would relaunch as a 24-hour news channel. Radio 5 as it was meant to be was in real peril.

A relative of a Radio Sport producer and a parliamentary colleague alerted me to the danger in July 1993 and I immediately slammed down an Early Day Motion (12 July 1993). It stated:

that this House recognises the important service that Radio 5 provides for some 5 million listeners each week and regrets the proposal to replace it with a news network depriving them of many sporting events, dramas and other programmes for children and young people; further believes that, whereas the BBC has a duty to provide an adequate comprehensive news service, this should not be achieved at the expense of the only national sports network available in the whole of the United Kingdom which has increased its coverage threefold in the last three years; urges the governors and the Director-General of the BBC to abandon any plans they might have which could particularly jeopardise the coverage of major sporting events which have a massive following throughout the United Kingdom and beyond; and believes it is the duty of the BBC to guarantee and maintain these important aspects of the nation's culture.

There was huge cross-party support for my motion – it was signed by 151 MPs, from Neil Kinnock to Ken Livingstone to David Mellor. Even Peter Mandelson signed it! Immensely valuable support was also given by former Olympic athletes-turned-politicians Seb Coe and Menzies Campbell. In order to ensure maximum press coverage for our campaign, we arranged a press conference and photo-call alongside Will Carling, Terry Venables, Peter Scudamore and Kriss Akabusi. We were rewarded with column feet rather than inches. On the face of it, the response from BBC bigwigs was gratifying, as they gave assurances that the future of sports coverage on the radio, and the BBC as a whole, was guaranteed. More than 2,000 hours of sports coverage annually was promised on the new, revamped Radio 5. But serious concerns remained, thanks largely to Director-General John Birt's ambitions. In a speech to the Radio Academy he said: 'There is one service the BBC as yet does not provide: a continuous news service available all day and all night ... following the developments in a major breaking story.'

The big fear was that news priorities would interrupt supposedly guaranteed sports coverage. As the great Frank Keating wrote in *The Guardian*:

> Whose finger will be on the button? The sports editor's or the gaffer on news? How many gunshots in a high street bank raid, for example will be needed to take precedence over a goal in an FA Cup final? How many billions in the monthly trade deficit will it take to interrupt hysterically the whispered final putt in the Open?

John Birt clearly intended to create the kind of news service in which a short cycle of news bulletins is continuously updated, and obviously that would be completely incompatible with such things as all-day live coverage of Wimbledon, or live coverage of matches, whether they were football or rugby, or Formula One races, and so on. We feared that major matches and tournaments, to which sports viewers would have their ear glued to the coverage of, would be interrupted. The head of BBC radio sport, Mike Lewis, insisted that sport would not come out second best, saying: 'This is a partnership of equals.' But other BBC executives admitted that there would be some clashes of priorities. The doubts and fears remained.

As shadow Sports Minister I wrote regularly to Marmaduke Hussey, then the chairman of the BBC Board of Governors. His assurances were not clear cut. In one response he said: 'We do not intend to reduce our sports coverage', adding: 'Both the Director-General and I are great sports enthusiasts.' But, in another, he said: 'No firm decisions have yet been taken.' However, Leighton Andrews, the BBC's head of public affairs, told me in a letter: 'The high-quality sports programmes will remain and the new network will enhance the role of sports journalism on radio so that the excellent events coverage is supplemented by proper explanation, analysis and debate on topical sporting issues.' In other words, the future was rosy, and we had nothing to worry about. But worry we did.

I pulled out all the stops to ensure that everyone was aware of what was at stake. A key weapon in my armoury was the BBC's own mission statement, *Extending Choice*, which sought to 'reflect all the dimensions of both popular and minority culture that makes us different as a nation'. In a letter to the Prime Minister, the cricket-mad John Major, I pointed to that statement and said: 'I cannot possibly see how the chairman of the Board of Governors and the Director-General can justify a proposal which could jeopardise such a wide variety of programmes.' I went on:

> While I am well aware that the BBC does have a duty to provide a comprehensive news service, I am sure that you will agree that this should not be achieved at the expense of the only national sports network available to this country, which, incidentally, has also increased its sports coverage threefold during the last three years. Indeed, as you know, the BBC already provides extensive news coverage on two other radio frequencies. You will understand that any plans to discontinue this service will be met by profound disapproval throughout all sections of the community, including blind people who rely a great deal upon the radio community for their enjoyment of sport.

I am not sure if, or how, Mr Major influenced things, but my appeal to him cannot have hurt!

Throughout the campaign we were heartened by the reaction to the proposals from within the BBC from men and women who risked their jobs to join in with the public outrage. They included Radio Sport editor Bob Shennan who, while supporting a 24-hour news network, did not believe it should be done by 'robbing Peter to pay Paul'. In letters to me he spoke of his 'feeling of outrage that we may be aiding and abetting a small, but nonetheless powerful, section of society to ride roughshod over the rights of less vocal licence fee payers'. Under the proposals, he wrote, 'In terms of its audience profile, probably the most varied network would be dismantled and its creative talent scattered to fight for its airtime.' Bob pointed out that, under the proposed regime, the previous night's resignation of Northern Ireland Minister Michael Mates after a scandal involving his links to fugitive businessman Asil Nadir would have scuppered Wimbledon coverage. He asked how rolling news would impact on the following year's World Cup and Commonwealth Games. He said:

Not to cover these events fully would also endanger our ability to procure contracts for such major events as Wimbledon and Test Match cricket. It would certainly mark the death-knell of Test Match Special as we know it. The morning sessions are currently broadcast on Radio 5, as is ball-by-ball commentary of all England's overseas tours plus the cricket World Cup. Neither of these two events is available on BBC Television. They can never be accommodated on the News Network.

Meanwhile, the listening public were voting with the 'On' switches of their radios – perhaps because of the threat that sports coverage would be the main victim when Radio 5 as we had known it was axed. In October 1993, *Radio Joint Audience Research* reported that, over the previous year, Radio 5 had increased its audience share by 47 per cent, rising to more than 4 million who tuned in for more than thirty minutes each week. By contrast, Virgin 1215, Richard Branson's rock station seen as the main threat to BBC radio, had dropped by 1.4 million to 3.28 million, well below Radio 5. Michael Green, deputy head of BBC Radio, conceded: 'The growth in Radio 5's share comes from its sports coverage; sport will be an essential part of the new news and sports network.'

We remained unconvinced, and for good reason. At the time I said in a memo to interested parties:

We need to ask how the BBC intends to reconcile the needs of the two different groups of listeners (news and sports). They have promised us a 'partnership of equals' and that is exactly what we must get. We need to make sure that priority is given to the kind of sports coverage that we have done so much to protect. Otherwise we might well see coverage of sports events being interrupted or cancelled simply because the news editors think they have a major story and want to run with it.

Our fears and doubts about the sincerity and integrity of supposedly sports-mad BBC executives were reinforced by reports of a meeting involving the new boss of the new news and sports station, one Jenny Abramsky. No sooner had she assured her team that she was a 'great sports fan' than two strangers walked into the room, prompting her to ask who they were. George Best and Terry Venables were not amused by her ignorance. It might have been a gap in her knowledge at the time, but she must be congratulated for the support she gave us after she was convinced that the Director-General was on the wrong track.

One of my chief concerns was that sports reporters and editors are often reticent to cover sports stories that aren't directly related to incidents on the pitch. The lack of reportage of the Galatasaray issue mentioned in a previous chapter was one horrific example. But some progress was being made in this arena, notably by the programme *Sport in Question* on Carlton TV.

At the same time, a new dimension was added by the launch of Sky TV, which added to the competition for the coverage of sporting events. First to go was the Premier League, in a development that probably did more than anything else, before or since, to boost the profits of the big breweries, as everyone in the country without a satellite dish went down the pub to watch the football. Next was the Ryder Cup, poached from the BBC, while a great deal of cricket coverage also went to Sky. Even Wimbledon looked like it was under threat. All of which underlined the importance of maintaining good, comprehensive sports coverage on the radio, including live matches.

I and, thankfully, the BBC itself, was hit by a tsunami of letters from the listening public. One, from Richard Scott of Fishguard, stands as a flavour of them all. He wrote that 'sport on radio is threatened by the fanaticism and determination of a small clique in the BBC'. He predicted that 'conflicting interests will lead to a news-dominated network with the continuity and spontaneity of sports broadcasts lost for ever'.

The demise of sport on Radio 5 will undermine the BBC's claim that 'the role of radio will be particularly critical not only in maintaining national institutions such as Test Match Special but also in guaranteeing universal access to a wide range of sports.'There is a desperate need for someone to tap the huge reservoir of support for Radio 5 and to demonstrate that any attempt to destroy one of the finest sports services in the world will not be tolerated. The case is unanswerable.

Then, as now, I continuously paid tribute to all those at the BBC who consistently produced the best sports coverage in the world. At events like the Barcelona Olympics they showed us all how sports coverage should be handled, and they earned a number of prestigious awards, including the Golden Ring of Lausanne from the International Olympics Committee, which made it all the more important that radio sports coverage should not be down-graded.

Eventually, the BBC listened to the concerns of myself, other campaigners and millions of sports listeners. After an eight-month research project headed by Phil Harding, including analysis of more than 6,000 letters from the general public and open meetings up and down the country, in October 1993 the board announced details of the new Sport and News Network on what was to become Radio 5 Live. The BBC governors issued a statement, which promised: 'The high quality sports programmes will remain and the new network will enhance the role of sports journalism on radio so that the excellent events coverage is supplemented by proper explanation, analysis and debate on topical sporting issues.'

In a letter to me, Head of Sport Mike Lewis said that the new station would be 'a very long way removed' from the original concept of a continuous news channel and that the campaign I led had 'a very significant influence' on the final outcome. He went on:

The efforts that you, Seb Coe and Menzies Campbell made to rally support in the Commons not only met with a spectacular response, but stimulated many leading figures in the sports world to write in and express their own concerns over the future of the sports output. Because of your efforts no one in the senior BBC Management or on the Board of Governors was left in any doubt that the radio sports service was both immensely popular and highly valued. The final result is that we have ended up with a powerful voice on the new network rather than being just junior partners or even left out in the cold.

I issued a press release that acknowledged that the new replacement for Radio 5 was 'potentially exciting'. But, I added:

Clearly, we in the House of Commons, along with millions of sports lovers, will be monitoring the new network of sport and news to ensure that it will be a 'partnership of equals'. Until then, we wish the new programme every success and hopefully it will build on the great success story of Radio 5.

Radio 5 closed down at midnight 27 March 1994, and five hours later its replacement, Radio 5 Live, was born. The news of the first day was dominated by a fatal stabbing at Hall Garth School in Cleveland, the first of many major incidents that the network covered live as they unfolded. Its news-gathering and presentation quickly established a reputation for slick professionalism.

We still kept an eagle eye on its sports coverage, however, and that, with a few quibbles, has indeed proved impressive. During the course of its history, BBC Radio 5 live has broadcasted some of the biggest sporting events including Live Premier League Football, the Six Nations and Grand Slam tennis tournaments.

While commercial stations continue to acquire the vast majority of television broadcasting rights in the UK, the BBC remains dominant in radio sports.

Would any of that have happened if John Birt's initial 'vision' had prevailed? I very much doubt it. I am exceptionally proud of the leading role I played in saving radio sports coverage for the millions who appreciate it, and ensuring that the elitism that all too often prevails did not ride roughshod over ordinary licence-payers who, like me, are passionate about sports.

Ten years later I was invited to celebrate the new Radio 5 on its ten-year anniversary at a hotel near Broadcasting House. I attended with my son Dominic and before meeting Jenny Abramsky, Bob Shennan said: 'You are to get a special mention tonight.' And so it turned out that those assembled – the great and the good of sport – heard Jenny in her welcome say we would not be here tonight to celebrate our ten years of success if the fight had not been led by someone 'who is with us tonight, Tom Pendry MP. Together with others, he deserves our thanks and appreciation for their efforts to bring us together here tonight to celebrate.'

During its peak in 2013, Radio 5 Live had 6.12 million listeners, while its Sports Extra feature regularly pulls in up to 850,000 each week. That is an extraordinary achievement, especially given the original intention to pull the plug.

CONCLUSION

O n editing the previous pages I am struck by the thought that, although writing one's memoirs is bound to be a bit narcissistic, it is almost impossible to avoid the accusation that there is too much 'I, I, I' and perhaps not enough 'we'. To that I do plead guilty, but I found it difficult to master the craft without achieving that result.

My wartime evacuee days and my first encounter with the coalminers of Durham – hearing of the terrible treatment that was meted out to them by the 'wicked colliery owners' – forged my belief in democratic socialism. I decided to do whatever I could to change things for the better, which is why I started my career by joining the Labour Party at fifteen years of age after a chance meeting with Bessie Braddock MP in 1950. I still remember Bessie telling my mother that if I wanted to have a career in the Labour Party I should raise my ambitions and become a Labour Member of Parliament like her.

The journey for me was far from steady, but the unpleasant parts did not outweigh the pleasurable ones. Most certainly the most important 'up' moment was when I became a Labour MP, although there were of course some less than happy moments along the rocky road before and after that breakthrough. Paramount among those was the disappointment of not getting the Sports Minister job after five years of hard toil and after presenting what many thought was a laudable set of policies for the 1997 general election for both sport and tourism. Tony Blair, despite my role in giving him his chance to start his political career, decided to find another to fill my spot. Nevertheless, I am proud of my successful efforts to push sport towards the top of the political agenda. When I started, sport had been relegated to the side-lines, particularly by successive Tory governments. During the 1987 general election, for example, a top commentator said: 'The air above Britain is dark with political footballs at the moment; it is a shame that sport is not one of them.' All that has now changed. Today, all major parties recognise its vital importance to the health and well-being of the nation, to the economy, to the hopes and aspirations of young people, to education, to community cohesion, to the tourism and hospitality industries, to the environment, to national and regional pride, and to international diplomacy. As Nelson Mandela once said,

Sport has the power to change the world … it has the power to inspire. It has the power to unite people in a way that little else does. It speaks to youth in a language they understand. Sport can create hope where once there was only despair. It is more powerful than government in breaking down racial barriers.

After my election success in 1970, my maiden speech prompted the Chief Whip, Bob Mellish, to put me on the front bench – the first of the 1970 intake of Labour MPs to be promoted. From there my career was an up-and-down affair. It began well with my appointment as Lord Commissioner of the Treasury in both the 1974 elections, but my career really picked up after my resignation from the government, when I was appointed as the Under Secretary of State for Northern Ireland from '78 to '79 by James Callaghan.

Other things I am proud of include forming the All-Party Group on Football and a Jazz Appreciation Group. But most important of all, I feel, is introducing the Carers and Disabled Children's Act 2000 after winning a spot in the Private Members' Ballot, and pushing it through with all-party support. The progress of that legislation, which has helped many thousands of carers and their families, showed Parliament at its very best.

However, my biggest misjudgement was not resigning as a government whip earlier, as my career was not likely to be advanced all the time I was there. But, out of loyalty and recognising the perilous state of Labour's small majority at the time, I hung on until the situation eased itself with an unofficial Lib–Lab pact.

Politicians are not always at the top of the popularity charts, but I think over the years I have had the greatest of admiration for the vast majority of politicians of all parties who enter parliament with an overriding desire to help their fellow citizens.

I despise those, especially those in the press, who seem determined to undermine the sincere efforts of politicians. I believe we are currently seeing the effect of such actions with the declining numbers who turn up to vote.

It is not unique, of course, for people to change their political allegiances, Winston Churchill was a Liberal before becoming a Tory after all, but one memorable occasion for me was recalling when I was a union official at the time of the 1964–66 general elections in Nottingham. I was a warmup speaker for the Labour candidates in those two elections. One candidate was Jack Dunnett and the other one was Michael English, both were Nottingham's Members of Parliament at the time and were defending their seats. I did my warm-up speech, but my most persistent heckler was a young man who I remembered well – he always looked very dapper, always with an umbrella, smartly dressed, and I think I coped with him fairly well. However, years later, when in the House of Commons having a meal with some of my Labour colleagues, to my astonishment one of them was boasting how he had 'cut his teeth' in the elections of 1964 and 1966 in Nottingham on 'Slab Square'. The moment I heard him say that I realised that he was the one who was giving me trouble by heckling me during my speeches at that time. I turned to him and said, 'I remember you well, Dale, you were the Conservative heckler who heckled me when I was making my speeches' and of course he couldn't deny it – that was Dale Campbell-Savours, who was at that time the Labour Member of Parliament for Workington and now a very active and very conscientious Labour peer in the House of Lords.

I've always believed that the sinner who repents is someone that the Lord above would put a gentle hand on and give entry into the kingdom of heaven and certainly in the case of Dale it will be a very gentle hand.

I am proud to have served to the best of my abilities the good people of Stalybridge and Hyde for so long. They are in my heart always. The greatest thing about constituency work is that you can often see the results in the faces of those you help.

I am proud, having witnessed as a youngster the Attlee government creating the National Health Service and introducing welfare reforms, to have played a modest part in successive Labour administrations that have changed people's lives for the better. Their achievements span the Wilson, Callaghan, Blair and Brown premierships and include immensely better treatment of the old and infirm, the disabled, the disadvantaged and the deprived. They have resulted in an NHS that remains the envy of the world, despite Tory-led efforts to undermine it, the national minimum wage, relative peace in Northern Ireland, the replacement of crumbling schools, the Open University, the return of sporting excellence internationally ... the list goes on and on.

I have referred to the important day in the lives of both my wife and myself, when against what we thought would never happen, we were blessed by having our daughter Fiona. However, the arrival of young Dominic, two years later, was truly the icing on the cake.

Dominic made history by being the first Roman Catholic to be christened in the crypt of the Palace of Westminster since the reformation. The priest who performed the baptism was the padre of Manchester United. Little did he know then that at the age of ten Dominic would become a mascot to the rival north-west team Liverpool FC and has remained a true 'red' ever since.

Both my children have enriched my life in every respect, not least being active members of the Labour Party and by so doing carrying on the family tradition.

However, the football rivalry between my two children was such that Dominic's zeal for Liverpool FC was evenly matched by Fiona's ardent loyalty to Manchester City and being an ardent supporter of Derby County FC myself, one can imagine the healthy punch-ups in the Pendry household as far as football was concerned. In the case of Dominic, his love of football is such that he is streets ahead of me in the knowledge of the beautiful game and he is certainly a very lucky young man to have been able to accompany me as a privileged guest to many football matches over the years.

There always is another side to the overall picture of a person's life and I am no exception to that rule.

I have always acknowledged those of my parliamentary colleagues who have experienced difficulties squaring up to their responsibilities as an elected member of the House of Commons and their family commitments in either a marriage or partnership.

In my case, when I was elected to the Parliament, my wife knew of my ambition to become a Labour MP before we were married. Indeed, she was instrumental in achieving that goal.

Moira herself became the Labour chairman of education in the borough of Derby and vice-chairman of education in the county of Derbyshire. Such were her own political capabilities she was made Alderman at the age of twenty-six – the youngest on record at that time (and probably of all time given that the role no longer exists!)

When I moved to the county of Cheshire (of which Stalybridge and Hyde constituency was then a part), she had to forgo her positions in neighbouring Derbyshire. This was not planned, nor something either of us had envisaged, but an unfortunate consequence of my selection for Stalybridge and Hyde and promise to live in the constituency.

Clearly it was a blow to her as she was making great political strides in her own right. The pressure built up and became more intense when our children came on the scene. A 'normal' husband, working away from home during the week, could be expected to relieve the work-load endured by their partner. Unfortunately, this did not marry well with the reality of life in Westminster. I, like many other MPs, had no time to totally relax at the weekends. Then there were surgeries, six per month in my case, party meetings to attend, fetes to be opened…

I liked to think, however, that through it all I always found time to enjoy the limited family life I had with Moira and our children. Unfortunately, that wasn't enough and in 1984 Moira petitioned for judicial separation. Amicably we have continued to have a loving relationship with our children and I am proud that both Moira and I were able to provide the love and support they needed, despite the vagaries of a life in the political spotlight.

When our separation was officially announced, Moira put it best in a statement, which read:

> Tom and I are concerned that the children are not affected. We shall continue to exist as a family unit, the only difference being that Tom and I are friends rather than a married couple. Marriage to a Member of Parliament is difficult due to the demands made by the House of Commons and the constituency.

This statement was endorsed by the Stalybridge and Hyde Labour Party, which said that 'the couple were very much liked and respected and the situation did not affect Mr Pendry's professional ability'.

I would like to thank both of my children, Moira, and the rest of my family who have supported me throughout what has been an extraordinary political journey. One can see that my life and career has been a bit of a roller-coaster, but the 'downs' by comparison cannot be compared with the 'ups'. Where would I find a job that gave me access to meet such people as Harold Wilson, Michael Foot, James Callaghan, Pope Paul VI, John Paul II, Henry Kissinger, Muhammad

Ali, Nelson Mandela, Kris Kristofferson, Stanley Matthews, Johnny Dankworth, Tom Finney, Mikhail Gorbachev, Alec Douglas-Home, John Major, Richard Attenborough, Robin Gibb of the Bee Gees and many others too numerous to mention? So to think that the important meeting with my mother and Bessie Braddock in 1950 at the Margate Labour Party conference, where Bessie told me to raise my sights, put into action my political journey. Bessie was an inspiration and it was a pity that she was not able to be around to see that sprightly fifteen-year-old end up as a Labour MP. However, growing up in a family of five Catholic boys, it was my mother's determination not to raise one to become a priest, but rather a Labour MP, that really set the course of my incredible political life – and for that I must thank her.

INDEX